P9-BTX-882

THE STORY OF THE SURVIVORS

Linda Morgan, a teenager who fell asleep on the *Andrea Doria* and woke up on the *Stockholm* . . .

Ruth Roman, a beautiful Hollywood star who spent desperate hours searching for her missing son . . .

The Boyers, who stayed in the bar for a nightcap, then returned to their cabin to find nothing but a gaping hole . . .

Dr. Thure Peterson, who worked furiously to free his trapped wife as time ran out on the doomed liner . . .

Robert Hudson, who awakened from a drugged sleep to realize he was utterly alone on a sinking ship . . .

Captain Calamai, dazed and unable to take command as his crew pushed aside panic-stricken passengers to save themselves . . .

Baron Raoul de Beaudéan, captain of the *Ile de France,* faced with an agonizing decision on which 1,706 lives depended . . .

"The individual stories lure the reader page by page."
—*Los Angeles Herald-Examiner*

"Excellent . . . a classic sea adventure."
—*Baltimore Sun*

"As entertaining and significant as *A Night to Remember.*"
—*Boston Herald*

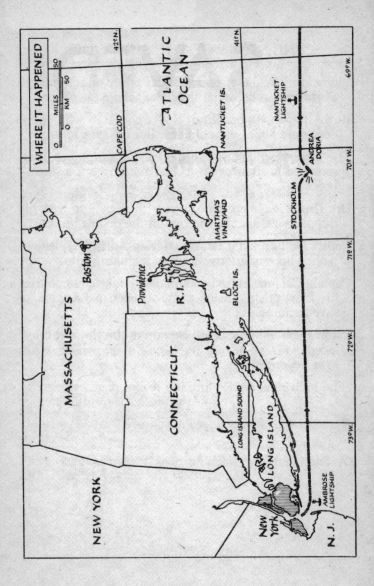

WHERE IT HAPPENED

MILES
0   50   150
KM
0   50

42° N.

41° N.

MASSACHUSETTS

Boston

CAPE COD

ATLANTIC OCEAN

NANTUCKET IS.

Providence

R.I.

MARTHA'S VINEYARD

NEW YORK

CONNECTICUT

BLOCK IS.

NANTUCKET LIGHTSHIP

LONG ISLAND SOUND

LONG ISLAND

STOCKHOLM

ANDREA DORIA

New York

N. J.

AMBROSE LIGHTSHIP

73° W.   72° W.   71° W.   70° W.   69° W.

SAVED!

The Story of the *Andrea Doria*— the Greatest Sea Rescue in History

William Hoffer

BANTAM BOOKS
Toronto / New York / London

*This low-priced Bantam Book
has been completely reset in a type face
designed for easy reading, and was printed
from new plates. It contains the complete
text of the original hard-cover edition.*
NOT ONE WORD HAS BEEN OMITTED

SAVED!
The Story of the Andrea Doria—
the Greatest Sea Rescue in History

*A Bantam Book/published by arrangement with
Summit Books*

PRINTING HISTORY
*Summit edition published July 1979
A Dual Main Selection of the Literary Guild
Serialized in* Ladies Home Journal *and by*
The New York Times Syndicate
Bantam edition/September 1980

*The excerpts from Edward P. Morgan's commentary
on pages 194–196 and 203–204 are reprinted
by permission of ABC Radio Network.*
Life Magazine Photos © 1956 Time Inc

ISBN 0-553-13938-X

Published simultaneously in the United States and Canada

*Bantam Books are published by Bantam Books, Inc. Its trademark, consisting
of the words "Bantam Books" and the portrayal of a bantam, is Registered
in U.S. Patent and Trademark Office and in other countries. Marca Registrada.
Bantam Books, Inc., 666 Fifth Avenue, New York, New York 10103.*

PRINTED IN THE UNITED STATES OF AMERICA

0 9 8 7 6 5 4 3 2

ACKNOWLEDGMENT

The author wishes to express his grateful appreciation to the survivors of the *Andrea Doria*, and to the officers and crew of the *Andrea Doria* and the *Stockholm* for their cooperation in recounting the tragic night of July 25, 1956.

To My Father

. . . Her name is *Andrea Doria*, and she is as beautiful a new piece of marine construction as I ever saw.

. . . A ship is a wonderfully solid thing, making sense in a shaky world. A ship doesn't hurry too much. It's nearly impossible to sink one or set it painfully afire. It works faithfully for its master, and takes on a portion of his personality. The man, in turn, is influenced by his vessel, and comes to be like her.

. . . it is ladies like the *Andrea Doria* that I kiss in print.

—from a column by Robert C. Ruark,
after seeing the *Andrea Doria*
in New York Harbor in April 1953

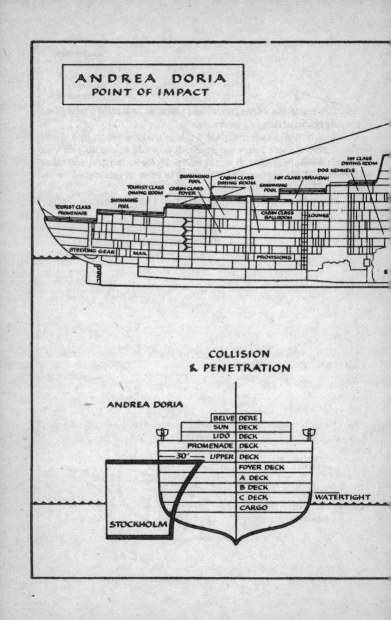

ANDREA DORIA
POINT OF IMPACT

1ST CLASS
DINING ROOM

SWIMMING POOL
TOURIST CLASS
DINING ROOM   CABIN CLASS
CABIN CLASS   DINING ROOM   1ST CLASS VERANDAH
SWIMMING   FOYER   SWIMMING
POOL   POOL   DOG KENNELS
TOURIST CLASS   CABIN CLASS
PROMENADE   BALLROOM   LOUNGE

STEERING GEAR   MAIL

                                                        PROVISIONS

COLLISION
& PENETRATION

ANDREA DORIA

BELVE	DERE
SUN	DECK
LIDO	DECK
PROMENADE	DECK
30' ──► UPPER	DECK
	FOYER DECK
	A DECK
	B DECK
	C DECK
	CARGO

WATERTIGHT

STOCKHOLM

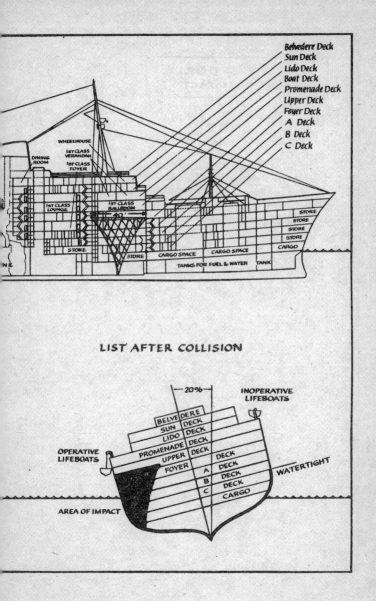

Belvedere Deck
Sun Deck
Lido Deck
Boat Deck
Promenade Deck
Upper Deck
Foyer Deck
A Deck
B Deck
C Deck

WHEELHOUSE

DINING ROOM

1ST CLASS VERANDAH

1ST CLASS FOYER

1ST CLASS LOUNGE

1ST CLASS BALLROOM

STORE

STORE

STORE

STORE

STORE

STORE

CARGO SPACE

CARGO SPACE

CARGO

TANKS FOR FUEL & WATER

TANK

LIST AFTER COLLISION

20%

INOPERATIVE LIFEBOATS

BELVE DERE
SUN DECK
LIDO DECK
PROMENADE DECK
UPPER DECK
FOYER
A DECK
B DECK
C DECK
CARGO

OPERATIVE LIFEBOATS

WATERTIGHT

AREA OF IMPACT

PREFACE

MEN AND WOMEN, in the routine of their lives, are rarely tested to a point near the limits of their courage and endurance. Yet in each of us lies the question: what would I do *if*? For most, the question remains unanswered, for the test never comes. To be sure, there are moments of anxiety as when the airplane encounters turbulence or the tire goes flat on the interstate. But these usually are unreasonable fears that subside as soon as the brief tension has ended.

Except for war, there are few true opportunities for us to measure the level of courage or cowardice within us. Most of us, therefore, can never know what we would do *if* . . .

At 11:10 P.M. on Wednesday, July 25, 1956, 1706 human beings of varied hopes and backgrounds were suddenly forced to answer the question. There was an element of fate at work that night in the coastal waters of the Atlantic Ocean near Nantucket, as two small, bean-shaped pips on a radar screen representing two great ocean liners somehow met each other at the edge of the world's second largest ocean. The billion-to-one shot came in. It was as though an unseen force contrived to pull 41,478 tons of steel together at a combined speed of forty knots while the skilled men in command stood by in impotent frustration.

The *Andrea Doria* was a beautiful, even sensuous, maiden of the sea, whose fate was to be encountered alone on a foggy night, first raped, then abandoned to die slowly in the dark.

Fate was no less evident on a personal scale. For the passengers the difference between survival and death was sometimes no more than the decision to linger in a lounge for a last cup of coffee before bed. Minor choices assumed monumental dimensions to those who remained alive to contemplate them.

It is the individual dramas of human beings reacting to stress that make the study of tragedy so compelling. While the collective story of the *Andrea Doria* is as mammoth as the 697-foot ship, it is also an unparalleled collection of personal stories. An editorial in the *New York Post* on Sunday, July 29, 1956, put it this way:

> No matter how far we press against the outer limits of time and space with the science and engineering we take for granted, there will always come a time when the ultimate test faces us in stark and simple terms: man against nature with nothing to aid him but his fellow man.
>
> Wednesday night was such a time. The original dispatches that all aboard were safe and/or accounted for were much too slick and easy to be believed. It is only now, when one tragic epic story begins to break down into two thousand short stories, that courage and valor take shape in a manner one can recognize and thrill to.

Courage and valor were present in abundance, but so was fear, so was cowardice. There were heroes and heroines, but there were villains, too. And no one can say what he or she would have done *if* . . . except for those who lived through it.

Deep, untested aspects of the human character surfaced during the worst hours of the *Andrea Doria*'s travail. One man risks death by plunging beneath the sinking decks to gather life jackets for strangers; another tries to steal them. One crewman works for hours in a destroyed cabin to free the trapped occupants; another flees the ship before the passengers.

The telling dramas of that evening, when taken collectively, add up to a greater whole. It is one which is at the same time tragic and near-comic, painful and rewarding, and all very human.

To record the most compelling of the individual stories, I have traveled thousands of miles throughout America and Europe and personally interviewed scores of survivors. Everyone, though almost a quarter century has passed, retains a detailed memory of that incredible night. Many shared their once private, and often painful, recollections with me.

Equally vital to the accurate reconstruction of the story are the recollections of the crews of both ships. In Italy, Sweden, and France I interviewed those officers and crewmen of the *Andrea Doria* and the *Stockholm* who played a major role that evening, along with the captain of the *Ile de France*. All except the master of the *Andrea Doria* have survived. The personal interviews were augmented by an exhaustive research of the events, including study of the 6217 pages of pretrial depositions taken from crewmen.

It will prove inevitable for the reader to compare this tale to the sinking of the *Titanic*. There are multiple similarities but also intriguing differences. The *Titanic* crashed into an iceberg in 1912, and went down with the loss of 1513 lives. Shipbuilders learned from that disaster and important modifications were made in ship design and safety procedures that, in theory, should have prevented much of the agony that took place on the *Andrea Doria*. Perhaps the most significant change was that ships were required to carry enough lifeboats to accommodate a full load of passengers and crew. The *Titanic* had a lifeboat capacity of 1178 and carried 2207 persons. The *Andrea Doria* had a lifeboat capacity of 2000 and carried only 1706 persons, which *should* have been sufficient to rescue all aboard.

The forty-four years between the two disasters also witnessed the invention of radar, an achievement that supposedly could prevent collisions at sea and in the air. The *Titanic* was forced to rely on a lookout in the bow who spotted the killer iceberg only in time to give the captain thirty-seven seconds to react. The *Andrea Doria* picked up the *Stockholm* on its radar miles ahead.

While the *Titanic* crashed into an inanimate block of frozen water, the *Andrea Doria* collided with another ship directed by intelligent, experienced human beings. This set up controversies—legal, moral, and emotional—that could never be argued out with an iceberg.

Though both ships rest today in the dark, salty muck beneath the Atlantic Ocean, they met their ends in quite different ways. The *Titanic* was involved in a primitive contest between man and nature. The *Andrea Doria* was, and is, the protagonist in the most incredible modern drama of the sea—the collision of two sophisticated behemoths which almost seemed to search each other out in the treacherous Atlantic fog.

But the most striking difference between the two incidents is found in the casualty figures. On the *Titanic*, 1513 persons died, while only 705 survived. That story can only be viewed as a great tragedy. Many lives were also lost on the *Andrea Doria* and the *Stockholm*. But the most telling fact of this epic is the large number of passengers and crew members on the *Andrea Doria* who, after facing imminent death, were heroically, and fortuitously, saved.

Theirs is the story of the most inexplicable disaster and the greatest rescue in the history of the sea.

1

THE DRILL

THE WHISTLE, high atop the bridge, screamed out six short blasts, followed by a single long moan.

The ship's loudspeaker crackled with static, then called out its orders. "All passengers are directed to report to their muster stations at once, with their life jackets," an authoritative voice announced, first in Italian, then in accented English. "Wait there for instructions."

Throughout the ship, passengers hurriedly gathered bright orange life jackets from their cabin closets and rushed to their assigned stations. First-class passengers went to the front of the Promenade Deck; cabin-class passengers to the cabin-class Ballroom farther back on the same deck; tourist-class passengers, most of them Italians emigrating to America, to various posts aft on the Promenade Deck.

They queued in small groups, seeking out family and friends, helping one another with the unfamiliar straps and buckles of the life jackets. The scene in the cabin-class Ballroom was typical of what was happening at all the muster stations. Here, three nuns laughed at their appearance as they slipped the orange jackets awkwardly over their billowing

17

black habits. Sister Angelita Myerscough of Ruma, Illinois, had difficulty pulling the jacket over the broad white collar of her habit. She made a mental note not to wear the stiff collar if there should ever be a real emergency.

"Where is the crew?" Sister Angelita wondered aloud.

Her friends shrugged. "They told us to wait," said Sister Marie Raymond Baker of Marywood, Grand Rapids, Michigan. "Surely someone will come around to give us instructions."

The passengers grew restless. One of the men who seemed knowledgeable about ships explained how the lifeboats worked. The Promenade Deck where they were standing was enclosed on all sides by sliding glass windows. Looking out through them, Sister Angelita could see above to the Boat Deck where the lifeboats hung.

"When they prepare the boats, they lower them on those winches," the man explained. "They drop them right here to our level, and all we have to do is step out through the windows to the boats. Then they just lower them to the sea."

It looked simple enough. Was it so simple that the crew did not have to conduct a dry run? Sister Angelita waited in the Ballroom with her friends for about an hour, but still no one from the crew showed up. "When you think about it," she said, "traveling on a big ocean liner is probably the safest. You never hear about these things sinking anymore."

The others concurred. Danger was a remote eventuality on such a giant ship, and the gentle waves seemed to mock any suggestion of concern over the listless lifeboat drill.

"I guess the drill is over," someone said.

Gradually the crowd of passengers dispersed. It was Wednesday, July 18, 1956, and the ship was sliding easily through the bright waters of the Mediterranean, running between Naples and Gibraltar, her last port of call before heading across the Atlantic to New York. Everyone was eager to enjoy the recreational facilities. They had a full week of play ahead of them, but few wanted to waste additional time on this needless drill. As they drifted off to their pleasures, no one was overly concerned that the crew had failed to give them instructions.

They all knew that the *Andrea Doria* was unsinkable.

2

THE FOG

At three o'clock on the afternoon of Wednesday, July 25, 1956, Captain Piero Calamai stood on the bridge of the great Italian luxury liner, the *Andrea Doria*, staring to the west. The afternoon sun was headed toward a nebulous haze on the western horizon, the unmistakable precursor of a July fog off the Massachusetts coast.

Fog. The quiet killer of the sea. It enshrouds a ship like a dark blanket, robbing a navigator of his single most treasured tool: vision. The *Andrea Doria* was equipped with the latest radar—two scopes, in fact—but Calamai was a traditional captain who preferred the evidence of his eyesight. He would rely on the radar when he had to, but he would keep his own senses vigilant. Fog destroyed more ships than storm winds, coral reefs, or icebergs.

Calamai was confident, if cautious. Dressed in his daytime whites emblazoned with the proud insignia of the Italian Merchant Marine, he felt at ease on the bridge of the *Andrea Doria* as no one else could. The ship and her master were almost a single personality, having traveled the North Atlantic together for three and one-half years. He was the only captain the ship had ever known.

Calamai stood six feet tall on the bridge, his uniform covering more muscle than would be found on most fifty-eight-year-olds. His bulbous nose overlooked a weathered face that testified that he had been at sea almost constantly since the age of eighteen, when he graduated from the Nautical Institute at Genoa. He came from a seafaring lineage, his father, Oreste, having founded a magazine called *La Marina Mercantile* and his brother Marco ranking as an admiral in the Italian navy. Piero himself served with distinction during both world wars. As master of the thirteenth largest passenger vessel in the world, Piero Calamai earned a salary of $625 per month.

He stared into the haze, trying to gauge its depth, contemplating the orders he would issue to protect his ship against this respected antagonist. When Calamai gave an order he rarely, if ever, raised his voice.

Calamai was a mild-mannered, almost antisocial master. He seemed happier on the bridge scanning the open sea than socializing with passengers. He never drank. Although he often dined with fellow officers at a special table in the first-class Dining Saloon, he never invited a passenger to join him. As Senior Chief Officer Luigi Oneto described him, Calamai was "dignified but distant."

He was secretive by nature, particularly toward the passengers. Once, early in the voyage, the ship made a ninety-degree turn in order to raise the starboard side slightly to repair a leaking drainpipe. A passenger visiting the bridge asked the captain why the ship was swinging. Calamai answered, "We saw a big whale in front and turned to avoid it." Perhaps the captain felt the layman would not understand a technical explanation, especially when delivered in his patchy English. This tendency to keep passengers uninformed would later be the source of intense controversy.

Calamai knew this would be his last voyage on the *Andrea Doria*. After his round-trip crossing he was due for his annual vacation, then was in line to take command of the *Doria*'s younger sister, the *Cristoforo Colombo*. Calamai was sometimes saddened at the thought, for a master develops a sense of union with his ship that few others can ever know. Piero

Calamai and the *Andrea Doria* had been through so much together. Leaving her for another ship would feel like an act of infidelity.

There was that troublesome maiden voyage in January 1953, when in these same waters near the eastern coast of the United States the *Andrea Doria* encountered a vigorous storm. A swell caught the ship broadside and she took a sudden twenty-eight-degree roll that sent passengers and crew tumbling to the decks. Twenty persons were injured. Since that time, however, the *Andrea Doria* had successfully crossed the Atlantic Ocean an even hundred times. On this voyage, the hundred and first, the ship left Genoa on July 17, stopped at Cannes, then Naples, and Gibraltar before heading out past the Azores and across a sunny summer route toward New York. She was estimated to arrive at her pier the next morning, Thursday, July 26, at 9:00 A.M.

Like every ship's captain, Calamai had issued standing orders that he was always to be summoned in the event of fog. This Wednesday afternoon he appeared on the bridge before he was called, perhaps sensing an impending haze. The suspicion was based more on experience than on mysticism, for the area off Nantucket Island is often foggy, particularly in July, when warm currents from the Gulf Stream collide with icy northern waters.

The captain walked out on one of the bridge wings, observation platforms that extended out on either side of the Sun Deck beyond the edges of the hull. Here, some eighty feet above the surface, he could view the horizon best. There was no mistake. A bank of fog stretched ahead of the bow. Calamai turned, strode back to the wheelhouse, and issued his orders.

He called to the engine room, relaying the information that they were in fog. "Reduce the speed," he said.

The engineers knew their duty. They reduced pressure in the boilers from 40 to 37 kilos per square centimeter, which dropped the speed of the ship from its cruising velocity of 23 knots to 21.8 knots. This was only a token reduction. In theory, a ship should be able to come to a stop in half the distance of its visibility. But in practice few captains choose to lose time

21

that way. Every extra minute spent at sea burns up additional fuel oil, and every hour late into harbor produces more disgruntled passengers. A ship's captain is evaluated partly on his ability to meet schedules. At its slightly reduced speed the *Andrea Doria* would reach the Ambrose lightship, the last major checkpoint before New York Harbor, at 7:00 A.M., only one hour behind schedule.

Reinforcements arrived in the engine room to stand by in the event that fast maneuvering became necessary. Stopping, or even slowing, a great ship is a difficult job requiring many sets of muscles to twist cumbersome valve wheels. Even with extra manpower the task cannot be done quickly.

Calamai, alert on the bridge, was confident that he could guide the ship safely through despite the excessive speed.

"Close the watertight doors," he ordered, and an officer pressed the switches that activated the safety partitions. Twelve green lights on a control panel changed to red, indicating that the massive steel doors had slammed shut, locking the ship into eleven separate compartments below A Deck.

Watertight compartmentalization was the feature that gave the ship the label "unsinkable." The *Andrea Doria* theoretically could remain afloat if two adjacent compartments were flooded. The watertight doors would keep the remaining nine compartments dry. Only one of the passenger levels, C Deck, rode beneath the waterline, but for safety the watertight doors stretched up past B Deck to the bottom of A Deck. The ship would have to list more than twenty degrees to either side in order for seawater to pour in above the sealed-off sections.

The theory of watertight integrity was a good one, but more useful on a cargo ship or a military vessel. On a passenger liner, designers must always consider the comforts of paying customers. The use of more, smaller compartments would have been safer, but they would inhibit the movement of people through the lower decks. Fewer stairways were also preferable in case water penetrated above the compartments, but passengers flowed up and down the ship in a constant restless dance. They were on vacation. Competition for tourist dollars was important; recreational luxuries must be accessible. Thus, safety was compromisible.

Unconcerned with such theoretical engineering issues at the moment, Calamai continued with his fog precautions.

"Sound the whistle," he ordered. The ship's foghorn began to bellow its six-second blast every one minute and forty seconds, a necessary but always foreboding symbol of a blinded ship steaming through fog.

Calamai sent a seaman up front to the forecastle on the tip of the bow where there was a telephone for quick communication with the bridge should the man spot an approaching hazard.

"Radar," Calamai said. First Officer Carlo Kirn switched on one of the two radar screens and checked to make sure that it worked properly. A bright green line of light swept around the circular scope in synchronization with the antenna on top of the bridge. Serious-faced officers stood ready for critical actions. The *Andrea Doria* was rigged for running in fog.

The 29,082-ton ship had been launched in Genoa at the Ansaldo shipyards on June 16, 1951, after nine million man-hours of labor. Because she was built only three years after the 1948 International Convention for the Safety of Life at Sea, she was equipped with the most modern safety devices available. The *Andrea Doria* had magnetic and gyrocompasses, an automatic pilot, a new device known as loran (*long-range* n*av-*igational instrument) for determining position at sea, radio direction finder equipment, two radar screens, and a complete meteorological station.

The 697-foot hull had a double bottom for extra strength. Various tanks in the deep holds could store nearly four thousand tons of fuel oil, three hundred tons of lighter-grade diesel oil, and four thousand tons of fresh water, all of which could be shifted around to maintain stability.

Throughout the ship, interiors were lined with nonflammable materials. A special fire-resistant insulation separated the steel hull from the cabin paneling. The decks were divided into thirty-three fire safety zones that could be sealed off by automatic doors. The ship had its own automatic sprinkler system, numerous fire extinguishers, a special carbon-dioxide fire-smothering system, and its own hook and ladder company.

The 572-person crew was schooled in emergency procedures. When the *Andrea Doria* had stopped at Naples to embark passengers, the crew had conducted an abandon ship drill. Small groups of crew members received additional safety instructions daily, and every crewman was issued a booklet of regulations that included a personal emergency assignment.

In the event of a catastrophe, the *Andrea Doria* carried sixteen aluminum lifeboats with a capacity of two thousand persons, more than enough to accommodate a full load of passengers and crew. Two of the boats had marine engines and two-way radios.

All of the equipment was inspected and certified by the Registro Navale Italiano and the U.S. Coast Guard.

Thus, when the *Andrea Doria* slid silently into the wall of fog, Calamai and his officers exhibited no special concern. They and their ship were prepared.

She was on a heading of 267 degrees, aiming directly for the Nantucket lightship, a small, red-hulled Coast Guard vessel anchored off the hidden shoals near the coast. The lightship served as the first point of contact with North America for ships approaching from Europe at this critical juncture of shipping lanes, some two hundred miles east of New York. So many ships converged in this area that some veteran seamen referred to the Nantucket coast as "The Times Square of the Atlantic." In 1934, the Greek liner *Olympic*, running in a heavy fog, crashed directly into the lightship, killing all hands on the Coast Guard vessel.

After an hour or so of hushed tension, the officers saw the fog lift suddenly. Calamai relaxed, stopped the foghorn, and allowed the ship to regain speed. He left the bridge to go to his cabin one deck below and write up the logbooks. But the respite was short. The fog rolled in again as rapidly as it had lifted, and Calamai was called back to the bridge.

As he prepared for his duty as a waiter in the cabin-class Dining Room, Giovanni Rovelli saw the fog close in on the ship once more, and it brought with it a premonition. Rovelli remembered similar fog conditions when he had been working on the *San Miguel*. Sailing through a Norwegian fjord, the *San Miguel* had rammed the *Binna*, which sank in fifteen minutes.

The shroud seemed to grow even thicker as evening approached. Sometimes the bow of the ship, two hundred feet forward, was not visible from the bridge. The atmosphere at the command headquarters was still one of professional vigilance, however, rather than alarm. The fog was a challenge these men had met many times in the past, and Calamai's officers considered him one of the best at handling a ship in delicate situations.

There were, in fact, four licensed masters on the bridge that evening. In addition to Calamai, Senior Second Officer Curzio Franchini, thirty-six, stood watch over the radar screen, which was set to a range of twenty miles. He also checked the ship's position frequently with loran. Tall, with heavy black hair, Franchini had graduated from the Italian Naval Academy as a reserve officer, finishing sixteenth in a class of eighty. Tonight he felt the usual excitement generated by the approach to New York.

Third Officer Eugenio Giannini, twenty-eight, assisted Franchini at the radar and frequently went out onto the wings of the bridge to keep watch with Calamai. A stocky man with wavy brown locks and energetic eyes, Giannini knew his role that night was to help wherever needed.

The fourth master present on the bridge was the second in command, Staff Captain Osvaldo Magagnini, who offered to relieve Calamai after his hours of anxious command.

At 8:00 P.M., just as the sun was setting as an undefined glow in the haze, Calamai allowed himself a short break. He left the bridge briefly to change from white into a fresh blue nighttime uniform with gold epaulets on the shoulders, topped by a natty beret. He stopped for a moment in the Belvedere Lounge, located just beneath the bridge, where the first-class passengers gathered nightly for drinks and dancing, and said hello to a few acquaintances. It was a rare social gesture for the shy captain.

He ate his dinner that night on the bridge. Despite the presence of the other officers, Calamai knew it was properly his job to command.

The evening was punctuated by moments of excitement as

WHAT THE ANDREA DORIA SAW

FRANCHINI TESTIMONY:

At 17 miles distance, the pip was 4º north.

At 3½ miles distance, the pip was 15º north.

At 1 mile distance, the Andrea Doria saw the Stockholm 35º - 40º north

CALAMAI TESTIMONY:

At 17 miles distance, the pip was 4º north.

At 5 miles distance, the pip was 14º north.

At 1.1 miles, the Andrea Doria sighted the Stockholm visually 22½º north.

the *Andrea Doria* encountered and overtook several other ships. Franchini or Giannini kept them under radar observation until they steamed safely past. The ships were crossing north or south, or they were slower westbound ships that the speedy *Andrea Doria* overtook from the rear. None of them was eastbound, heading directly toward the *Andrea Doria*, and no one on the bridge expected to discover such a ship. Captains sailing to the east near Nantucket were supposed to take a route twenty miles to the south, thus reducing the hazard of meeting other ships head to head.

About 9:30 P.M., Giannini spotted a pip on the radar, seventeen miles distant from the ship. Franchini took a loran fix of the *Andrea Doria*'s position, then listened with the radio direction finder for the signal sent out by the Nantucket lightship. He plotted the bearing of the signal and then reported to Calamai, "We are headed directly toward the lightship."

"Change to two hundred and sixty-one degrees," Calamai ordered soon after. Giannini relayed the command to the helmsman, and watched as he shifted the spoked wheel slightly to the left until the compass needle rested on 261. The new course would take the ship safely to the south of the Nantucket lightship, with an estimated passage distance of one mile.

At 10:20 P.M., the telephone rang on the bridge. The forecastle lookout reported that he could hear a foghorn off the starboard bow. At the same time Franchini tracked a pip on the radar screen. He followed its movement as revealed by the sweeping flasher. He told Calamai that they were passing the lightship at a distance of one mile.

"Steer two sixty-eight," Calamai commanded, and Giannini ordered the helmsman to swing seven degrees to the right. The *Andrea Doria* now headed almost due west, directly toward New York.

Calamai's feet traced a path on the bridge wing. He looked up at the ship's masthead lights, fuzzy and dim in the heavy fog. Periodically he caught glimpses of stars and the full moon, and he knew that the fog was patchy, rather than a continual dark haze. He shivered slightly in the cool breeze created by the ship's forward motion. The whoop of the foghorn lent an air of solemnity to the misty night. Calamai and Giannini remained out on the wings, their eyes alert for the lights of any approaching ship.

It was 10:45 P.M., Eastern daylight time, when Franchini yelled out to the others from the chartroom, where he was crouched over the dim radar screen.

"It's a ship. We can see a ship," he said.

Giannini went to look. The men watched as the bright green sweep line of the radar moved around the circular screen several times. Each time it revolved it illuminated the small, bean-shaped pip. Franchini noted the change of location with each sweep.

"What's the distance and bearing?" Calamai called out to Franchini.

"Seventeen miles distance and bearing, four degrees on the starboard bow." The unknown ship was almost directly in the line of the *Andrea Doria*'s course. The radar screen showed the pip to be off to the north by a matter of only a few millimeters.

Calamai joined Franchini at the radar while Giannini returned to keep watch on the wing. Franchini studied four indicators on the round cathode ray screen. The first, a series of concentric circles, with the *Andrea Doria* at the center, showed the distance of any foreign body from the ship. A luminous green sliver of light called the *flasher* rotated constantly with the antenna, and with each revolution illuminated the ominous pip in its new location. The *heading flasher* was a stationary line set on the course of the *Andrea Doria*. Another line, the *cursor*, could be manually adjusted. Franchini set the cursor on the position of the pip and could then read the bearing. By comparing the location of the cursor with each new pip, he could follow the progress of the other ship as it moved through the sea.

For his calculations to be valid, Franchini had to be sure that the heading flasher correctly reflected the exact course of his own ship. This was not the bearing ordered by the captain but the precise direction steered by the helmsman at the moment. Even the best helmsman allowed the ship to yaw back and forth slightly. To monitor the course, Franchini glanced at the gyro repeater attached to his radar screen, which reflected the actual compass bearing.

A few sweeps of the flasher told the officers that the ship was not merely a slower one moving west, such as others they had passed that evening. This ship was moving east, toward the *Andrea Doria*. It was disconcerting since the oncoming ship was twenty miles north of the recommended eastbound route.

"I think it is unusual for a ship to be coming eastbound in these waters," Franchini told Captain Calamai.

"Yes, it is very unusual," the captain replied.

Franchini knew his duty was to watch closely and keep track of the bearing of the pip. If the bearing continually increased to the north, it meant that the other ship was on a course that would allow it to pass safely on the starboard side of the *Andrea Doria*. If the bearing decreased, then the ships were on a dangerous course and would have to take evasive action.

Calamai, now back out on the starboard wing, called out, "How's the bearing?"

"It's increasing," Franchini reported. If both ships held

their courses, they would pass safely starboard-to-starboard. When two ships meet head-on in the open sea, they are supposed to pass port-to-port, unless that would force them into a crossing course. Since the other ship was already on the starboard side, to the north, there seemed to be no reason to swing to the right for   normal port-to-port passage. Franchini decided that a starboard-to-starboard passage would be equally safe. Several times Calamai returned to the radar screen to check the pip himself. It was a fast ship—not as speedy as the *Andrea Doria,* but fast nonetheless.

When the other ship was about seven miles ahead, Franchini switched the radar to a range of eight miles. Immediately the pip retreated toward the edge of the screen and grew to more than double its previous size. On the screen it was closing faster now, for the relative sizes and distances had increased.

Franchini did not take the precaution of plotting the progress of the pip on the Marconi Locater Graph that sat nearby in the first drawer of the plotting table. Franchini had not used the device since the ship left Gibraltar five days earlier. To use the plotter, Franchini would have had to note the location of the pip each time the sweep revealed it, correct for any course error shown on the gyro repeater, then transfer that location to the plotting board. By connecting the dots he would be able to monitor the course of the ship and would note any changes. Instead, he set the cursor each time the pip reappeared, so that he could follow the progress only from one reading to the next.

Each reading seemed to confirm his observation that the other ship would pass safely on his starboard, or right, side.

Calamai approached Franchini at the radar. "How close will she pass?" the captain asked.

"About one mile to starboard," Franchini replied.

The captain returned to the bridge wing and searched the horizon. Five minutes later from the wheelhouse, Franchini called the newest radar data. "Bearing fifteen degrees. Range three and a half miles."

Calamai responded with an immediate order. "Steer four degrees to port."

Calamai reasoned that the slight swing to the left would open the gap between the two ships and allow them to pass starboard-to-starboard even farther than the one mile estimated by Franchini. It was also his way of telling the helmsman not to allow the ship to yaw to the right. But the course change was not dramatic enough to be readily apparent to anyone who might be watching a radar screen on the other ship.

The change of course seemed to bring the *Andrea Doria* to an area where the fog was not quite so dense, but Calamai still estimated visibility at less than half a mile. The *Andrea Doria*'s fog whistle continued to send out its wail every hundred seconds.

Calamai and Giannini watched the horizon carefully on the starboard wing. It was important to make visual contact with the other ship at the earliest possible moment, for radar is at best an imprecise aid to navigation. Eyes are more trustworthy. Calamai did not expect to see the other vessel until it was close, because of the fog, but he was puzzled that he did not at least hear its foghorn.

"Why don't we hear her?" Giannini asked the captain. "Why doesn't she whistle?"

Calamai did not reply. His forehead furrowed as he stared into the night. It was a few minutes after 11:00 P.M.

Giannini left the wing to check the radar screen once more and fix in his mind the position where the other ship should appear. "We can't hear the fog whistle," he commented to Franchini. He quickly studied the radar and saw the other ship at a distance of one and a half miles and at a bearing of thirty to thirty-five degrees to the right. He came back outside and searched to starboard with his binoculars. Suddenly he saw a blur of lights some thirty-five degrees off to the right, just as the radar had indicated.

"Did you see?" Giannini said, pointing to the glow.

"Yes, I see," Calamai replied.

Franchini, hearing that the men had made visual contact, abandoned his radar screen and joined the other officers on the right wing of the bridge.

The ships were about one mile apart when the vague glow of the approaching vessel separated into visible masthead lights. The officers studied carefully to determine the course of the other ship. There are four signal lights that reveal the direction of an oncoming vessel. A bright green light glows from the starboard side of the bridge, indicating that the right side of the oncoming ship is visible; or a red light from the port, or left side, indicates the opposite. Two white masthead lights are also key indicators. The lower light is situated forward of the higher light. If the lights are aligned vertically, then the other ship is heading directly toward the observer. If the lower light is to the left or right of the higher light, then the ship is heading in that particular direction.

Giannini pointed his binoculars at the glow and strained to see the masthead lights. There were two white lights, the lower one slightly to the right of the other.

For an instant, Calamai thought the other ship would pass safely to the right. It was perhaps the last serene moment Captain Piero Calamai would ever experience.

Then Giannini focused his binoculars once more on the lights of the approaching ship. He was suddenly confronted with the ghastly realization that the lower masthead light of the other ship was rapidly swinging to the left of the higher masthead light, and the red light on the port side of the other ship was now visible for the first time. Incredibly, unbelievably, the other ship was turning directly toward the *Andrea Doria.*

"She is turning! She is turning!" Giannini exclaimed. "She is showing the red light. She is coming toward us."

Calamai looked anxiously at the approaching ship and verified Giannini's alarm. He had to act quickly, but there was little time. The master's decision was one of desperation. When collision is unavoidable, a ship should turn *toward* danger to minimize impact. A head-on collision of streamlined vessels is more likely to result in a glancing blow. But Calamai could not bring himself to concede the inevitable. His choice was made instantly, but it was the product more of his intense affection for his glorious ship than the hard judgment of years at sea.

"Hard left!" he yelled at Helmsman Giulio Visciano. Even the Italian word for "left," *sinistra,* was foreboding. It was a last daring attempt to outrun a disaster, by turning the *Andrea Doria* to the left faster than the unknown vessel was turning to the right. But in doing so Calamai risked turning the *Andrea Doria* broadside to the other ship.

Visciano swung the wheel to the left with all his strength, using both hands to maintain pressure on the rudder and accelerate the turn. Giannini jumped on the ledge of the middle window in the wheelhouse for a better view of the onrushing ship.

Calamai seemed suddenly immobilized. Franchini knew that they should signal their turn to the other ship.

"The two whistles?" Franchini reminded.

Calamai nodded, and Franchini disconnected the foghorn in order to blow two short blasts, indicating a left turn.

"The engines?" Franchini suggested, wondering whether they should be shut down to lessen impact.

"No," Calamai said. "Don't touch the engines. It turns more rapidly." Still he clung to the hope of outrunning his attacker.

Straining under the hard left rudder, the *Andrea Doria* slid forward for perhaps half a mile before the turn took effect.

"Is she turning? Is she turning?" Giannini asked Visciano imploringly.

"Now," the helmsman replied, "she is beginning to turn." Giannini heard the click of the gyrocompass recording the change of direction. But instead of easing the *Andrea Doria* away from the menacing ship coming toward them, the turn exposed the broad mass of the *Doria*'s side, like a target, to the onrushing bow of the other vessel.

"She is coming against us!" Calamai yelled in amazement.

The captain instinctively drew back from the railing of the wing. The bow of the intruder seemed to point directly at him on the bridge, though he knew it would hit much lower, probably no higher than the Upper Deck, some forty feet below. For an instant Calamai wished he was down there, where the impact would crush him. It would be an act of mercy, for the captain saw in the approaching bow a more horrible destiny. He was a captain! This was his ship! How could this happen to him?

Never in all his years at sea had Piero Calamai felt so alone.

3

THE SHIP

By 1956, the golden age of the transatlantic passenger liner was in its dotage. Civilization was switching gears. The time-is-money generation threatened the end of an era. Still, there were holdouts: those with air-travel phobias, emigrants carrying their possessions to a new land, those who obstinately refused to hurry, and those with the discretionary money to purchase pampering.

The 1134 passengers on board the *Andrea Doria* were a cosmopolitan lot, not unlike the diverse occupants of a large city. Among the 190 first-class passengers were two movie actresses, two celebrated ballet stars, the mayor of Philadelphia, a former general manager of the Atomic Energy Commission, the Madrid correspondent of *The New York Times*, the circulation director of the *San Francisco Chronicle*, and many prominent businessmen and their families.

The 267 cabin-class passengers were largely middle-income families enjoying a rare vacation. Tourist class was quite different. Most of the 677 tourist-class occupants were Italian families from poor country villages huddled in relatively small cabins. Though tourist class was, in effect, the ship's ghetto, it was still comfortable, and the emigrant children gaped at modest conveniences that would be delights back home.

Segregation was practiced on a cash basis. Vigilantly class-conscious, the *Andrea Doria* was the first transatlantic liner to provide a separate swimming pool for each of the three classes of passengers. Separate ballrooms, lounges, dining rooms, cardrooms, gymnasiums, movie theaters, and deck promenades were maintained. The security was often violated by curious teenagers, but for the most part the passengers kept to their own. Only the chapel and the hospital were open to all.

There were ten passenger decks. Topmost was the small Belvedere Deck crowned with a single stack that proudly displayed the red, white, and green colors of Italy.

Below that, on the Sun Deck, was the command center. Here in the wheelhouse Captain Calamai and his officers directed the ship. Then came the Lido Deck, a first-class area (except for a portion devoted to officers' cabins), with a children's playroom, gymnasium, solarium, massage parlor, and a swimming pool surrounded by buffets and bars.

Below that was the Boat Deck, where the sixteen aluminum lifeboats hung from davits, a conspicuous reminder of the remote perils of the sea. On the front of the Boat Deck, directly beneath the bridge, was the Belvedere Lounge, the favorite late-night gathering spot for the first-class passengers. The Boat Deck was circled by an open promenade, where many strolled in the fresh air.

Next came the Promenade Deck, the social heart of the ship, housing the ballrooms and lounges for the first- and cabin-class passengers. At the rear was the popular village square for the emigrants, the tourist-class swimming pool. Walkways, closed in from the sea by large windows, circled the Promenade Deck.

Below, on the curiously named Upper Deck (there were five levels above it), were the majority of the spacious first-class cabins. Then came the Foyer Deck, the ship's Main Street. It featured a row of specialty shops, clothing stores, a bank, and the purser's office. Just forward of the main foyer was the Gothic chapel with Romanesque columns and original frescoes. The *Andrea Doria* was a favorite of the many priests and nuns who traveled between Rome and the United States.

On either side of the chapel were four deluxe first-class suites, each appointed by a different Italian designer. The suites were the largest, costliest accommodations on board. Amidships, on the Foyer Deck, where the rolling motion of the ship was least noticeable, was the first-class Dining Room.

A Deck housed cabin-class passengers as well as the ship's ten-room hospital, staffed by two doctors and five nurses.

Tourist-class cabins were jammed into the fore and aft sections of B and C Decks, split in the middle by the cavernous engine room where the power of fifty thousand horses spun two thick axles, each turning a three-blade propeller that was nineteen feet in diameter. B Deck housed the garage, where nine automobiles were stored, including a Rolls-Royce that belonged to Miami Beach socialite Edward Parker and a $150,000 experimental car built by Ghia in Turin, Italy, for the Chrysler Corporation.

Below C Deck, cargo holds were filled with silks, woolens, cottons, furniture, olive oil, wine, Olivetti business equipment, and Necchi sewing machines. Below the holds were the deep tanks for fuel and water.

The *Andrea Doria* was a world of her own, and for a full week passengers forgot that Gamal Abdel Nasser was claiming the Suez Canal for Egypt, that Vice President Richard M. Nixon was fighting to remain on the ticket for President Eisenhower's reelection bid, and that a singer named Elvis Presley was exposing his new young fans to explicit sexual gyrations.

No, the world could take care of itself for a week. There were more important considerations, such as swimming, sunning, table tennis, volleyball, shuffleboard, gymnastics, trapshooting, bingo, cards, and shipboard horseracing. There were leisurely walks to take on the open promenade of the Boat Deck, elegant dinners to eat in the quiet dining rooms, parties and dances to attend in the ballrooms.

Though the threat was then clear, shipping companies refused to capitulate easily to airliners. They fought back with vessels that reflected the personalities of the flags they carried. The *United States*, built in 1952, was considered antiseptic by some, but could cross the Atlantic in a record three and one-half days. The *Queen Elizabeth*, refurbished in 1946 after carrying troops during World War II, was the largest passenger ship in the world, but was cumbersome and already obsolete. The *Ile de France*, built in 1927 but completely refitted in 1949, was the sophisticated grande dame of the fifties, old but freshly powdered.

Italy could not compete on the basis of size nor speed, but could tap into a classical heritage second to none. When the *Andrea Doria* was outfitted for transatlantic service in 1953, she was big, nearly seven hundred feet long from bow to stern, but not the biggest; fast at twenty-three knots, but not the fastest. What she was, was beautiful. Some said she was the prettiest ship in the world. Her black hull held a gleaming white superstructure. All her vertical lines were angled backward, creating an illusion of movement even when the ship was at rest.

It was the interior decor, however, that made her unique. Stepping inside the ship brought a sudden encounter with Renaissance glories. The Italian Line had commissioned scores of artists to decorate the ship with a wide variety of original canvases, murals, frescoes, tapestries, sculptures, and mirrors.

The focal point of its artwork was the first-class Lounge on the Promenade Deck. Here, artist Salvatore Fiume had created a giant mural that surrounded passengers with a tribute to Raphael, Michelangelo, and other Italian masters. Near the mural was a massive bronze statue of a sixteenth-century admiral, clad in battle armor, a huge sword at his side. It was Andrea Doria himself.

Overhead hung a large silver crest, the coat of arms of the man who was perhaps the second-most famous Italian admiral (after Christopher Columbus), having been the father of Genoese independence. The crest hung for centuries in the admiral's Genoese mansion and was donated to the ship by the Marquis Giambattista Doria.

Many a passenger, seeing the display for the first time, suddenly realized that the great ship was named after a man, not a woman. "An-*dre*-a," the Italian sailors politely corrected when someone said "*An*-dre-a."

The first-class Ballroom was the site of the traditional Captain's Ball, normally held the night before arrival in port. But Captain Calamai scheduled the event for Tuesday evening, July 24, because the ship was scheduled to arrive in New York so early Thursday morning. He reasoned that many passengers would want to retire early on Wednesday. On Tuesday night Calamai had grudgingly put in an appearance at the party, fixing a polite smile and muttering greetings in standard English phrases.

Wednesday morning, July 25, dawned bright and warm, but there was a new mood discernible among the passengers. The voyage was nearly over, and some of the leisurely pursuits gave way to the packing of luggage, exchanging addresses with new acquaintances, and the emotional gear-shifting necessary to move back into normal routine.

Robert Young sat near the first-class swimming pool that afternoon after a buffet lunch and indulged in a critique of the ship and her crew. He was on vacation with his family, but could not ignore his professional interest. He was principal surveyor, or inspector, for the Western European division of the American Bureau of Shipping, one of the two major organizations that certified ships as seaworthy for insurance purposes. He became concerned as soon as the fog rolled in about three o'clock that afternoon. It was not one solid cloud of moisture, but rather that peculiar kind of patchy fog that would suddenly lift for a few moments, then close in again rapidly. That, Young knew, was the most dangerous kind because it created sporadic conditions. He hated fog at sea.

Once during the afternoon the ship emerged suddenly from the haze and Young was shocked to see a cargo ship cutting sharply across the wake of the *Andrea Doria*, much too close for comfort.

He tried unsuccessfully to hide his anxiety from his family. His trained ear knew that the *Andrea Doria* had not slowed her engines significantly. Young knew the ship was making at least twenty knots, almost top speed, probably twice as fast as she should be traveling.

Young also knew that the *Andrea Doria*, like other liners, would be more vulnerable to danger near the end of a voyage. The ship's fuel and freshwater tanks were low. The captain could order the empty tanks filled with seawater, but this was generally not the practice. It would be an expensive and lengthy job to pump the water out in New York before the ship could refuel.

The ship was "tender," almost top-heavy. Young knew that if for some unlikely reason the ship took a list, it would be difficult to stabilize her. But Young dismissed the concern from his mind. He would leave the safety of the *Andrea Doria* to Captain Calamai and his crew. After all, he was on vacation.

The previous night's social event made Wednesday evening seem anticlimactic to some. The fun was over, and life ashore was to begin again the next morning. As Calamai had predicted, by ten o'clock many tired couples began drifting out of the social rooms toward their cabins on the layered decks below. By eleven, about half the passengers were in bed.

There remained, however, a stubborn corps of dedicated partygoers who were not yet ready to let the voyage end. Fun-lovers gathered in the tourist-class Social Hall on the Upper Deck, one level higher in the cabin-class Ballroom on the Promenade Deck, or still higher in the first-class Belvedere Lounge just beneath the bridge.

All, of course, were unaware that the decision to party or not to party, to sleep or not to sleep, was not one of those trivial choices that abound in normal circumstances. In a short time, some would see clearly how the mystical workings of chance would order their lives.

Others would never know.

4

THE PLAYERS

THE WHEEL OF FORTUNE spun quickly, the staccato click of its pointer generating excitement throughout the ornate first-class Ballroom on the Promenade Deck of the *Andrea Doria*. Gradually the wheel slowed and the pointer came to rest on number three. Winners grinned and losers tore up their betting tickets as a steward stepped up to move a large wooden horse head, number three, forward one square across the finish line of a multicolored pattern spread out on the dance floor. Even though the crowd was fascinated by the gaming, their numbers were thinner than usual.

It was slightly past ten o'clock that Wednesday evening. Many of the gambling devotees had gone to their cabins below in anticipation of an early-morning arrival in New York. Others had forgone the festivities for a quiet refreshment in the lounges above deck, or lingered in the dining rooms.

From her seat at one of the tables in the first-class Dining Room, Beverly Green chatted with her friend Jean Ruth as she sipped an after-dinner drink. Mrs. Green, an attractive, petite woman, hoped that the ship would dock in New York Harbor on time. The next morning she and her husband, Alfred, planned to drive out to Jamaica Race Track to see their four-year-old colt, Hartsville, run in the seventh race.

The Greens were veterans of ocean travel. Each summer Alfred took time away from his New York garment-manufacturing business for a long vacation. This was, however, their first voyage on the *Andrea Doria*, and, unlike most of the other passengers, Beverly Green was not delighted with the ship. Dressing for dinner that night, she told her husband, "I prefer the French Line. Next year let's take the *Ile de France*."

"Fine," Alfred agreed. Unknown to the couple, the *Ile de France* at that moment was passing the *Andrea Doria* in the opposite direction on her way to Le Havre, France.

Jean and Donald Ruth were prior acquaintances who had encountered the Greens in Capri. They were delighted to learn that they were returning from their vacations on the same ship. Donald Ruth was a Long Island, New York, realtor. The Greens invited the Ruths to join them for late drinks in the Belvedere Lounge, high up on the front of the Boat Deck.

About 10:30 P.M., as the Greens and Ruths were finishing dinner, a third couple approached the table. Colonel Walter G. Carlin and his wife, Jeanette, were considerably older than their friends. Walter Carlin, a man in his sixties, was enjoying semiretirement. For years he had been a successful attorney and a potent political boss in his Democratic ward in Brooklyn. Jeanette Carlin was a heavy woman with long, red-brown hair that hung down to her shoulders. She had an easy sense of humor that delighted Beverly Green. The Carlins roomed in cabin 46 next to the Ruths' cabin 48 in the first-class section on the Upper Deck. By coincidence they were also assigned deck chairs next to the Greens, so the three couples became frequent shipboard companions.

"Will you join us in the lounge for a drink?" Jeanette Carlin asked Beverly Green.

"We've already invited Jean and Donald," Mrs. Green replied. "Why don't you join us?"

Mrs. Carlin appeared ready to accept the invitation, but her husband looked tired and doubtful. "Why don't we just go up, pack, and get ready for bed?" he said.

Carlin extended his arm to his wife and together they

walked out of the dining room. Beverly Green smiled at them and nudged her husband. "When I grow old," she said, "I want to be just like Mrs. Carlin."

The Carlins made their way to an elevator near the middle of the ship. They rode up one level to the Upper Deck, then walked forward through the hallway past the Ruths' empty cabin, to their number 46. It was on the starboard side, about one-third of the way back from the bow and almost directly beneath the Belvedere Lounge. The cabin was spacious and comfortable, with two single beds separated by a dressing table.

Meanwhile, the Greens and Ruths left the dining room and rode an elevator three levels up to the Boat Deck, and walked forward to the Belvedere Lounge. The elegant lounge was decorated with tapestries, paintings, and wood carvings set against glossy blond paneling—all accented by soft, indirect lighting. Fresh flowers garnished the room for this last night. Windows on three sides normally provided a panorama of the open sea ahead of the ship, but tonight the view was obscured by a thick fog.

It was slightly past 11:00 P.M., when, about thirty feet below the Greens and the Ruths, Jeanette Carlin selected a book from her luggage and pulled the covers of her bed over her to escape the air conditioning. Walter Carlin walked down a narrow passageway of the cabin that extended back toward the corridor. The bathroom was located at the end of the passageway. Just as he pulled out his toothbrush, he steadied himself against a sharp left turn the ship seemed to be making.

Dinner was to have been a special event for Linda Morgan that night. As the slender, brown-haired fourteen-year-old walked with her family along the open promenade high up on the Boat Deck, she clutched her Camp Fire Girls' autograph book to her side. Tonight the family was to dine with the captain, and Linda wanted his signature in the book that already contained the names of Jimmy Stewart, Gregory Peck, Cary Grant, and John Steinbeck. Linda was no stranger to celebrities—her father was Edward P. Morgan, whose nightly newscast on the ABC radio network was popular throughout the United States.

Linda's parents were divorced in 1946 and her mother, Jane, forty, was now married to Camille Cianfarra, forty-nine, the Madrid correspondent of The *New York Times*. After four years in Spain, The *Times* had granted Cianfarra a furlough, and he was bringing his wife, Jane, their eight-year-old daughter Joan, and Linda back to America. He had earlier reservations on the *Leonardo da Vinci*, another Italian Line ship, but business had forced him to postpone the trip.

A stroll on the deck before dinner was a ritual for the Cianfarras, but tonight the usual carefree mood was absent. "I feel like I'm in an envelope," Linda commented to Joan.

A thick vapor encased the ship. Linda could not even see across to the other side, ninety feet away. The glow of artificial lighting from the interior rooms mixed with the fog like a yellow shroud. The deep bass of the methodical foghorn accented the gloom.

Camille Cianfarra suggested that they cut short their walk and go directly to dinner. The family climbed into an elevator that took them down to the first-class Dining Room.

The maître d' greeted them at the doorway with an apologetic expression. "I'm sorry," he said, "the captain will not be able to join you for dinner this evening. He must remain on the bridge. Because of the fog." Calamai probably would not have joined them in any event, but obviously felt he could not even spare a subordinate.

Disappointed, Linda set her autograph book next to her dinner plate and hoped that the captain might at least stop by to say hello.

While the family waited for dinner, the newsman in Camille Cianfarra surfaced. "Wouldn't it be fantastic if the *Andrea Doria* crashed in the fog?" he asked rhetorically. "Think of the exclusive we'd have for The *Times!*"

The *Times* correspondent's dark eyes danced, but his wife saw the girls' concern at the jest. "Don't worry," she reassured, "the captain is doing his duty."

After dinner, the Cianfarras could not decide whether to stay awake or go to bed early. They played the horse-racing game for a while in the first-class Ballroom. During the trip Cianfarra had won $95 at bingo and another $45 for making the closest estimate of the length of a day's voyage. But tonight his good luck had ended. After losing at the races he yawned and decided he was sleepy. "Let's go to bed," he suggested, and the others agreed.

Linda Morgan followed her family down to the Upper Deck and along the corridor to cabins 52 and 54. These adjoining rooms had originally been booked by George P. Kerr, the European Manager of Proctor & Gamble, his wife Matheson and their daughter Kyrie. The Kerrs were on their way from their home in Rome to a holiday in Mexico. They had boarded the ship in Naples. "I don't want to be with you all the time," thirteen-year-old Kyrie had complained to her parents. "I'm grown up now." Kerr had his daughter moved to a single cabin high up on the Boat Deck, while he and his wife switched to cabin 67 on the port side of the Upper Deck. When the Cianfarras boarded the ship in Gibraltar, cabins 52 and 54 were available.

Linda and Joan were in 52. The two half sisters chatted excitedly about the morning. Joan brushed at her dark bangs. Linda set her autograph book onto a table next to her bed and slipped into her yellow pajamas decorated with Chinese writing.

The doorway adjoining their parents' cabin opened and the Cianfarras walked in to say good night.

"No talking," the father admonished. "We have to get up early, so you two get right to sleep."

"We will," the girls promised.

Linda moved her head firmly into her three pillows on her bed next to the porthole. "I'm glad we brought these extra pillows," she said. "They're so comfortable."

Linda reached for the light switch and the stateroom went dark.

Dr. Thure Peterson ordered a half bottle of champagne with dinner. "We'll celebrate," he said to his wife, Martha; "it's our last night out."

A white-jacketed steward brought the champagne in a silver ice bucket that mirrored the reflected light of massive crystal chandeliers overhead. The Petersons talked softly together as they ate their dinner. Martha had been right. The relaxing voyage was just what they needed, instead of two weeks of busy sight-seeing in Italy.

The couple was returning home to Upper Montclair, New Jersey, after a month-long vacation in Sweden, Denmark, and Switzerland. Thure Peterson, a burly man with a high hairline exposing a pink scalp, and iron gray temples that gave him the distinguished appearance of a "Dr.," was endowed with great energy. But his frantic schedule had worn him out. As president of the Chiropractic Institute of New York, he had been persuaded to lecture to a chiropractors convention in Switzerland. The unscheduled work cost the couple a week of their vacation.

Guilty that he had taken the time away from Martha, Peterson had tried to extend the trip two weeks so they could tour Italy. He attempted to change their reservations from the *Andrea Doria* to another Italian Line ship, the *Cristoforo Colombo*, scheduled to sail two weeks later. But the *Cristoforo Colombo* was fully booked. Instead, he made airline reservations for July 26. Martha finally persuaded him that a week on an ocean liner would be more relaxing than foot-wearying sight-seeing. The Petersons decided to honor their original reservations and had boarded the *Andrea Doria* at Cannes, France, on July 17.

Thure Peterson sat back in his chair in the dining room, lit his pipe, and sipped at the last of his champagne. At fifty-seven he knew that it was good for him to slow down. The effect of the sumptuous late dinner, the champagne, and the twenty-five-hour days (as the ship crossed into new time zones) brought on premature sleepiness. Dr. Peterson checked his watch. It was 10:30 P.M.

"Let's turn in early," he suggested.

The couple left the dining room on the Foyer Deck and walked past the fashionable ladies' dress shop where mannequins behind plate glass displayed the latest Italian fashions.

They stepped through the main foyer area and up a flight of stairs to the Upper Deck. They found their cabin, 56, next to the Cianfarras.

The chiropractor and his wife had no way of knowing that their room had previously been assigned to two other families. Robert Young, the shipping inspector, was concerned about his wife's sensitive stomach, and had asked to be switched from cabin 56 to a room back toward the middle of the ship where the rolling motion would be less discernible.

Cabin 56 was then assigned to Nora Kovach, twenty-four, and her husband, Istvan Rabovsky, twenty-six, Hungarian ballet dancers who had been granted asylum in the West in 1953. Having completed a European dancing tour, they were returning to their new home in the United States. But when they boarded the *Andrea Doria* at Genoa they complained that cabin 56 cost $60 more than they wanted to pay. They were switched to cabin 77, a smaller, less expensive room about midships on the portside. The seemingly unpopular cabin 56 was then given to the Petersons.

Dr. Peterson slipped the key into the lock, and as the door opened he noticed immediately that the maid had confused their beds. She had placed Martha's white nylon nightgown on Thure's bed near the porthole, and put Thure's bathrobe on Martha's bed.

The doctor asked his wife if she wanted to change beds. "No," she answered. When they had first seen the cabin, Martha had walked over to the porthole to look out. She discovered that she was too small, only five feet three inches, to see out. There was no reason for her to sleep next to the water. She chose the bed against the corridor wall, adjacent to an elevator shaft.

The couple prepared for bed. Martha turned on the reading light over her bed and opened a book. Thure Peterson threw off his robe and crawled nude into his bunk. Cabin 56 grew quiet.

Father John Dolciamore, thirty, and Father Richard Wojcik, thirty-three, had planned to go to bed right after dinner. But as they ate in the dining room a third priest approached them. He was fifty-six-year-old Father Paul Lambert, pastor of St. Philomena's Catholic Church in Lansdowne, Pennsylvania, whom they had befriended during the voyage. Every night since leaving Naples the three priests had played a game of Scrabble.

The middle-aged priest presented a sharp contrast to the two slim, younger clerics. He always wore a long black priestly cape to cover his immense body. His extraordinary girth and clerical garb made him stand out among the *Andrea Doria* passengers.

"How about a farewell game tonight?" Lambert asked. He was a friend to the two younger priests, and they did not want to disappoint him. But they wanted to be fresh in the morning for their train ride back to the Chicago archdiocese.

"We plan on getting up pretty early tomorrow," Wojcik said. "Maybe we should forget it for tonight."

Lambert's face drooped. "Come on," he said, "it's our last chance."

"Perhaps we could play quickly," Dolciamore suggested.

Lambert agreed to hurry through his dinner and join them soon. Dolciamore and Wojcik left the dining room, took the elevator up to the Boat Deck, and found a table in the quiet cardroom just behind the Belvedere Lounge. Lambert soon joined them, appearing like a huge apparition, with his snowy white hair.

"It's a long walk up here," Lambert complained good-naturedly. "My feet hurt." The man's great bulk caused chronic circulation problems.

He eased himself into his chair with a grateful sigh. "I'm glad this cruise is almost over. I'll tell you a secret," he said, lowering his voice, "I'm scared to death of water."

As they arranged the letter tiles for their game, the three men talked about the fog, and of the difficulty in navigating the ship in such blinding conditions. "I guess they've got radar," Lambert said nervously. "I hope they know how to use it."

The Scrabble game dragged. Dolciamore checked his watch

and saw that it was already past 11:00 P.M. He hoped the game would end soon. He and Wojcik could then go to sleep in their cabin, number 58, next to the Petersons.

Among the sleepier passengers sitting in the Belvedere Lounge was Marion W. Boyer. For three years he had held one of the most demanding jobs in the postwar world, general manager of the Atomic Energy Commission. Now he was a director of Standard Oil Company of New Jersey. He sat at a table with other Standard Oil officers and directors who had been traveling through Europe on a study tour and vacation.

After dinner that night, Marion Boyer had said to his wife, "Let's not bother to go up to the Belvedere Lounge. We have to get off the ship early tomorrow morning. If we're smart, we'll be at the head of the line."

Mrs. Boyer frowned. "This is our last night aboard. Maybe they'll put on a good show."

Reluctantly, Marion Boyer followed his wife up to the elegant lounge. She was a night person, still alert in the early hours of the morning. He was not. He sat drinking *Faching-wasser* while Mrs. Boyer happily watched the passengers dance.

Boyer stifled a yawn. He found the active leisure of shipboard life exhausting. Shortly before 11:00 P.M., he nudged his wife. "Let's go get some sleep now. We have to get up early."

"First, I'd like to have another cup of coffee," Mrs. Boyer insisted.

Boyer reluctantly ordered the coffee. Mrs. Boyer suddenly turned to watch a vivacious woman dance past their table, smiling at her partner. Every eye focused on the woman in the bright sheath evening gown who had become the center of conversation in the ship's first-class section. She was Ruth Roman, at age thirty-two a veteran actress in more than twenty motion pictures. Miss Roman was returning from a European vacation accompanied by her three-year-old son Dickie Hall and a nurse-companion, Grace Els. Dickie was born during Miss Roman's marriage to Mortimer Hall, a Los Angeles

47

radio station owner. The child was asleep in cabin 82 on the Upper Deck, while Grace Els sat patiently with him.

It was getting late. Many of the guests had begun to leave. Marion Boyer wanted to join them; he could not stay awake. The Boyers occupied room 178 on the Foyer Deck, directly below the Carlins and the Ruths. Boyer waited with growing impatience as his wife drained the last of her coffee.

"All right, now let's go," he said, rising up from his chair. "It's past eleven."

"Wait till I finish my cigarette," Mrs. Boyer retorted.

Her husband, annoyed, sat back down.

The voyage had been an absolute fantasy for thirteen-year-old Peter Thieriot. Every year his parents took a grand vacation, but this year he, too, had been invited as a reward for his graduation from grammar school. Ferdinand Thieriot, thirty-five, was circulation director of the *San Francisco Chronicle*, a newspaper owned by his socialite family. He and his wife, Frances, thirty-six, had flown with Peter to England, where the boy stayed on a friend's farm while his parents ran with the bulls at Pamplona. Then Peter rejoined them for the rest of the vacation.

The Thieriots originally planned to fly home, but Frances persuaded her husband to try a voyage. At a Madrid travel office they were informed that the *Andrea Doria* would stop at Gibraltar. Thieriot asked for a suite with adjoining rooms, but none was available. Instead Ferdinand and Frances reserved one-half of deluxe suite 180 for themselves, knowing they would have to share it with another couple. Peter was assigned to a small room by himself about fifty feet farther aft.

The *Andrea Doria* did not dock at Gibraltar, but anchored offshore, forcing the Thieriots to take a tugboat out to board the ship. As they approached the liner the elder Thieriot, a Phi Beta Kappa scholar who thrived on detail, looked up at the ship. "See that doorway?" he asked Peter. "That leads to the foyer where we'll board. And see that porthole to the right of the door? That's our suite."

"Terrific," Peter said dryly. He was more fascinated by the vast hull of the ship. He had built many models of ships like this, but his young imagination never dreamed of the reality. The *Andrea Doria* was longer than two football fields.

Peter quickly made friends with some of the other teenagers on board, and spent most of his days with them. In the evenings, however, he grumbled when he had to dress for dinner in the formal dining room.

After dinner that Wednesday evening, Peter sat in the first-class Ballroom fascinated by the spinning wheel of fortune which determined the outcome of the horse-race game. The last spin was a disappointing moment, a sign that the voyage was practically over. As stewards cleared the horse-racing paraphernalia, Peter knew his parents would feel it was time for him to be in bed.

As if to confirm his suspicion, Ferdinand Thieriot glanced at his watch. "Time to hit the sack," he announced. Peter started to protest that it was the last night out, then he saw that his parents, too, were ready to leave. "We all have to get up early," Ferdinand Thieriot said. He turned to the couple seated with them.

"Coming?" he asked.

"No. I think we'll go up to the lounge and have a drink," said Max Passante, a pleasant, forty-four-year-old geologist, who had become a shipboard grandfather to Peter. "We'll be down to bed later. See you in the morning." Passante was president of a Denver research firm known as Geotech, Inc. He and his wife had reserved half of suite 180 before Ferdinand Thieriot had booked passage.

The Thieriots left the Passantes in the Ballroom and walked two levels down to the Foyer Deck. Frances Thieriot walked Peter to his room across from the ladies' dress shop.

"Now you go right to bed," she instructed kindly. "We're going to have to get up at six."

Frances Thieriot then walked forward to deluxe suite 180, located on the starboard side of the ship directly across from the chapel and beneath the Cianfarras and Petersons. Each time she entered the rooms she marveled at their elegance.

Frances Thieriot had taken many cruises, but she was particularly impressed with the *Andrea Doria*.

Ferdinand was waiting for her. Frances undressed and joined him.

One of the passengers absent from the Belvedere Lounge that evening was fifty-seven-year-old Richardson C. Dilworth, the mayor of Philadelphia. He had been in office for six months, winning the post after a tiring campaign. By the summer of 1956, both he and his wife, Ann, were ready for a vacation. They had toured France and Italy and had stopped off in Monaco for an audience with Princess Grace. Unfortunately, the audience was canceled when the princess was detained in Paris.

A fastidious gentleman with a professorial air, Dilworth had authored a remarkable political story. His campaign benefited from his World War II record as a Marine Corps Reserve major (he was badly wounded at Guadalcanal) and his local renown as a formidable trial lawyer. But in an era when marital scandal normally spelled political death, Dilworth had won the mayor's job despite an earlier divorce.

Dilworth had overcome an even greater political debit than divorce. He was a reformed alcoholic, a fact known to the local press but professionally ignored in those pre-Watergate days. During the voyage, he devoted hours to his two favorite pastimes, reading and dining. He had been delighted to find Ruth Roman on board and, in fact, in the adjacent cabin. During the cruise he and Ann introduced themselves to the actress, who invited them to visit her in California.

That Wednesday night, the Dilworths were tired. The mayor knew that his vacation would end at the dock in New York. His driver would be there to propel him to Philadelphia and the business of the city.

Before dinner he asked a ship's officer if the fog would delay their arrival. He was assured that the *Andrea Doria* could make almost top speed in fog. They would arrive only an hour or two late.

"Tomorrow's going to be so busy," he said to Ann as they finished dinner, "let's go to bed now."

"OK. I want to get up early anyway. I want breakfast before we get off."

The Dilworths walked to cabin 80, on the starboard side of the Upper Deck, down the corridor from the Carlins, Cianfarras, and Petersons. The mayor began to undress. "I guess I'll just leave my clothes here tonight," he said, arranging his suit neatly on a hanger near the foot of the bed. "There's no sense in packing them away in the wardrobe if we're going to get back into them so early tomorrow."

In the tourist-class Social Hall, Paul Sergio presided at an impromptu party for his extended family. He watched with open pride as his playful nephews and nieces devoured their ice cream. Several other passengers had brought concertinas into the hall and couples danced, while others sang. The mood was one of festivity mixed with apprehension, as the emigrant families prepared for their arrival on the legendary shore of America.

Paul Sergio knew that the United States was a good country. Originally from a poor village in Calabria in southern Italy, Sergio had traveled to New York as a young man. Already an accomplished cobbler, he easily found steady work. He saved his wages until he could afford to return to Calabria in 1927 to marry his girlfriend, Margaret. Two years later he brought his wife and infant son, Tony, to South Bend, Indiana, where they settled. Eventually Sergio opened a shoe repair shop directly behind the Golden Dome on the campus of Notre Dame University. He became a fixture at the school.

Meanwhile, as often happens in small European villages, Paul's younger brother Ross married Margaret's sister Maria. Ross journeyed to South Bend to live with his brother while he saved enough money to bring Maria and their four children to the United States.

By 1956 Margaret was anxious to return to Calabria to visit her aging mother. Brother Ross's family could travel back with them. Ross's wife, Maria Sergio, was supposed to bring her children to the United States in April, but her oldest daughter contracted a cold and immigration authorities would not allow her to make the trip. Now Paul and Margaret Sergio were shepherding the young mother and her children across the Atlantic on the *Andrea Doria*.

Paul Sergio opened his pocketbook this last night out for the special treat of ice cream for Maria's four children: Giuseppe, thirteen, Anna Maria, ten, Domenica, seven, and little four-year-old Rocco. "How beautiful the children are," he said to Maria. "How lucky they are to be traveling to America so young, with their whole lives to live."

At 10:30 P.M., the Sergio family left the Social Hall and went down to Maria's cabin, number 656, on the starboard side of C Deck. Paul and Margaret Sergio helped Maria prepare the children for bed.

Little Rocco, dressed in fresh pajamas, jumped into his uncle's arms. "Can I sleep in your room tonight?" he asked. "Please, Uncle Paul?"

Paul shook his crew cut in kindly refusal. "No. You've got to get your sleep tonight," he said. "You can't stay up too late. We're going to dock in only a few hours. We'll see you in the morning."

"You come and get me, Uncle Paul," Rocco said.

The gentle man tossed Rocco onto his bed. "OK."

Paul and Margaret Sergio left. A sailor on duty opened a doorway and let them through the watertight door back into the compartment where their cabin was located. In their cabin, Paul stepped over to the washbasin. Margaret slipped into her nightclothes and began to say her rosary.

An attractive young Italian woman in a low-cut red evening gown was among the most exuberant passengers at a table in the bar near the tourist-class swimming pool. For 24-year-old Liliana Dooner the excitement had built each day of the voyage. She spoke to her friends about her husband, George, a handsome young U.S. sailor she had met when he was as-

signed to the naval air station in Naples. After he was trans-
fered back to the United States, Liliana had to wait years for
permission to join him. Their daughter, Maria, only six days
shy of her third birthday, was asleep down in cabin 641 on C
Deck, in the care of a baby-sitter.

Mrs. Dooner could have flown to America, but airplanes
frightened her. She had sought passage on the *Andrea Doria*
but was told at the ticket office in Naples that the beautiful
liner was fully booked. Two days prior to sailing, the office had
called back. Space was now available due to a cancellation.
When the young mother informed the ticket agent that her
daughter was subject to seasickness, he arranged a cabin on
the lowest deck, where the motion of the ship was less noticeable.

Mrs. Dooner spent much of the voyage caring for her child,
who suffered severely from nausea during the trip. Liliana
used the few minutes available to herself each day to swim in
the tourist-class pool. She was an expert swimmer and a champion 800-meter runner. In Naples, she had worked as a nude
artist's model and had appeared as an extra in an Italian
film.

Just before 11:00 P.M. on Wednesday night, Liliana suddenly rose from her table in the tourist-class bar. "I have to go
down to my room and check Maria," she explained to her
friends.

"Why?" an older woman responded. "She's OK. If she gets
sick, the baby-sitter will call you."

"No, I must go." Liliana could not explain the impulse, nor
the anxiety that suddenly engulfed her. The two previous
nights she had dreamed that the *Andrea Doria* had sunk.

It was a long, mazelike journey down from the bar to cabin
641. On the port side below the waterline, the cabin was a long,
narrow room with beds at either end and a large wardrobe in
the middle.

Maria was sleeping peacefully. Liliana could not understand why she had raced down. She was thinking of returning
to her friends when she suddenly felt the ship lean into a sharp
left turn. Liliana steadied herself against the wardrobe.

The passengers this night could be evenly divided between those who chose to celebrate on the higher decks and those who chose to sleep in their cabins in anticipation of the morning's arrival. Of the sleepers, none rested more soundly than a young merchant sailor from New Orleans, Robert Lee Hudson. Hudson was a passenger on the *Andrea Doria,* not a crewman, but he was hardly enjoying the voyage. He had signed onto the freighter *Ocean Victory,* but was injured in two separate accidents which left him with two painful herniated discs in his back, an eight-inch cut on his right hand, and a nearly severed index finger. He was put off at Gibraltar to await the next ship to America. That ship was the *Andrea Doria.*

Hudson was assigned to a cabin near the men's ward of the ship's hospital. But his injuries were so painful that he spent most of the voyage in a hospital bed, rather than in his cabin. Feeling better late this Wednesday afternoon, he decided to explore the ship. Walking slowly, he shuffled through the A Deck corridor from the center of the ship to the stern, a distance of three hundred yards. Then he climbed up three levels to the Promenade Deck, where a trapshooting contest was in progress. Hudson slumped wearily in a deck chair.

An hour later, he retraced his steps. He had not slept well in the ship's hospital. He felt he would rest more soundly in the cabin and decided to retire early, at about 7:00 P.M. For the first time during the voyage, Hudson pulled himself up into the small upper berth of the cabin he shared with an Italian emigrant. He swallowed a painkiller prescribed by the ship's doctor and fell into a deep sleep.

As the *Andrea Doria* cut through the foggy waters off Nantucket, Hudson slept so soundly he did not hear the two shrieks of the ship's whistle signaling a left turn. Had he been awake, the veteran seaman would have immediately recognized it as a sign of possible danger.

Two women met in an elevator. One of them, Ruby Mac-Kenzie of Canon City, Colorado, confided that she was afraid of the fog.

"Why?" asked her friend. "There's nothing to worry about."

Mrs. MacKenzie shivered. "I just finished reading *A Night to Remember*." The book, published the year before, was Walter Lord's classic tale of the sinking of the *Titanic*.

"Oh, my goodness!" the friend exclaimed. "What a book to read just before an ocean voyage."

Fifteen-year-old Martin Sedja left his parents in the cabin-class Ballroom and walked out on the deck for some air. The heavy fog blanketed the deck. As he felt his way in the darkness toward the rail, he heard the ship's whistle scream out two short blasts. Something caught his eye. There seemed to be a soft glow off the starboard bow. Could there be something out there, so close?

Suddenly he saw the white shape of a ghostlike ship looming out of the darkness, her sharp prow angled toward a spot on the *Andrea Doria*'s hull about a third of the way back from the bow on a line with, but lower than, the Belvedere Lounge.

Forward in the lounge the party was livening up. Laughter and spirited conversation filled the room. In one corner Morris Novik, president of New York's Italian-language radio station WOV, and his wife smiled at each other as the band once again struck up its favorite tune, "Arrivederci, Roma."

Ruth Roman, swinging happily around the dance floor, sang the words of the tune softly to herself.

Marion Boyer watched his wife snuff out her cigarette and he rose to leave.

Grace McLean of Norfolk, Virginia, got up from her table to dance, leaving her purse, which contained a letter to her husband telling him what a wonderful voyage she had. She looked across the shoulder of her dancing partner and saw a blaze of light coming closer.

Down in her cabin on A Deck, Frances Aljinovic of Cleveland glanced out of her porthole and saw the same lights. "Oh, my God, Mary!" she screamed to her friend asleep on the other side of the cabin. "I can see a boat next to us. Get ready to pray. We're going to be hit!"

It was ten minutes past 11:00 P.M.

5

THE STOCKHOLM

AT 8:30 THAT EVENING, Johan-Ernst Bogislaus August Car-stens-Johannsen (everyone called him Carstens) had climbed to the bridge of the Swedish-American liner *Stockholm* to begin his watch, which was scheduled to last until midnight. The twenty-six-year-old third officer had served on the *Stockholm* for little more than two months. He had nine years' experience on other ships, first as an apprentice and later as an officer.

The handsome, curly, brown-haired mate, his shoulders prominent under his uniform, approached his evening's duties with an ingratiating grin. He was happy. At home in Sweden his young Alsatian wife, Liliane, was five months' pregnant with their first child. Carstens worked hard to support her. His salary was about $225 a month, counting overtime, and he was pleased with his swift rise in responsibility. As watch officer he would be in charge of navigation whenever the captain was not on the bridge. Someday, he believed, he would command his own ship.

Before coming on watch Carstens ate a heavy dinner and took a relaxing steam bath. Now the evening air freshened his good mood.

His first actions were to check the logbook, the chart, and the weather report. The sea was smooth with only a slight swell. The wind was from the southwest at two knots. There were reports of fog in the vicinity of the Nantucket lightship, but at the *Stockholm*'s present position the sky was merely overcast, the horizon somewhat hazy, a condition the Swedes referred to as "sun smoke." The young officer estimated visibility at six miles.

He checked the progress of the ship along the course marked out on the navigation chart. Thirty-year-old Senior Second Officer Lars Enestrom, whom he was relieving, told Carstens that the ship was more than a mile north of the planned route and that radar conditions were very good. Enestrom also explained that he had been unable to check the ship's gyrocompass for accuracy a few minutes earlier. This is normally done by obtaining a position fix on the sun at its true horizon, which occurs when two-thirds of the setting sun's diameter is still visible. As sunset approached Enestrom had readied his equipment for the reading, but just as he was about to take the fix a cloud obscured the sun.

After reporting all this to Carstens, Enestrom left the bridge and went to bed.

Three seamen worked with the third mate to keep the ship safely on course. They were Ingemar Bjorkman, twenty, Sten Johansson, eighteen, and Peder Larsen, twenty-six. They rotated their duties between helmsman, lookout, and a standby to keep watch on the bridge whenever the mate went into the chartroom to check the ship's position. Unlike the *Andrea Doria* and most other large liners, the *Stockholm* did not employ enough officers to have more than one on duty during routine watches. Whenever the third mate wanted to step into the chartroom behind the wheelhouse, he had to rely on the eyes and ears of one of the able-bodied seamen on duty with him. At certain of these times, the liner was effectively in the hands of a teenager.

Smaller and less pretentious than the *Andrea Doria,* the *Stockholm* was still a comfortable, serviceable passenger ship. Stretching 524 feet long and weighing 12,396 tons, she was the largest passenger vessel ever built in Sweden. The sleek racing lines of her white hull gave her the appearance of a massive luxury yacht. She was launched in 1948 with a capacity of 395 passengers, and despite being large for a Swedish ship, she was the smallest passenger vessel operating in the North Atlantic. Because of this, she had been rebuilt in 1953 to accommodate 580 passengers. She boasted specially strengthened bulkheads and one-inch-thick steel plating on the bow to enable the ship to follow icebreakers through the frozen seas of Scandinavia.

The *Stockholm* had six double watertight doors to protect it from flooding in the event of an accident that pierced her skin. She offered all the usual amenities of shipboard life, plus some Swedish specialties such as saltwater baths and luxurious massage parlors. Her seven decks were comfortable, if not ostentatious. Reflecting her northern routes, her single swimming pool was located indoors.

In command of the *Stockholm* was sixty-three-year-old Harry Gunnar Nordenson. The captain was born in Quincy, Massachusetts, but soon returned with his parents to their native Sweden. He first went to sea in 1911 at the age of eighteen. He passed the examination for his master's license in 1935 and since that time has commanded a variety of ships for the Swedish-American Line. For three years during World War II, he commanded the *Gripsholm*, under charter to the U.S. Government for diplomatic exchange service, and received numerous citations for his work. He commanded the *Stockholm* for four months in 1954, then transferred to the *Kungsholm*, which he directed on a round-the-world cruise. He again took command of the *Stockholm* on September 14, 1955. He maintained a home in Gothenburg with his wife, two sons, and a daughter.

A small, balding man with blue eyes, Nordenson was genial and given to hard work, but was sometimes thought to be a stern disciplinarian. The atmosphere on his bridge reflected his Scandinavian sense of order.

Captain Nordenson had ordered a course of ninety degrees, due east. The *Stockholm* routinely passed about one mile south of the Nantucket lightship whether it was going east or west.

This was against the recommendation of the 1948 Convention for the Safety of Life at Sea, which advised an eastbound course twenty miles to the south of the lightship. Several shipping lines had an agreement to follow the southern route, but the course was voluntary and, in any event, the Swedish-American Line was not a party to the agreement. Nor, for that matter, was the Italian Line. Captain Nordenson was not accustomed to wasting time by swinging twenty miles out of his way to the south. He had crossed the Atlantic 423 times, and always followed this route. He wanted to get his 534 passengers to Gothenburg on time.

The *Stockholm* had left pier 97 in New York at 11:31 that morning, but not before two of its passengers had experienced premonitions. Ernest Swenson, forty-nine, a landscape gardener from Reading, Pennsylvania, was going to visit relatives in Sweden. He called his wife, Miriam, from the dock and told her he was overcome with an eerie feeling of approaching danger. He said he was thinking of calling off the trip, but Miriam persuaded him to go ahead.

Paul and Jennie Anderson of Birdsboro, Pennsylvania, were leaving on a six-month tour that would take them to Sweden, then north of the Arctic Circle. When it was time to board, Mrs. Anderson was seized with a dark fear that something terrible was going to happen. Her husband laughed off the feeling.

By nightfall the *Stockholm* was well away from New York, cruising ahead at its top speed of eighteen knots. Nordenson, as was his custom, walked leisurely on the wings of the bridge, his white uniform contrasting against the darkening horizon, his head bowed in contemplation.

Third Officer Carstens went about his duties quietly, methodically. He checked the compass in front of the helmsman to make sure he was holding course steady at ninety degrees. He stepped outside to the wing and glanced up at the crow's nest to assure himself that the lookout was alert at his post. Simultaneously, he looked for signs of fog. At intervals he rang for the standby sailor to come from a room just off the bridge to keep watch while he stepped into the chartroom to plot the position of the ship.

The *Stockholm* was not equipped with the new loran system. Instead, Carstens used the older radio direction finder (RDF) method. Turning to the known frequency of a broadcasting station such as the Nantucket lightship, he obtained the bearing of the radio source, then drew a line on the map to indicate the position of the signal. By obtaining two or three bearings from different sources, he could plot the approximate position of the ship at the point where the lines intersected. This position was then confirmed by noting the depth of the water as reported by the ship's echo sounder, and checking that against a depth chart.

Carstens also monitored the radar scanner, one of two on board that had been inspected the day before by a service technician. It was set at a range of fifteen miles.

It was a busy schedule for a young third mate to follow, but Stockholm officers were expected to be capable of handling all duties.

At 9:40 P.M. Nordenson came in from the wing and checked his mate's position plottings.

"Change to eighty-seven degrees," he ordered.

Carstens stepped up to the helmsman and ordered the change. The helmsman adjusted the wheel slightly to the left. The new course would take the *Stockholm* to a position approximately one mile south of the Nantucket lightship.

A few minutes later the third mate once again stepped into the chartroom to fix the position of the ship, this time by dead reckoning. He read the SAL log, a nautical odometer that measured the ship's passage through the water. Carstens laid out the progress along the course drawn on the map, though he knew the ship to be slightly north of this point. Nordenson again came in from the bridge and spoke to Carstens. "I will be down in my cabin. If there is fog, call me." The captain then went below to work on the omnipresent pile of paperwork and to make an entry into his personal diary.

The navigation of the ship was now completely in the hands of the young third mate, who did not need to be reminded of the standing orders of his stern captain. He was never to leave the bridge without using the standby sailor as a lookout. He was never to pass another ship closer than one mile. And in the event of mist, fog, snow, sleet, or any unusual occurrence he was to put the engine telegraph on standby and notify the captain immediately. Nordenson always stressed that he would rather be called to the bridge too often than not often enough.

At 10:00 P.M., Carstens took RDF bearings from Block Island and the Nantucket lightship. In addition to its regular directional signal, the Nantucket lightship was broadcasting a special signal of four dashes in one minute, followed by two minutes of silence. It was a coded warning that there was dangerous fog in the area. Though the meaning of the radio signal was recorded in a manual on board, Carstens seemed to be unaware of it. The third mate merely used the signal to help fix his position. His plotting at 10:04 now showed the *Stockholm* to be two and one-half miles north of its intended course. He consulted the tide timetables and noted that there was a northerly current.

Carstens walked out on the bridge and automatically checked the weather. His masthead lights were clear, not obstructed by any kind of fog. The breeze seemed to have abated slightly. Above him and slightly to starboard the third mate could see the nearly full moon. Below him he could hear the assuring throb of the engines, sometimes drowned out by the laughter of passengers enjoying the first night of the cruise. Carstens paced the bridge, alert but calm, pleased with the position he had achieved in only twenty-six years of life.

At 10:30 Carstens took another position fix. The *Stockholm* was now farther off course to the north, 2.7 or 2.8 miles from its intended route, still drifting in a strong current. Carstens did not feel the error was serious enough to notify Nordenson. He merely ordered the helmsman to shift course two degrees to the south to compensate.

A few minutes later the three seamen rotated their duties for the final segment of their watch. Johansson climbed to the crow's nest, Bjorkman came down to act as standby, and Peder Larsen took the helm.

"Eighty-nine," the third mate said to Larsen, indicating the ship's new course.

Carstens felt he should keep a close watch on the compass

with Larsen at the helm. The Danish sailor, Carstens believed, sometimes let his attention wander from strict observation of the compass needle. Carstens checked the compass heading at irregular intervals, but the pressure of his other duties kept him from supervising Larsen as often as he would have liked.

Larsen had been going to sea for eight years and always worked at the more common-laboring jobs on board. He was unfamiliar with the *Stockholm*. He had journeyed from his native Denmark to Sweden and signed onto the ship only eleven days before.

The extra supervision required of Larsen added to Carstens' roster of responsibilities. He moved constantly in a busy circle from the chartroom, forward to the wheelhouse, and out to the wings on either side of the bridge. The night was still clear.

In the bow, where their modest cabins were located, several crew members relaxed after the hard work of the first day of the voyage. Alf Johansson, Kenneth Jonasson, Sune Steen, and Karl Elis Osterberg slept peacefully. All were stewards and kitchen helpers. Arne Smedberg undressed and sank into bed with a grateful sigh. But many of the bunks in this forward area of the ship were empty tonight because most of the kitchen personnel had been ordered to work overtime.

About ten minutes to 11:00 P.M., Third Mate Carstens rang the bell summoning Bjorkman from the standby room. "Bjorkman, take the lookout while I go inside and take some bear-

WHAT THE STOCKHOLM SAW

At 10 miles distance, the Stockholm saw the pip 2° north of its course heading.
At 6 miles distance, the Stockholm saw the pip 4° north.
At 4 miles distance, Carstens estimated a passage distance of 0.6 to 0.7 miles.
At 2 miles distance, the Stockholm sighted the Andrea Doria visually, 20° north.

MILES	0		2		4		6		8		10
STOCKHOLM									STOCKHOLM	HEADING 91°	

ings," he ordered. Bjorkman glanced at the radar screen, saw that no ships were in the area, and went out to the wing.

Carstens stepped back into the chartroom, where he took RDF bearings. The ship was now three full miles off course to the north. The mate went forward to the wheelhouse and ordered Larsen to shift course an additional two degrees south, which would put the ship on a heading of ninety-one degrees. Then Carstens checked the radar. During the several minutes he had been busy in the chartroom a pip had appeared on the screen.

The third mate adjusted the instrument in an attempt to brighten the pip, but it remained fuzzy. He estimated the unknown object to be twelve miles away from the *Stockholm*, and slightly to its left.

As the beam swept around the screen, Carstens transferred the changing position of the pip to a plotting board with a red wax pencil. This gave him a continuing record of the location of each pip, so that he could track the other ship's course. If his calculations were to be valid, he had to be sure that the *Stockholm* itself was on course. There was no gyro repeater at the radar screen, so Carstens could not check the compass himself without leaving his place. He called out to the helmsman. "Larsen, the compass reading." Larsen yelled back, "Ninety," or one degree to the north of the set course.

His eyes intent on the radar screen and his dimly lit plotting board, his brow knotted in concentration, Carstens traced the pip to a point now ten miles away. It appeared to be a fast ship, heading at full speed almost directly toward the *Stockholm*, but it was about two degrees off the port bow, or left side. Carstens had no way of knowing the name of the other ship, nor did he realize that its own radar showed it to be on the right, or starboard side, of the *Stockholm*, not to its left.

Carstens ordered Bjorkman out to the bridge to search for the lights of the approaching ship off the port bow. The standby sailor did as he was told. Carstens, the only officer on the bridge, was kept busy plotting the changing position of the pips. He saw that the other ship's bearing seemed to be increasing slightly to port—now it was four degrees to the left. The ships were now six miles apart. If both vessels held course they would pass in the prescribed manner—port-to-port—Carstens thought.

"Larsen," the mate called, "again, the compass reading."

"Ninety-one," Larsen replied, indicating that he was holding steady on the course set by Carstens a few minutes earlier.

The mate, using a ruler for a straightedge, connected the dots on his plotting board and calculated that the ships would pass at a distance of 0.7 to 0.8 miles, slightly less than the minimum of one mile ordered by Captain Nordenson.

At the helm Larsen glanced at the clock, then he reached up and pulled on a cord, ringing six bells—eleven o'clock. In the crow's nest Johansson heard the signal and repeated it on his own bell. Down at the desk in his dayroom underneath the bridge, Captain Nordenson heard the bells and knew that the *Stockholm* would soon be approaching the Nantucket lightship and he would need to set a course for the open sea. He carefully put away his logbooks and his diary and prepared to go back up to the bridge.

Carstens looked at his radar, then back out through the windows of the wheelhouse, a puzzled expression on his face. He searched futilely for the lights of the oncoming ship. Radar showed the unknown vessel to be only four miles away now, and closing fast, yet neither he, nor Johansson in the crow's nest, nor Bjorkman on the bridge had spotted her running lights. Perhaps the ship, though fast, was small, he speculated. The thought that her lights might be obscured by fog did not occur to the young mate at the moment, for he could see that his own running lights were clear. Besides, he believed that the other ship was traveling too fast to be in fog.

He switched the radar screen to a range of five miles, and the pip of the unknown ship swelled in size and continued to bear down on the *Stockholm*.

Out on the bridge wing, Ingemar Bjorkman peered intently toward the blackness off the port bow. The bright moon to starboard still seemed to obscure the horizon to port. The pip on the radar screen was only two miles away when Bjorkman pointed to the north and called, "Light on port."

"OK," Carstens answered.

Carstens quickly abandoned his radar screen, grabbed his binoculars and stepped out to the wing to see for himself. The ship was about twenty degrees off the port bow and less than two miles away. Both Carstens and Bjorkman read her lights easily. The forward, lower light was to the left of the higher masthead light, meaning that the ship was on a course that would take it safely past on the portside. A weak red light, indicating that the other ship's left side was facing the *Stockholm*, confirmed the position. They would pass "red on red," or port-to-port. Nevertheless, the passage would be closer than one mile, which would contradict not only Captain Nordenson's orders but the commonsense rules of the sea. Carstens decided to turn the *Stockholm* to the right to give the other ship more maneuvering room.

"Starboard," he called out to Larsen. The helmsman swung the wheel two full turns to the right. When the compass indicator had moved twenty degrees, the mate then ordered, "Amidships." In response, Larsen brought the wheel back to center. "Steady so," the mate next ordered, instructing Larsen to hold fast to the new course. Carstens did not order a blast of the ship's whistle that would have signaled his sharp right turn to the other vessel.

The telephone suddenly rang in the wheelhouse. Carstens turned his back on the approaching ship and left the bridge wing in order to answer the telephone.

It was lookout Johansson calling from the crow's nest. "Light twenty degrees on port," the lookout reported.

"All right," the mate said. Carstens hung up the phone and glanced once more at the radar screen, before picking up a pair of binoculars and heading back out to the wing.

In the crow's nest Johansson's attention shifted from the lights on the *Doria* to the blazing moon. Its movement in the sky made him realize that his own ship was turning to the right. He looked back at the oncoming vessel and saw that the forward light had suddenly swung to the right of the rear light, a sign that the ship was veering directly across the path of the *Stockholm*. Johansson did not pick up the telephone to relay the new information to Carstens. As he understood his orders, it was his job to report a ship sighting but not necessarily to keep track of its course.

While on the telephone, Carstens could not see the other ship begin to swing across the *Stockholm*'s path.

Now a moment later, on the bridge, both Bjorkman and Carstens simultaneously saw a dramatic change in the unknown ship's navigational lights, and stared into the darkness in disbelief.

Horror etched across Carstens' face. He could see the other ship swinging into a hard left turn that was bringing it into a direct line with the *Stockholm*'s course.

Carstens was incredulous. Soon, he saw the entire starboard side of the other ship in front of him. The glow from rows of portholes indicated to him that the unknown ship that suddenly materialized like a giant apparition was a large passenger liner. Carstens could see the sharp steel bow of his ship headed directly for the vulnerable broadside of the giant in front of him.

Two ships approaching from opposite directions had maneuvered carefully to avoid each other. One had turned to its left, the other to its right. Now, they seemed drawn by fate to meet at the edge of a fogbank no matter how carefully their officers calculated.

But Carstens had no time to speculate. The mate pulled hard on the engine telegraph indicator to FULL SPEED ASTERN, thinking to lessen the force of the impact as much as possible by reversing the engines. At the same moment, he decided to turn the ship's bow away from the looming target.

"Hard starboard!" he yelled at Larsen. Larsen turned the wheel five full revolutions to the right and held it firmly in place.

Carstens heard the unknown ship's whistle shriek a protest into the night.

Captain Nordenson heard the ring of the engine telegraph and knew that his third mate had encountered a serious situation. "What the hell is this?" he muttered to himself. He grabbed his hat and walked quickly toward the stairway up to the bridge.

In the engine room Second Engineer Güsta Harold Svensson reacted quickly to the order on his telegraph, for it could only mean that the *Stockholm* was in grave danger. Quickly he ordered Motorman Alexander Hallik to open the air valves to brake the engines. Then he lunged for the telegraph and answered the bridge, confirming that the order was being carried out. He struggled with the throttle valves, closing down first the starboard engine, then the port. Pressurized air from the brake valves flowed into the cylinders to check their forward motion. But the ship's propellers continued to turn forward due to the motion of the ship in the water. When Svensson saw that the starboard propeller had finally stopped, he opened its throttle valve and fed oil back into the cylinders. The engine started up and the starboard propeller spun in reverse, causing the entire ship to shudder with a sudden backward pressure. Then Svensson hurried to the port engine, where Hallik was beginning to start its propeller in reverse.

On the bridge Carstens could hear the starboard screw finally spin backward, but he knew that it was too late. He braced himself for the impact, and watched helplessly as the white bow of his ship took aim on the starboard side of the black hull of the *Andrea Doria*.

6

THE CRASH

THE BOW OF THE *Stockholm*, angled forward on top like a sharpened blade, cut first into the Upper Deck of the *Andrea Doria*, slicing in at the partition separating cabins 52 and 54. The shriek of steel scraping against steel pierced the solitude of the ocean night. A fireworks shower of white and orange sparks flew toward the sky. Heat from the friction immediately smoldered the fire-resistant lining that separated the steel hull of the *Andrea Doria* from her interior paneling.

Shock waves of destruction vibrated outward from the point of contact, collapsing cabin walls, crushing beds, hurling debris to either side, and transforming the comfortable, spacious rooms of the Upper Deck into death traps of mangled metal, splintered lumber, and flying bits of jagged glass. Disintegrating even as it penetrated, the bow smashed a hole in the Upper Deck of the *Andrea Doria* from cabin 42 back to cabin 58, thrusting aside any obstruction with merciless authority and filling the deck with gagging smoke.

One level below on the Foyer Deck the full power of the blow hit directly on deluxe suite 180, crushing the luxury appointments of the designer rooms, and pushing the far wall of the cabin flat against the other side of the corridor. The bow of the intruder stopped just short of the chapel.

Just below on A Deck, the even-numbered cabins from 202 to 238 were instantly demolished, their furnishings splintered and thrown into the hallway. Load-bearing girders snapped, pulling walls out of line and jamming the doors of nearby rooms.

Down on B Deck the bow knifed into cabins 424 to 432 as well as the garage, mangling automobiles stored there and collapsing a steel bulkhead, opening two once-watertight compartments.

Though penetration was less on the lower decks, the smaller, crowded cabins on the starboard side of C Deck from number 642 to 670 were smashed open. And here, below the surface, salt water poured in immediately, stinging the fresh wound and flooding the two compartments on either side of the demolished watertight bulkhead, challenging the *Andrea Doria*'s safety features to the limits of engineering design.

Below the passenger decks, fuel tanks and deep ballast tanks ruptured, splashing hot flammable oil above into the polished hallways. Water cascaded into the electrical generating room. All along the point of impact the fire-resistant lining smoldered now, sending heavy smoke through the corridors.

The tough steel skin of the *Andrea Doria* finally stopped the intruder when it was thirty feet inside her belly. The V-shaped gash, conforming to a cross section of the *Stockholm*'s bow, was fifty feet wide at the Upper Deck and narrowed to a point deep below in the water. Tremors shook the writhing victim. The shock disrupted the electrical connections to the ship's whistle and from the bridge a long, sharp, involuntary shriek of agony screamed across the ocean.

With the forward motion stopped, the *Stockholm*'s engines, set in reverse, immediately pulled her back out to the sea, revealing a dark, open wound in the side of the *Andrea Doria*.

The forward motion of the Italian liner continued to force the side of the ship against the broken nose of the *Stockholm*. The mashed bow of the Swedish ship bumped hard at least twice more against the *Doria*, shattering windows on the

Promenade Deck and sending more showers of sparks into the night.

The *Andrea Doria* tilted toward her right side as the weight of floodwaters filled her bowels. The edges of A Deck sank beneath the surface of the ocean as the *Doria* listed, destroying the watertight integrity of the ship. Water poured over the top of A Deck and rained down into nearby compartments that were theoretically sealed off by the watertight doors but were now exposed to the onslaught of the ocean.

In cabin 46 on the Upper Deck, Colonel Walter Carlin, his toothbrush in hand, was knocked to the bathroom floor. He scrambled to his feet, bruised and uncomprehending. Instinctively he staggered back toward the bedroom for his wife. Through eyes clouded by smoke and swirling dust he could see the top edge of the *Stockholm*'s shattered bow inside his cabin, hovering over the inert, bloody body of his beloved Jeanette.

A cry of agony stifled in his throat; the stunned man stood immobilized, incapable of understanding the scene before him. He watched hypnotized as the white bow of the attacker slipped backward, the suction of its retreat tugging at Jeanette's broken bed. Suddenly the bunk tore loose from its moorings and slid toward the sea. The colonel cried out, but there was no one to hear, no one to help, no way to save his wife. Almost in slow motion, the bed carrying his wife disappeared from the cabin, and when it was gone Colonel Carlin could see nothing but blackness.

Two doors aft, all that remained of cabin 52 was a huge black hole, filled by the death screams of passengers in the lower decks. But there was no one in cabin 52 to hear those pitiful sounds. The beds of its occupants, fourteen-year-old Linda Morgan and eight-year-old Joan Cianfarra, had simply disappeared into the void along with the two sleeping girls.

Their parents in cabin 54 were pushed aft by the *Stockholm*. Camille Cianfarra was thrown into the Petersons' cabin next door, his body smashing into torn wall studs and the jagged edges of ripped paneling. He tumbled wildly through cabin 56, finally coming to rest in the bathroom hallway, where he lay, mangled and disfigured, his head smashed, but still alive and thrashing in agony. Jane Cianfarra was hurled fifteen feet and came to rest in cabin 56, where she was enmeshed by the wreckage. Her left leg was broken, twisted under her and caught in a tangle of bedsprings. She was trapped in a strange crouch, half-seated, half-standing. Blood covered her face and matted her hair.

In cabin 56, Martha Peterson was thrown sharply against the elevator shaft that backed up to her cabin. She was only a few feet from Jane Cianfarra, lying on her back, her body bent around the corner of the shaft. Even if her frail body had been strong enough to lift the heavy debris that held her in a vise, she would have been unable to flee. Her spine was shattered and her legs broken. She was paralyzed from the waist down.

Her husband, Dr. Thure Peterson, woke for an agonizing instant to the sensation of a loud, tearing noise. He looked up and saw the white bow of the *Stockholm* enter his cabin. He felt himself flying through the air. His naked, muscular body was thrust from his bunk in cabin 56, underneath the wall paneling into cabin 58, where he landed beneath the remains of Father Wojcik's unoccupied bed. As the paneling snapped neatly back into place, leaving no trace of a hole between cabin 56 and cabin 58, Thure Peterson's mind went dark.

Below on the Foyer Deck the elegant furnishings of deluxe first-class suite 180 were flattened as though a trash compactor had compressed the rooms from the hull to the interior corridor. Somewhere in the tangled mess lay the bodies of Ferdinand and Frances Thieriot.

In cabin 236 on A Deck, three-year-old Rose Marie Wells cried out for help. Her left hand was pinned to her bed by an upper bunk fallen from its mooring.

Nearby, a nude woman stumbled into the corridor, her shocked gaze trying to comprehend the blood flowing from her mangled arm and her ripped side. As others ran toward her, the woman tottered on her feet, then fell softly into the ocean.

Several emigrant families in the tiny cabins of tourist class on C Deck were instantly killed by the impact, others drowned within moments as water poured in over them. In cabin 656, Maria Sergio drowned quickly, along with her children, Giuseppe, Anna Maria, Domenica, and little Rocco. Only minutes before the boy had pleaded futilely with his Uncle Paul to let him sleep in his room farther down the hallway.

The collision wracked the *Stockholm* as well. Thirty feet of her bow was gone, its wreckage jammed in amid the torn steel and wood of the *Andrea Doria.* The ship looked like a gladiator whose nose was sliced off in one blow. The impact smashed the chain locker, sending the huge iron anchor chains spinning to the bottom some 225 feet below. The anchors themselves were embedded uselessly in the misshapen steel bow.

The *Stockholm*'s fire sprinkler system was activated by the shock, showering the front portion of the ship. Barrels of gray paint, stored in the bow, burst open, spewing their stinging liquid into the crew cabins. The forward crew quarters were smashed to a portion of their original size or ripped open to the sea.

The impact shattered the protective collision bulkhead near the bow. Water flooded the number 1 hold, surging against the second watertight bulkhead. Its weight pulled the nose of the ship down, bringing the sea precariously close to the top of the watertight bulkhead at the bottom of A Deck.

Casualties on the *Stockholm* were confined to those unlucky crewmen assigned to the foremost cabins. Injuries would have been more numerous if many of the crewmen had not been working overtime in the kitchen. On the Main Deck, Karl Elis Osterberg, a mess boy, was killed on impact. His roommate, Sven Ahlm, was seriously injured. The bodies of two young crewmen, Kenneth Jonasson and Sune Steen, disappeared into the sea from their cabins on A Deck. Thirty-year-old Alf Johansson was thrown to the floor of his cabin, his legs and skull fractured. Evert Svensson, in a forward cabin torn open by the collision, was caught up in the iron links of the anchor chain. It twisted around his body like a python and pulled him, screaming in agony, down to the bottom of the ocean.

The trim indicator soon showed the *Stockholm* to be down

three feet seven inches in the bow. Captain Nordenson, arriving on the bridge immediately after the collision, called to the engine room to straighten out the ship. "Start the ballast pump," he ordered. Engineers sent the pump roaring, but water was flowing into the number 1 hold as fast as they pumped it back out to sea. In a few moments, the bow was down another seven inches.

On the bridge, Third Officer Carstens, shocked by the collision, turned plaintively to Second Officer Lars Enestrom. "Why did she turn to port?" he asked. Enestrom, who had been fast asleep only moments before, could not comprehend the question. He shook his head. For several minutes Carstens wandered around the bridge, confronting each of the crewmen with his unanswerable query.

Chief Officer Herbert Kallback ordered several men to pry open the doors of the collapsed crew cabins to free sailors whose wails carried through the metal partitions. The rescuers cleared some debris by hand, then prepared acetylene torches to burn their way in.

Kallback then moved down to A Deck and looked below. The water in the number 1 hold now reached the eleven-foot mark, perilously close to the top of the watertight door. Fortunately, number 2 and 3 holds were still tight. The forward list must be corrected, Kallback knew, or water would soon overflow the top of the bulkhead.

The trim indicator now showed the *Stockholm* heeling toward its bow more than four feet two inches. Second Officer Enestrom then reported thirteen feet of water in the number 1 hold. The list must be halted, rapidly, or the *Stockholm* was doomed.

Chief Engineer Gustav Assargren set his men to work pumping out to sea the ninety-five tons of fresh water stored in the forward tanks. Twenty-five tons of fuel in the starboard tanks were pumped over to port to balance the ship. The bridge crew waited tensely to see if these new efforts would succeed. All eyes were fixed on the trim indicator.

Chief Purser Curt Dawe completed a quick accounting that showed that all the passengers had miraculously been spared.

One crewman was dead. Three more were missing and presumed dead. Alf Johannson was in critical condition in the ship's hospital. Several other sailors were seriously injured.

But up on the bridge Nordenson and his officers soon broke into restrained smiles. The trim indicator was edging backward. Slowly the forward list decreased to only seven inches, then held steady. The *Stockholm* would survive.

There was little panic among the *Stockholm* passengers. Some returned to the lounges to resume their first-night parties. But most stood out on the open decks, listening. Across the quiet water they could hear the frightful wails of people trapped on the other stricken ship that stood somewhere off from them in the thick Atlantic fog that had once again closed in.

Death came speedily to about forty of the *Andrea Doria*'s passengers who were either asleep or in their cabins preparing for bed. The surviving passengers and crew members, however, now faced a battle against extinction that would test each of them to his or her limit this night. Some would see the dawn; some would not. Stranded in the fog on a ship tilted perilously to starboard, its crippled hull shuddering spasmodically, the list increasing with each frightening heave, they were forced face to face with destiny. Gone were the superficial class distinctions that placed human beings in well-defined compartments. Everyone was, quite literally, in the same boat.

In a tourist-class cabin at the edge of the gaping hole on C Deck, fourteen-year-old Antonio Ponzi of Italy, on his way to join his mother in Newark, New Jersey, was trapped in his upper bunk by debris from the crash. "Help," he screamed out to his roommate, a somewhat older man with the same name, Antonio. The roommate reached up and pulled the boy from his bunk. Black water swirled in the cabin, rising rapidly. His roommate tugged frantically at the cabin door, but it was jammed, and would not open. Suddenly an iron beam fell from the ceiling. The elder Antonio grabbed it and smashed away at the cabin door until it gave the two passengers enough room to work their way through the water to the safety of the higher decks.

Three-year-old Maria screamed in cabin 641 on C Deck. Her mother, Liliana Dooner, was thrown wildly about the cabin. The straps broke on her red evening gown and the dress fell to her waist as she stumbled bare-breasted around the room, calling for her daughter amid a choking white smoke. She tried to reach Maria's bed, but a tall wardrobe had fallen the length of the room, blocking her way. Liliana struggled over the obstacle and grabbed her child.

She thought of their life jackets, but they were jammed underneath the wreckage of her bed. Liliana decided to abandon them and race with Maria to the upper decks. Suddenly aware of her nakedness, she tugged at the purple half slip at her waist, pulling it up over her body.

With Maria in her arms, she ran to the stairway next to her cabin door. The ship was tilted on its side, and the odd angle made climbing up the stairwell difficult. Liliana realized that, in order to find her way to an open deck, she would have to retrace her steps all the way to the tourist-class bar where she had been sharing a drink with friends only minutes before. It was long but it was the only route she knew that led upward.

As she moved further up the decks, the number of passengers rushing to safety increased, and she became enmeshed in a mob of men, women and children screaming out prayers and curses as they fought their way through. People stumbled and fell to the floor. Fearing that Maria would slip from her grasp and be trampled, Liliana pushed her back against the wall and slid sideways through the crush of people.

Finally, they reached a stairway where the fleeing mob funneled almost to a standstill. Panic exploded as passengers fought one another for a chance to live. Men struggled unheedingly past women and children; one woman pushed aside a frightened little child. The only possible way up the stairs was to grasp the stairway railing and hold on determinedly. The polished bar became a desperate prize.

Liliana fought to reach the railing, but the wailing crowd in the narrow hallway pressed her back repeatedly. With a final effort, Liliana reached the stairway rail, graspd it with iron fingers and pulled herself and Maria toward the upper deck. Laboriously they made their way up several flights through the hysterical mob.

At last, she reached the rear of the Promenade Deck where men formed a human chain to pull her up to the open area on the high side of the stern. Little Maria, sleepily confused through it all, complained that she had to go to the bathroom.

Paul and Margaret Sergio rushed into the hallway in their pajamas.

"My sister! My sister!" Mrs. Sergio cried. "The poor kids are probably scared to death."

But the corridor that led to her sister's cabin was already clogged with shrieking people in various states of undress, some covered with oil, water, and blood, and all rushing for a stairway away from the direction of Maria's cabin. Prayers for mercy were screamed heavenward in Italian. Paul Sergio, with Margaret at his side, tried to fight his way against the flow. The couple slipped and slid on the floor, making slow progress. Paul tried to judge the rate of the onrushing water and wondered if they would reach the children in time.

As they arrived at the doorway that led to a forward hallway and Maria's cabin, a sailor appeared and pulled Margaret back.

"You can't go in there," he shouted to the anguished couple. "There's no way you can get in there." A door blocked the Sergios' passage forward.

The old cobbler's face collapsed into tears as he tried to explain about his nephews and nieces. He remembered little Rocco's plea to sleep with him.

"They'll be all right," the sailor reassured them. "They'll go up another stairway toward the front of the ship. Go on up." He tried to push Margaret toward the stairs, but he was no match for the hysterical woman though she was less than five feet tall. Water swirled around her but she refused to move.

Her husband tried to remain calm. He could see that it was impossible to get to Maria's cabin, so he pleaded with Margaret to go upstairs before the water rose. "We'll find them up above," he said.

In his own mind he was not so optimistic. He thought of his six children at home in South Bend. *I'll never see them again,* he told himself.

Sister Callistus Arnsby of London, Ontario, snapped on the light in her cabin on A Deck. "What's the matter?" Sister Marie Raymond Baker asked from her lower bunk.

"Something's happened. We better get up," Sister Callistus replied. She sat up and reached her leg out in search of the ladder down to the floor. At that instant, the ship gave a sudden lurch, propelling Sister Callistus to the floor with a shriek.

As soon as they recovered their equilibrium, the two nuns pulled their habits over their nightclothes. Sister Raymond saw her alarm clock slide across a table and she paused to push it back into place. Again it slid down the table; again she pushed it back. When it slid down a third time she said to herself, *Sister, you're wasting valuable time. This ship's in trouble.* Sister Callistus was already dressed and had gone out into the hallway to learn the cause of the confusion.

"What did you find out?" Sister Raymond asked when her friend returned.

"Nothing. Come on. Let's get up to our muster station."

Carrying their bright orange life jackets, the two nuns headed for a stairway. Because of a congenital limp, Sister Raymond had difficulty walking at the odd angle of the slope, but she managed the journey despite the mobs that jammed the stairway.

Across the hall, a third nun, Sister Angelita Myerscough, was vaguely aware that she had heard a grating, crunching noise, as though a large crate had broken loose and was bumping against the back of the cabin. When she realized that she had slipped down toward the foot of the bed, she pulled herself back up to her pillow. She turned over to go back to sleep, but her roommate, a woman named Giovanna, tried to shake her awake. Feeling groggy from the effects of a Dramamine pill, Sister Angelita wanted nothing more than to fall back into oblivion.

"Wake up!" Giovanna yelled. "The motors have stopped."

Sister Angelita sat up, awakened now by the absence of the comforting throb from below.

Giovanna was dressed and ready to leave the room, but she stopped near the door and pulled open a closet. She pointed inside and said, "Don't forget your life jacket." Then she left Sister Angelita sitting in a chair, trying to clear her fuzzy head.

In cabin 80 on the Upper Deck, Mayor Dilworth jumped out of his bed. "I think there's been an explosion," he said to his wife Ann.

"No, that was just like the way they describe what happened to the *Titanic*," she replied.

Dilworth assured her there were no icebergs on the approach to New York City. He pulled open the cabin door and was confronted by dense smoke and the chaotic scene of screaming men and women running wildly about. "We'd better get upstairs," he said.

Ann dressed quickly, for her clothes were laid out at the foot of the bed. The fastidious mayor pulled on his dark suit, then leaned over to struggle with his garters, mumbling absent-mindedly about what pair of shoes to wear.

"For Christ sakes! We've got to get out of here," Ann yelled, tugging at him.

Their eyes tearing from smoke, the Dilworths groped their way to a stairwell. The wet linoleum floors, always kept highly polished by the crew, were like ice under their feet. The tilt of the ship made climbing difficult. They tugged at the handrails and cautiously made their way up to the Promenade Deck where their muster station was located. Always a leader, Dilworth stood at the top of the stairwell for a while, helping others up.

A steward stood there also, guiding passengers along, assuring everyone in broken English that the ship could not sink.

Soon a crewman ordered everyone up to the high, port side of the deck, hoping that the human weight would counterbalance the increasing list. The mayor and his wife dropped to their hands and knees and crawled upward, painfully making their way to the rail where many had gathered.

When the Dilworths reached their goal, they held desperately to the rails, shivering in the chilled night, and looked out over the bleak Nantucket water. The fog seemed like a dense curtain. How, he wondered, could help reach them in such weather?

One hundred fifty people on the Foyer Deck were watching the film *Foxfire*, with Jane Russell and Jeff Chandler, when the screen went dark. A scream cut through the darkness, touching off panic. A Franciscan, Reverend Benedict Simon, was thrown to the floor where he twisted his foot. All around him, people were sliding off their chairs to the right, some of them crashing hard against the wall. As passengers scrambled toward the doorway, some nearest to the exit were thrown to the floor and trampled.

"Don't worry! Don't panic!" an authoritative voice shouted loudly.

The passengers suddenly grew subdued. Slowly they made their way out into the corridor, slipping and sliding on an oil slick that covered the floor. Passengers had to hold on to each other to make any progress.

Rosa Matrincola of Midvale, New Jersey, ran screaming from the movie down the crowded stairs to her cabin where her two children, Paddy, nine, and Arlene, eight, slept. The door was jammed shut, but she could hear the frightened children inside crying. The mother begged for assistance, but each person was caught up in his private struggle and no one stopped. When the door would not open, Mrs. Matrincola feverishly shook the knob, and threw her weight against the door. Finally, the door gave. Mrs. Matrincola grabbed her crying children and scurried to the deck above.

When the shock occurred, nineteen-year-old Melania Ansuini, an attractive young woman from Italy emigrating to California, was dancing to the music of an impromptu emigrant band with twenty-seven-year-old John Vali, a Canadian, in the tourist-class Social Hall at the rear of the Upper Deck. Suddenly dancers were thrust to the floor, tables turned, and drinks splashed across the room. The musicians tried valiantly to continue playing, but after a few notes the lights flickered and the room plunged into darkness. The ship shuddered toward one side, sending band instruments, chairs, cocktail glasses, and hysterical people crashing to the low side. When the lights came back on, hundreds scrambled for the doorway.

"Don't leave me!" Melania pleaded.

"I'll stay with you," Vali promised. With the terrified girl clutching his arm, Vali rounded up the rest of her family, located life jackets for them, and shepherded them to the high side of the open deck to await whatever was to come.

In the cabin-class cardroom on the back of the Promenade Deck, Ruby MacKenzie's first reaction to the impact was to scrape together the nickels she had just won from her friends. She threw the money into her purse, then calmly started to arrange the playing cards before she realized what was happening. "My God!" she exclaimed. "Ann's downstairs." She raced for a stairway accompanied by her friend Ruth Luder. They fought fiercely against both the list of the ship and the tide of people struggling in the other direction, until they reached A Deck. Half blinded by smoke, and hopelessly confused by the maze of passageways, Mrs. MacKenzie looked around. Mrs. Luder pushed in front of her.

"This way!" she yelled over her shoulder.

Someone opened a cabin door and sleepily asked, "What's happened?"

"We don't know," Mrs. MacKenzie yelled, not breaking stride now that she recognized the way to her cabin.

Her fourteen-year-old daughter, Ann, was sitting up in bed, rubbing her eyes. "What's the matter?" she asked.

"I don't know, but let's get our life jackets," her mother answered. She grabbed Ann by one hand and the life jackets in the other, and raced for the door. On the way out of the cabin, Mrs. Luder scooped up her coat in case it became cold.

The two women and the girl hurried down the smoky hallway and up the stairs that led to the decks above. They paused on a landing to pull on their life jackets.

"I can't get this thing buckled," Mrs. MacKenzie complained.

Ann laughed. "No wonder, Mom, you've got it upside down." She helped her mother with the life jacket.

Then Mrs. MacKenzie realized that Ann was dressed only

in a pair of skimpy panties. She grabbed Mrs. Luder's coat and clothed her daughter. "What in the world?" she scolded. "Why didn't you put your pajamas on?"

"Well, I couldn't find them," the teenager answered.

Suddenly Ruby MacKenzie realized what was important: that she and her daughter were together. The women continued on their way up to the Promenade Deck. Ann clutched the short coat tightly to her bare skin; it was tweed.

The Belvedere Lounge, site of carefree partying just moments before, was now solemn and quiet, the party atmosphere shattered by the sudden boom of what sounded to some like a giant firecracker. On a direct line with the collision but two decks above the highest point of contact, the beautiful lounge was spared the initial agony.

Quickly the rumor circulated—some had actually seen another ship. The *Andrea Doria* had been struck.

A white-haired waiter mopped up spilled drinks and calmly assured everyone in English, "Please wait here. There will be an announcement."

Minutes passed. Jean Ruth, sitting with her husband and the Greens, heard a garbled announcement in Italian that, she thought, was an instruction to abandon ship. The men snapped into their accustomed roles as protectors and organizers.

The couples moved toward the hallway, Jean Ruth stumbling because of the sudden list of the ship. The two men left the women at the top of the stairwell and went for their life jackets, climbing down past the Promenade Deck to their cabins on the Upper Deck. Donald Ruth threw open the door to his cabin 48. It was a shambles. The beds were crushed and splintered. Debris lay all around. The wall to cabin 52 was shattered. Had they not gone to the Belvedere Lounge for drinks with the Greens, they probably would have been maimed or killed on impact, he thought.

"Take this," a helpful steward said, thrusting a child's life jacket into the hands of the amazed man.

Ruth and Green hurried back to their wives. Donald Green strapped Jean into the undersized life jacket and the men ushered their wives to their muster station, the glass-enclosed Promenade Deck. Moments later Colonel Walter Carlin stumbled in, dazed, his pajamas torn and soiled. He was crying. "I want to offer a reward," he said in a shaky voice. "My wife has just floated out into the ocean. There's nothing I can do."

As gently as they could, the Greens and Ruths helped their grieving friend to a chair that was bolted to the sloping deck.

At the moment of impact, actress Ruth Roman's first thought was of her three-year-old Dickie, asleep in his cabin. She quickly kicked off her high heels and raced out of the Belvedere Lounge. A sailor tried to block her way but she pushed and struggled past him, down toward her cabin 82 on the Upper Deck. The sheath dress which tightly encased her body was restricting her movement down the now-tilted stairwell. She stretched around, then ripped it open up the back. Covered with oil splotches and dirt, she finally reached her cabin.

"What happened?" Grace Els, her child's nurse, asked sleepily.

"I don't know. We hit something. Quick! We must get Dickie upstairs."

They looked at the three-year-old boy, sleeping quietly. While Miss Els, a wiry, grandmotherly woman, gathered clothes for the boy, his mother awakened him. Dickie was grouchy and did not want to leave his warm bed.

Miss Roman's mind worked rapidly. "We're going on a picnic!" she said. The child became enthusiastic and jumped up. The women grabbed life jackets and blankets and carried Dickie up to the Boat Deck. The actress led them to the top of the sloping deck and built a barricade of blankets and life jackets to keep them from sliding down to the low side. She lay down and placed her arms over her head, consciously saving her strength for the next trying hours.

In the card room just behind the Belvedere Lounge, three priests were startled by the shock of impact and jumped up from their Scrabble game.

A steward thrust his head through the doorway. "Don't get excited," he ordered; "everything is all right."

The priests exchanged curious glances with other passengers in the card room. A second steward suddenly appeared. "Go to your stations and await further orders," he said.

Portly Father Lambert trudged toward his cabin for his life

jacket, while Father Dolciamore and Father Wojcik raced down to cabin 58 on the same mission. The trip down was difficult, for the stairways were waxed and the wall tilted by the severe list of the ship. At the Upper Deck, they were surprised to find the corridor deserted. Cabin doors were closed. Compared to the confusion that had gripped the upper decks, the priests felt as though the accident had not affected this area at all.

Wojcik opened the door to his cabin and switched on the light. The scene was a surrealist fantasy. Part of the outside wall had been cut through by an intruder, and was open to the sea. His bed next to the porthole had been sliced into strips of metal and wood. Smoking debris littered the floor. The priests lingered for a moment, contemplating the working of a Providence that guided them to an unwanted Scrabble game. They took their life jackets. Thinking of the fire danger, Wojcik switched off the cabin light, unaware that Dr. Thure Peterson lay only a few feet from him, unconscious and bleeding in the wreckage of his bed.

Marion Boyer and his wife rushed from the Belvedere Lounge out to the open forward end of the Boat Deck in time to see the *Stockholm* recede into the mist. They heard the long blast of the *Andrea Doria*'s whistle, followed by several short blasts—the signal to get life jackets and go to muster stations. Then they heard a garbled announcement, first in Italian, then in English, also calling them to their emergency positions.

"Let's go down and get our life preservers right away," Boyer said.

Hand in hand, they moved as quickly as they could down the sloping stairwells, past others racing up the stairs against them, past the Promenade Deck and the Upper Deck to the Foyer Deck where their suite was located. They came down a long, wide flight of stairs to the main foyer and turned forward toward their cabin, but the wall of the corridor was pushed flat against the side of the chapel.

"Mr. Boyer, you can't get in there," a steward said, pointing out the obvious. "There's been too much destruction. There's glass and debris from the collision everywhere."

The Boyers raced around the far side of the chapel and through it toward the other side of the hallway leading to their cabin. Shattered glass filled the corridor. The couple had to work hard to clear away wreckage until there was room to unlock the door and step into the interior corridor that led past the bathroom to the sleeping area.

"My God!" Marion Boyer said as he looked at the cabin. The corridor and the bathroom were intact, but the rest of the cabin was gone. In its place was a black hole overlooking the sea. Had it not been for the last cup of coffee his wife had insisted on, the couple would have been washed out into the ocean. The Boyers froze momentarily as they realized the extraordinary fortune that had spared them. Then Marion Boyer smashed into the jammed closet door and grabbed the life jackets. He locked up the cabin and pocketed the key. "Let's go up to our station," he said, his voice trembling in realization of what might have been.

Peter Thieriot woke up at the moment of impact with the sensation that he was falling out of bed. He switched on his cabin light and walked over to look out the porthole. He could see nothing unusual. He turned off the light and peered out at the ocean once more. Now he could see that the water level was much closer to the porthole than it had been before. He immediately recalled his mother's words early in the voyage: "We might run into a storm sometime and get hit by some heavy waves, but don't worry. It'll be all right."

It must be a storm, the boy told himself. *That's simply a wave washing up high on the side of the ship.*

Peter rubbed his eyes and eased back under the covers of his bed. Once more he felt himself falling out of his bunk.

Now awake, he sat up in bed. "If it were a storm, there would be two sides to the wave," he muttered aloud to no one. Curious, he returned to the porthole. The water was still high on the starboard side. It was obviously no wave, no storm.

Loud, excited voices filtered through from the corridor and Peter heard the sound of tinkling glass. Still dressed in his pajamas, he opened the cabin door. A mannequin had fallen through the window of the dress shop across from his room.

Someone scurried past and yelled to the boy, "Get your life jacket!" But the warning did not register in Peter's still-drowsy mind.

Maybe we're in New York already, he thought. *But why isn't it light outside?* Calmly he took off his pajamas and dressed for his arrival at the dock. He folded the pajamas neatly, packed them in his suitcase, zipped up the side of his bag, and placed it carefully next to the door. He wondered why he was so tired after a whole night's sleep.

Peter walked out of his cabin to find his parents. Broken glass crackled under his shoes. The furniture had toppled over in the foyer. *We must have had some sort of accident*, he reasoned.

Peter's eyes focused on the flattened corridor wall that led toward his parents' suite. He stopped. There was no path through to their door. Now alarmed, he ran around the far side of the chapel to approach from the other end of the corridor, but it, too, was blocked. He circled back around the chapel to the foyer at the base of a wide stairway, his body shivering. He stood motionless, searching his mind.

They must be upstairs, he said to himself. *I'll go look for them.*

As he climbed the long stairway toward the Upper Deck he encountered Max Passante, the kindly gentleman who shared his parents' suite. Passante was on his way down from the Belvedere Lounge for his life jacket. Peter followed him as he, too, tried to find a way into deluxe suite 180, but it was impossible.

"Where are my parents?" Peter asked anxiously.

The answer was clear to Passante. Both his parents were dead, killed at the second of impact, as the bow of the *Stockholm* knifed its way into their bedroom suite. But he could not bear to tell Peter. "I don't know," he said. "Let's go to our lifeboat stations and wait for them there."

He put his arm around Peter and guided him gently up to the Promenade Deck.

Professor Bruno Tortori Donati, the ship's physician, was drinking coffee and smoking a last cigarette before bed when he felt the shock of the collision. He donned his life jacket and moved quickly through the now-darkened, smoky hallways to the hospital on A Deck.

Rosa Carola, returning from her last visit to her native Italy with her daughter, Margaret, and her daughter-in-law, Christina Covina, had spent the entire voyage there. She was suffering from terminal cancer complicated by a heart condition.

"Where are my daughters?" Mrs. Carola nervously asked the physician.

"I'm sure they will be here soon," replied Dr. Donati.

With the aid of a nurse, the doctor began an arduous journey out of the hospital toward the safer Promenade Deck. They placed Mrs. Carola on a stretcher, then moved up tilted stairways, attempting to keep the stretcher level as they struggled for secure footings.

As they reached a landing, Dr. Donati looked at his patient and suddenly saw the characteristic signs of pulmonary edema. The woman was struggling for breath. Even in the dimness, Donati could see that her face was cyanotic. He quickly lowered the stretcher. While frightened passengers elbowed past him on their way upward, the doctor inserted a needle into his patient's vein, drawing off 250 cc of blood to reduce the pressure. In this impromptu aid station on the hectic stairwell landing, Donati hurriedly injected digitalis, diuretic drugs, and morphine into Mrs. Carola.

Dr. Donati and his nurse waited expectantly, convinced she was dying. But as minutes passed, her breathing eased, and she looked up. In a morphine mist, she called out for her daughters.

Donati and the nurse lifted their patient and resumed their journey up the narrow stairway. Soon after they began to move the stretcher, Mrs. Carola went into cardiac failure for the second time. Donati quickly stopped and administered another regimen of drugs to the dying woman. Once again, the patient rallied. The stretcher bearers moved her up to the Promenade Deck, where they found a quiet alcove on the portside, forward of the ballrooms. Dr. Donati checked his watch. The trip from the hospital had taken a full hour.

"Where are my daughters?" Mrs. Carola cried. Dr. Donati peered along the deck, now crowded with anguished passengers. The daughters, he realized, would have difficulty locating Mrs. Carola in this confusion. He had no way of knowing that Margaret Carola and her sister-in-law, Christina Covina, had been trapped in their cabin and had drowned moments after the crash.

Lying dazed and trapped in the darkness of cabin 56, Jane Cianfarra struggled to comprehend what was happening. Suddenly she heard a scream and a desperate sob from across the room. "It's better to be dead than to live like this!" Then the voice grew silent. Jane Cianfarra wept, for she recognized that it was the voice of her husband, Camille. And where were her daughters, Joan and Linda? What had happened? Blood trickled down into her eyes and mouth, mingling with her tears, and she realized she was probably dying.

She heard an anguished moan and saw in the dim light that someone was below her, also entangled in the debris. She called out. It was Martha Peterson from the next cabin, whose body, trapped in the same pile of wreckage, was almost touching her. Both women struggled to free themselves, but they were held tightly by the wreckage. How long, they wondered, before someone would find them? Every few minutes, they could feel the ship shudder and turn more precariously on its side.

Dr. Thure Peterson woke in darkness, immobilized. His first thought was of Martha. He called for her, but heard no reply.

Why was everything so quiet? Why had the engines stopped? There was no sound from the corridor. He tried to clear his head, then he heard a groan.

He called into the dark. His wife answered that her legs were caught. The voice sounded strangely distant, as though in a cave. Peterson implored her not to move. Using the full power of his muscular arms, Dr. Peterson pushed at the debris on top of him and finally managed to free himself. He could feel blood gushing down from his scalp. His whole body ached. As he staggered to his feet he tried to orient himself to the cabin, but something was wrong. The layout of the room seemed changed. He groped along a wall until he found a light switch, but the electricity had failed.

He called out to Martha and followed the direction of her faint reply, feeling his way in the darkness. Soon he came up against a wall and realized that Martha's voice was on the other side. He pushed open the cabin door and walked out into the corridor that was now bathed in the amber glow of emergency lighting. When he saw the number 58 on the cabin door he realized that somehow he had been thrown out of his own room and into the adjacent cabin.

He tried the door to his own cabin, 56, but it was locked and he had no key. Dr. Peterson saw that a bottom panel of the door was caved in. On his hands and knees, he crawled through, oblivious to the sting of cuts on his bare skin. Nothing mattered but Martha. Groping in the darkness toward the sound of his wife's voice, his hand brushed against an unresponding face, that of Camille Cianfarra. Dr. Peterson sensed that he was dead, but he was too intent on finding Martha to mourn others. Her quivering voice called out from behind an immovable pile of wreckage. There seemed to be no way he could reach her from his own cabin.

There must be a hole between the cabins, he thought, *and I was thrown through it.* Desperate, he went back into the corridor and next door to cabin 58. Calling regularly to his wife, and using her voice as a guide, he groped toward her in the darkness. But separating them was still the partition between cabins 56 and 58. Searching with his fingertips, he discovered that the bottom of the wall separating the cabins was loose. He jammed his fingers underneath and pulled the wall out with all his strength, creating a space barely large enough for a human body. He painfully squeezed his broad shoulders beneath it, moving his body into cabin 56. Dim light from somewhere below illuminated the scene of horror. Suddenly amid the wreckage, he saw Martha's trusting face staring up at him.

Then he saw another woman, Jane Cianfarra, entrapped near his wife. Peterson knew that he could not free the two women by himself.

He crawled back into cabin 58. Before leaving he remembered that he was naked. He tore down a curtain and modestly wrapped it around his waist. He rushed up to the Promenade Deck, imploring every man he encountered for help. But each was absorbed in his drama of survival. Finally he saw a young man in clerical garb who proved to be a Catholic seminarian from Pennsylvania. Encouraged, Peterson pleaded for help. The seminarian looked sympathetically at Peterson, streaked with blood, his massive body only half covered by a curtain, and agreed to help.

On the way down to his deck, Peterson explained the problem. The seminarian doubted whether his slender build would be much help in lifting the heavy debris, but he was willing to try. Peterson again lifted the partition and the two men crawled under the wall. It was obvious that they had to free Jane Cianfarra first, before they could reach Martha Peterson. The men struggled in the tiny space to lift the wreckage, but it was too heavy and solidly wedged in. They crawled back to cabin 58, where Peterson decided that he needed more help. He told the young cleric about Camille Cianfarra, who lay dead in cabin 56. While Peterson raced upstairs, the seminarian went to cabin 56 and recited the act of contrition. Then the young man raced off to find a priest to administer the last rites.

Peterson found waiters Giovanni Rovelli and Pietro Nanni, who were busy gathering life jackets to hand out to passengers. They agreed to help, and the three men returned to cabin 58. There was only room for two of them to slip under the wall, so Nanni gave Peterson his flashlight and returned to the Promenade Deck.

Peterson and Rovelli crawled into cabin 56. The chiropractor discovered that Martha had no feeling in the lower part of her body. Her back was probably broken. One of Jane Cianfarra's legs was shattered. Peterson knew that both women needed morphine, and he went off again, this time in search of a doctor.

Working stoop-shouldered in the tiny space, Rovelli cleared away the lighter debris, but knew that he and Peterson could not lift the bulk of the wreckage that was pinning down the women. *An automobile jack!* he thought, *that's what I need.*

He recalled seeing one in the paint locker near the bow on the Promenade Deck. Reassuring the women that he would return, he crawled back under the wall and raced upstairs.

Sister Angelita Myerscough sat in a chair in her cabin on A Deck, drowsily pulling on stockings and slippers. Having been awakened seconds after the crash by her roommate, she was still struggling against the hypnotic effect of a Dramamine pill, oblivious to the water rising in the lower side of the hallway outside her door. As she stood up, she found it strangely difficult to steady her legs. *I can't be that dizzy*, she thought. Then she realized that it was the ship that was heeling severely to one side. She rapidly drew the habit on over her nightgown, discarding the large white collar which would get in the way of her life jacket. Clutching at the precious jacket, she started out the door.

Death! The thought suddenly flashed through her mind. *I might die tonight, and if I'm going to die I want to be wearing my sash.* She stepped back into the cabin for the distinctive red sash of her order, the Adorers of the Blood of Christ. She put it on deliberately, reverently, and walked back out into the hallway.

The corridor was now deserted. As she hurried up the steps she found the climbing torturous. A childhood story flashed through her mind about someone paralyzed by hysteria. *That's happening to me*, she thought. *I can't move.* For one terrible instant the nun stood immobilized on the stairway, her will weakened, her feet obstinately declining to carry her up to safety. Death, which she had considered calmly a moment before, now seemed terrifying and very close.

Inexplicably, an inner determination returned. Sister Angelita pulled hard at the railing, commanding her body to move. She realized that it was the list of the ship, not her fear, that made climbing so difficult. On one flight of stairs she had to lean forward; on the next she was forced to bend backward in order to move. The sensation was not unlike being in a carnival fun house.

Slowly she rose to the Promenade Deck. She stumbled into the cabin-class Ballroom and collapsed against the lower wall. She saw small, apprehensive groups of passengers huddled there, waiting for information. No one seemed to know what to do. Four large pillars that supported the Ballroom leaned continually farther to the starboard in macabre imitation of Pisa's tower.

Everyone was disoriented, confused, deeply worried. Liquor bottles were taken freely from behind the bars and opened, their contents devoured by anxious passengers and crewmen.

An occasional scream or sob disrupted the night, but most passengers sat quietly, waiting grimly for what was to come. Few knew that the *Andrea Doria* had collided with another ship, but all knew she was in serious trouble. Surely a full announcement would be made soon. The *Doria*'s modern lifeboats would take them off to safety.

Professor John Pick of Marquette University encountered a crewman who was running in the direction of the starboard lifeboats. "We've been told to abandon ship," the sailor said. Pick was puzzled. He had heard no such order issued to the passengers.

About midnight, muffled, nervous conversations along the upper edge of the Promenade Deck were suddenly interrupted when an angry man stood up and shouted:

"Where is the captain? Who is in charge of this ship? What is happening here?"

7

THE DECISION

AT THE INSTANT of the crash Captain Piero Calamai groaned. Standing high on the wing of the bridge he was safely above and slightly forward of the point of contact. The sickening series of thumps as the *Stockholm* tore open the *Andrea Doria* caused Calamai to utter an involuntary, uncharacteristic, "Damn!"

As the *Stockholm* receded into the fog Calamai reacted by habit. He pulled the engine telegraph handle back to STOP. The power of the engines ceased quickly, but the ship continued to slide forward in the water. Finally, after several minutes, the broken ship stopped quietly, surrounded by the foreboding gloom of the fog.

Shortly after impact, the *Andrea Doria* heeled over toward her right side, scattering navigation maps and logbooks across the chartroom floor. The knowledgeable officers were aware that the list could be fatal.

The ship's whistle, set blaring by the impact, was adding confusion to the stunned atmosphere on the bridge. Second Officer Curzio Franchini walked to the controls and switched the whistle off.

Third Officer Eugenio Giannini leaped from the window ledge of the wheelhouse, where he had perched only moments earlier to view the approaching ship. He strode quickly to the inclinometer, the instrument that measured the severity of any list. He trained his flashlight on its dial. "Eighteen degrees," he reported to Calamai. Then quickly added ominously, "Now nineteen."

The threat was obvious. Any list greater than twenty degrees destroyed the watertight integrity of the compartments. Even now, the officers knew, the ocean was splashing against the tops of the watertight doors on A Deck. Unless they could decrease or at least stabilize the list, the ship would continue to take on water, continue to lean farther to starboard, until the end.

Calamai could not believe it. He stood for a moment trying to rewrite the scene he had just witnessed. He could not understand how the accident had happened. He had tried repeatedly to evade the other vessel. Why had she continued to turn directly at him? Pushing his mind back to the present, Calamai moved around the wheelhouse, speaking in a pained voice and ordering the necessary actions to save the ship.

The bridge, dimmed as always to provide better visibility at night, became the headquarters of a grim campaign to keep the *Andrea Doria* afloat. Each deck officer reported to Calamai without being summoned, then each was sent out on his mission.

"Check the watertight doors," Calamai ordered several men. "Check the damage. I need a report quickly."

Second Officer Guido Badano was one of those who reported to the bridge. "Order the crew to their lifeboat stations," Calamai commanded Badano.

Badano picked up a microphone and set the switches to carry his voice to all crew quarters but not to the passenger areas. "Deck crew to abandon ship position," he called in Italian. Simultaneously, Staff Captain Osvaldo Magagnini and First Officer Carlo Kirn hurried from the bridge to gather their rescue crews and station them at the lifeboats.

Calamai then issued another order to Badano. "Call the passengers to their muster stations," he said.

Badano reset the speaker switches to broadcast throughout the ship. He made the announcement first in Italian and then in English, "Passengers must go to their muster stations wearing their life jackets and keep calm." Badano knew his voice would carry loud enough to be heard even in the passenger cabins. Both he and Calamai assumed that the announcement was sufficient. They did not realize that panic and confusion had taken hold of the ship, so that few passengers would hear or understand the urgent message.

"Send an SOS," Captain Calamai then commanded the radio operator. Almost simultaneously, Calamai ordered Badano to fix the ship's position accurately. Franchini hurriedly took loran readings while Badano plotted the position on the nautical chart.

The radio operator flashed the universal distress signal, three dots, three dashes, and three dots. He reported the ship's location at 40°30' north, 69°53' west as measured by Badano.

One fact offered some hope. The captain learned that the fire tindered by the friction of the *Stockholm*'s hull had been contained in the lining between the ship's skin and the wood-paneled cabins. The smoke that had immediately filled some hallways was rapidly dying down. The immediate fire danger was over.

In the engine room, crewmen worked to pump the ocean water out of the *Andrea Doria*'s flooded starboard compartments, but it surged in faster than they could expel it. They pumped water from the starboard side of number 45 tank to the port side of the tank, theorizing that the added weight on the left would help stabilize the ship. But the starboard side, open to the sea, continued to take on water. Intake valves designed to flood other empty port tanks directly from the sea were useless. The tilt of the ship had lifted these valves above the waterline.

The electrical generating room was flooding fast, threatening to short-circuit the dynamos that normally provided power to the ship. The pumps were electrical. If the water continued to rise, the power supply would slowly dwindle, crippling further efforts to save the ship.

An employee of the shipboard bank, Credito Italiano, appeared on the bridge with his life jacket in one hand. The other hand was bleeding. Giannini took a bandage from the first-aid kit, tied up the torn hand, and assisted the manager into his life jacket.

Then Giannini stood by the captain, periodically shining his flashlight on the inclinometer. The needle continued to shift to the right of the dial. The ominous list increased quickly to twenty-two degrees and showed no signs of abating.

Calamai searched for a remedy. He could not bear the thought of consigning his beautiful ship to the deep. Perhaps he could save the *Andrea Doria* by bringing her to shallow waters where the wounded ship could be beached. Later, she could be salvaged or even repaired.

The captain checked with the engine room and learned that the starboard engine was useless, but that the port engine was unharmed. "Slow ahead on the port engine," Calamai ordered Giannini. He planned to examine the charts for a suitable landing spot to the north.

The telephone on the bridge rang. It was the engine room reporting water flowing into the boiler room and the engine room, both located aft of the collision zone. The *Doria*'s engineering design that was to keep the ship afloat with two adjacent compartments flooded had failed in the few seconds of impact. The *Stockholm* apparently had ripped open several smaller holes along the hull in addition to the primary wound. Water was now flowing into at least four compartments on the starboard side.

Despite all efforts, the ship continued to draw water, increasing the list with a frightening rapidity. The officers had heard reports of ships listing less than the *Andrea Doria*, which had suddenly capsized. Calamai knew that any forward motion would increase that danger. He was also concerned that the flooding of the engine room would make it impossible to move any sizable distance. If he continued to try to save his ship by grounding it, he might delay rescue operations and risk the lives of his passengers. Reluctantly, he ordered the port engine shut down once more.

Calamai was now resigned to the fact that the ship had to

be abandoned, and turned his attention back to the rescue effort. Each crewman had his assigned duty. Under normal conditions the ship could be evacuated with a minimum of risk. But the heavy fog surrounded the wounded liner, hiding her from the ships they hoped would soon be moving into these Nantucket waters. The fog would also make it difficult for the *Doria*'s lifeboats to find their way to rescue ships, and increase the chance of still another fatal collision.

Not a profane man, Calamai searched his mind for epithets against the fog.

Since the *Titanic* had gone down in 1912 while carrying lifeboats that could hold less than half of the passengers and crew, ocean liners had been required to carry an adequate number of lifeboats. The *Andrea Doria* had more than enough emergency capacity to accommodate everyone. The lifeboats were gravity operated. Winches held them in place ready to be lowered to the Promenade Deck where passengers boarded. When full, the boats would be lowered farther to the water. Though any lifeboat operation is necessarily hazardous, this procedure was designed to work automatically.

When the order to ready the boats was given to the officers, Giannini walked quickly toward his station on the port side, stopping briefly in his cabin for his life jacket and a crucifix his mother had given him when he first went to sea. On the portside of the Lido Deck he saw a group of sailors with their shoulders pressed against the wooden side of a lifeboat. The men grunted as they pushed. Giannini realized the problem immediately. The ship was tilted so severely that the davits on which the boats were suspended were angled upward. The boat would not slide down when its winches were released. Giannini threw his shoulder against the boat with the others, but the effort was ineffectual. The heavy boat would not move. All eight lifeboats wedged into place on the port side were useless.

There was a fatal anomaly in the design. The *Andrea Doria* could remain afloat unless she listed more than twenty degrees. But half the lifeboats became useless if the list was greater than fifteen degrees. The ship's list was so severe that it was endangering the lives of its passengers. But that same list was making it impossible to launch the lifesaving boats.

Soon Calamai received the report. Franchini went out to the port wing of the bridge and watched as sailors continued to try to push the boats free. It was obvious they would fail. No amount of manpower could push the boats uphill.

That left eight usable boats instead of sixteen. But even the normal procedure for launching the remaining lifeboats would not work, for the starboard boats were hanging too far out from the Promenade Deck. Sailors tried to pull them toward the deck with ropes, but the boats would not yield. They would have to be lowered into the water first. Passengers would somehow have to climb down to water level and then negotiate the gap of open space between the canted hull and the lifeboats. The area was particularly hazardous since the wound was sucking in water at a tremendous rate, creating dangerous undercurrents all along the starboard side.

When Calamai realized that the port side lifeboats could not be launched, he turned to Badano on the bridge. "Tell the passengers again to go to their muster stations," he ordered.

Badano repeated the order, then looked into the worn face of the captain. "Should I give the abandon ship signal?" he asked. Badano was referring to the signal posted in every passenger cabin: more than six short blasts of the siren followed by one long one.

Calamai pondered the dilemma of the lifeboats. The usable boats could hold less than a thousand people, but there were seventeen hundred on board. Such a signal, he thought, might create a panic and bring a crush of desperate people to the available boats.

The captain made his decision. He would not take the passengers into his confidence. He would make no announcement. Rather, his men would guide the passengers from their muster stations in small groups, the children, the old, the sick, and the women first.

The captain finally spoke. "No," he said to Badano. "No signal."

8

THE MIRACLE

THE GIRL WOKE UP staring at the night sky. She vaguely remembered a roaring sound and assumed it was part of a
dream. She was lying on her mattress, strangely stripped of its
sheets and blankets. Her yellow pajamas, embossed with
Chinese characters, were in tatters. Her left arm hung useless
at her side, though at the moment she felt no pain from it.
Confused and afraid, she cried out for her mother in Spanish.

Off to one side she heard a woman crying. Thinking it was
her mother, she called out, *"Madre! Madre!"* The woman
screamed incoherently, then sobbed for a few minutes, until
she became silent.

The girl could not understand what had happened to the
roof of her cabin. Instead of a ceiling overhead, she saw the
misty night sky. Wonder gave way to terror. *"Madre! Madre!"*
she screamed again. There was no answer. The girl was alone,
somewhere in the Atlantic Ocean, lying helplessly on the
wreckage of her bed.

Bernabé Polance García, the only Spanish-speaking
sailor aboard the *Stockholm,* was inspecting the damage at the
bow of the ship when he heard the girl's cry. He was surprised,

for he was unaware there were any Spanish passengers on board. He pushed aside the wreckage and approached the voice. "I'll help you," he reassured her.

García surveyed her injuries as best he could in the darkness. Her left arm was obviously broken. She could not sit up, and García assumed that she had also suffered internal injuries. Gently he cradled her in his arms and spoke softly to her in Spanish. The girl stared at him, grateful but uncomprehending. García stepped slowly through the debris on deck and carried her to the ship's hospital.

Chief Purser Curt Dawe was there. He asked for her name.

"Linda Morgan," she replied weakly.

Dawe checked the passenger list, confused. "There is no passenger with that name," he replied.

"Maybe it's listed as Linda Cianfarra, my stepfather's name," the girl ventured.

Again Dawe checked his records, but could find no mention of the girl. "Where did you come from?" he asked.

"Madrid."

Dawe was thoroughly perplexed.

The girl began to weep. "Isn't this the *Andrea Doria*?" she asked.

Dawe's face paled. His eyes widened with alarm. "No," he said, "this is not the *Andrea Doria*. This is the *Stockholm*."

Linda screamed. "It can't be. I'm on the *Andrea Doria*. Where is my mother?" She tried to wake herself from the improbable dream, but the images of sailors stumbling into the hospital, their bodies streaked with blood, oil, and gray paint, crying in anguish, were real. "Where is my mother?" Linda sobbed. "I want my mother."

Incredulous doctors treated her broken arm, but were more concerned about internal damage. They forced her to drink hot water, then salt water, trying to induce her system to retch. When they could find no symptoms of serious injury, they administered morphine to dull the pain of the broken arm.

Linda wavered for a time between merciful sleep and lucid moments of anguish. When conscious, she begged those around her to make sure her mother on the *Andrea Doria* was notified that she was safe. As the morphine took full effect, Linda fell into a deep trance.

Nearby, García hid his sadness. No one else in this girl's cabin could possibly have survived. She had been sleeping in the direct line of the crash. She should be dead. But on a night when conventional logic seemed suspended and unfathomable tales abounded, Linda's fate seemed perhaps the most incredible. The bow of the *Stockholm* had sliced into her cabin directly beneath her bunk next to the porthole, smashing her bed. It had hurled Linda's half sister, Joan, into the sea, where she perished. It had fatally torn her stepfather, Camille Cianfarra. It had thrown her mother, Jane Cianfarra into the adjacent cabin where she lay almost hopelessly trapped.

Then, as the *Stockholm*'s bow retreated from the *Andrea Doria*'s crushed innards, it lifted Linda and her mattress almost gently out of the doomed ship and deposited her safely on the Swedish liner. Without ever comprehending that there was a collision or that her cabin had been demolished and her family decimated, Linda lay unconscious on the deck without any apparent serious injury until the sailor heard her frightened plea for help.

"It's a miracle," García whispered solemnly.

9

THE WAIT

ON THE PROMENADE DECK of the *Andrea Doria* a woman suddenly collapsed. She lay motionless. A small girl clutched at the wet fabric of the woman's nightgown and screamed into an unresponding face, "Mommy, don't die! Don't leave me!" The girl's mother was dead, possibly a casualty of a sudden heart attack.

A dark apprehension snared the passengers. Would they succumb, one by one, until the ship rolled over and took its remaining victims swiftly? To many, it seemed that most of the *Andrea Doria* officers and crew members had disappeared into the same fog that cloaked the ship. They were human wreckage bobbing precariously close to the safety of New York Harbor, but agonizingly distant from immediate aid.

True, some of the crew could be seen working selflessly to assist stricken passengers, while others stood visible at their stations in a calm, professional manner. But the once omnipresent uniforms of the crew were suddenly scarce. People clutching for support on the slopes of the Promenade and Boat Decks had no way of knowing whether their protectors were incapacitated, busy trying to save the ship, or had abandoned ship. It was now apparent that they were going to receive little enlightenment from the ship's loudspeaker. Many passengers began to express open anger with their mute captain.

Rumors flashed along the decks from the Belvedere Lounge up front, through the ballrooms, corridors, and side rooms of the Boat Deck and the Promenade Deck to the open air of the stern where most of the emigrants huddled. Some were fanciful inventions. Others were grimly true.

"Someone saw a Russian submarine . . ."

"The captain has been killed . . ."

"We're going to capsize . . ."

"The lifeboats won't work . . ."

"The crew is leaving us . . ."

"There are sharks circling the ship . . ."

Reactions ran from calm acceptance through calculated action to emotional and physical collapse. Women gathered children to their bosoms. Husbands and fathers felt impotent, trapped in a situation beyond their capacity to control. The continual lurching to starboard was ominous. No one knew how long the ship would remain afloat and what, if anything, was being done to save them.

Standard Oil executive Marion Boyer reviewed it all in his mind—the watertight compartments, the double-bottom hull, the extraordinary engineering procedures that guaranteed the safety and stability of the *Andrea Doria*. Early in the voyage he had visited the bridge. His critical managerial eye was impressed by the discipline and professionalism of the Italian crew. After the crash, he and his wife, Malcolm, had returned from their shattered cabin with their life jackets and climbed to the port side of the Promenade Deck when the list was not very severe. They stood now at the sliding glass windows, holding onto a railing for support. Others in their group from Standard Oil of New Jersey sat in chairs nearby.

Boyer knew the ship was unsinkable. He grew only mildly concerned as the angled deck increasingly slanted toward starboard. "Sometime soon we'll reach an equilibrium," he said to his wife. "The ship will stabilize itself. Then they'll be able to right it."

Mrs. Boyer thought differently. The ship was heeling over too fast. She had seen for herself the gaping hole ripped into her own suite, and she knew the liner must have suffered greater damage below the waterline. But she confided her fears to no one. She did not want to create panic.

Dr. Stewart Coleman, leader of the Standard Oil touring party, approached Boyer. The two men quietly discussed the situation. "We're leaning over so fast," Coleman said, "I'm afraid we'll capsize."

"No we won't," Boyer reassured him. "They can pump fuel to the port side. Very soon now the ship will even itself out."

Coleman felt better after listening to his friend. When Boyer was general manager of the Atomic Energy Commission he had supervised the postwar production of an arsenal of nuclear warheads. He was an expert on engineering principles.

A shrill wail distracted them. An emigrant family from the tourist-class deck below suddenly appeared on the Promenade Deck, their half-clothed bodies smeared with black oil. Blood stained the leg of one of the children's pajamas. Crewmen helped the anxious Italian passengers up to the high side of the deck.

Boyer and Coleman realized they had not been exposed to the worst agonies of the night. Down below the waterline the Italian emigrants had suffered the most.

Coleman looked out the window at the dark surface of the ocean, growing ever more distant as the port side raised out of the water. "I wish we had life jackets," he said, staring at the orange vest securely strapped onto Boyer. "I forgot to get them. Maybe I should go back down for them."

Boyer placed a hand on his friend's shoulder. "Don't worry," he said, "we'll be all right."

In the darkness of A Deck, Mrs. Alba Wells of Birmingham, Alabama, screamed into a deserted and smoky hallway. "Help me! Someone please help me!" she wailed. She was answered only by the sound of water lapping across the doorway. Her eight-year-old daughter, Shirley, her bright blue Italian sailor dress blackened with oil, clung silently to her mother's skirt. Seeing that help was not available, Mrs. Wells went back to her cabin.

Inside, her three-year-old daughter, Rose Marie, whimpered in shock from the pain of the heavy upper bunk that pinned her tiny left hand to her crumpled bed. The girl screamed and struggled against her iron captor.

"Rose, oh, Rosie!" her mother cried. "I'm right here. I won't leave you. Ever." Mrs. Wells vowed to go down with the ship rather than to abandon her youngest child. But how could she also save Shirley, clinging so trustingly to her hem? And where was her nine-year-old son, Henry? She had not seen him since he went to a movie earlier in the evening.

The frantic mother pushed aside all problems except the immediate one. She must free her baby. Once again she tugged at Rosie's tiny body, but her efforts were useless. She could not move the iron bunk.

The ship lurched. Mrs. Wells caught her breath, waiting for the deadening onslaught of the sea. Once more the ship held steady. Once more the mother pulled vainly at her baby's arm.

It was Shirley who first saw the light of a flashlight beam bounce off the corridor wall. A man in a once-white uniform appeared in the doorway. Mrs. Wells recognized him as the dining room steward who always greeted little Rosie playfully.

"Mrs. Wells, I didn't see you up top. I thought I'd better check on you."

Mrs. Wells pointed to Rosie. The steward stumbled to her broken bed and tried to shove the top bunk away. The mother joined him and pushed strenuously, but the bed would not move.

The steward then tried to pull Rosie loose, but the hand was held too firmly. Rosie was now screaming continually, her cries echoing in the deserted hallway. The steward drew the mother aside. "If I cannot get it loose, we might have to cut her hand off," he said quietly.

"Anything is better than being dead," Mrs. Wells answered.

"I've got to get a crowbar," he said. "Stay here."

After the steward left, Alba Wells rested for a moment before returning to Rosie to push yet another time at the cursed bed.

Minutes passed as water continued to rise in the compartment. Finally, the steward returned, holding a flashlight and a crowbar.

Forty-five minutes, most of it spent futilely pushing against the bunk, had elapsed since the collision had pinioned Rose Marie to her bed. Before he could use the crowbar, the *Andrea Doria* suddenly gave a mighty heave. Metal clanged loudly as the fallen bunk slipped from Rosie's bed and splashed onto the watery floor. Rosie screamed. Mother and daughter reached out for each other. The little girl wrapped her right arm tightly around her mother's neck, still screaming. Her left hand was torn.

"Quickly," the steward said. "Take your daughters up to a top deck."

"Aren't you coming?"

"I'm going to see if anyone else needs help," he replied, and he moved out into the black hallway.

With Rosie screaming and clinging to her neck and Shirley grasping at her skirt, Mrs. Wells stepped into the corridor. Her feet slid on the oily floor and slipped out from under her. She tumbled, Rosie screaming even louder. Mrs. Wells gathered her children about her once more, and made her way toward a stairwell.

Now on her knees, she slowly crawled up the oily, tilted stairs. Up past the deserted levels of the Foyer Deck and the Upper Deck she moved, pausing at each landing to gather strength. She finally emerged on the Promenade Deck and moved far back toward the stern.

Mrs. Wells was stunned by the scene of frightened passengers and crew, waiting out in the open next to the tourist-class swimming pool that splashed water from its starboard side onto the overturned deck furniture. The rear of the Promenade Deck seemed like an island of castaways. Emigrant children screamed while their mothers prayed.

Mrs. Wells saw that most wore orange life jackets. Their

own were still down on A Deck, pinned underneath the wreckage of Rosie's bed.

In the enclosed area of the Promenade Deck, Margaret Sergio was lying down on the deck next to the glass windows. "My sister! My sister!" she cried. "Where are the children?"

The deck was covered with Italian emigrants, sitting or lying, grasping for support at anything bolted down. Paul Sergio, next to Margaret, felt helpless in the midst of the crowd. Throughout the voyage he had fulfilled his duties as surrogate father to his two nephews and two nieces. Now, when they needed him most, he could not find them. *Surely they must be somewhere up here on the deck*, he thought. *Perhaps they are closer to the front of the ship, for their cabin is in that direction.* Leaving Margaret in the care of others, Paul stumbled forward, searching the muster stations for Maria and the children. When he could not find them he knew he must go back down below.

He crawled his way toward a stairwell that led down toward his sister-in-law's cabin on C Deck, but a sailor held out an arm and stopped him.

"No!" the crewman yelled. "You can't go down there."

"But my wife's sister and her children are down there. I must save them!" Sergio cried.

The crewman took Sergio down a few steps and shone his flashlight into the dark hole. The cobbler could see nothing but water below A Deck. He felt he would retch. There was now little doubt about Maria's fate, as well as that of her four children. He sat on the stairs for a few minutes and cried. Then he composed himself. Margaret must not know of this. Somehow he would keep Margaret believing that Maria and the children were alive.

When he returned to the darkened spot on the deck where Margaret lay, he gently told her that the sailors would not allow him into the forward muster stations. "But they told me that passengers from Maria's section were safe there," he said. Margaret sobbed, unconvinced.

Sergio watched as a crewman threw open all the glass windows at the port side railing. "If we give you the signal," he told the frightened passengers, "just jump overboard into the water."

Sergio stared outside the open window. The edge of the great ship sloped in front of him. He knew he could never jump far enough to clear it. Neither he nor Margaret had a life jacket. In their haste to find Maria and the children they had forgotten to bring their own preservers.

A desperate man with huge bare shoulders streaked with blood, dressed only in a curtain, crawled up the four levels from the Upper Deck to the Sun Deck. He pushed his way through the officers milling around Calamai. Though several people were clamoring for his attention, the captain surprisingly remembered the strangely attired visitor by name. Dr. Thure Peterson had toured the bridge earlier in the voyage.

Quickly Peterson explained his predicament. His wife was trapped in cabin 56. With a distant expression on his features, Calamai replied, "I will send the doctor down to you." He ordered a cadet and other crewmen to help, and he sent a message to Dr. Bruno Donati.

Grateful, Peterson slid back down the stairways. The trip seemed to last forever. He was exhausted, but determined to save his wife. When he arrived back at cabin 58, he saw that Giovanni Rovelli had propped up the partition between the cabins.

Rovelli, who had failed to find a jack, had since returned to cabin 56. He was working in the cramped, sloping space, clearing loose debris. Peterson helped Rovelli free Jane Cianfarra's right leg, but the left one was still held solidly by a tangle of bedsprings. Peterson assured the women that the captain had promised assistance.

Peterson and Rovelli crawled back to cabin 58 where they met the young seminarian who had tried to help earlier. "I brought you some pants," he said. He held up a pair of black trousers borrowed from his roommate, Father Paul Lambert.

Thure Peterson threw aside the curtain and pulled the pants over his legs. Lambert's oversized pants hung loosely around him, though he was a large man himself.

A few moments later, Dr. Donati appeared with his medical bag. "I'm a doctor," Peterson informed him. "You can give me the morphine."

Dr. Donati prepared a syringe with a double injection for the two women. "Since you're a doctor," he told the chiropractor, "I'll leave a nurse with you in case you need something. I must go to help other people."

Peterson returned to cabin 56 and gave the shots first to his wife, then to Jane Cianfarra.

Peterson and Rovelli set to work once more trying to pull apart the bedsprings that entangled Jane Cianfarra's left leg. It seemed a hopeless task, when Peterson suddenly remembered something he had seen on the bridge, in the radio shack.

Wire cutters!

Minutes later, struggling for breath after climbing up four decks for the second time, Peterson appeared in the radio shack where the wireless operator was busily communicating with other ships. Peterson slid down the sloping floor toward the surprised radio officer, and asked for a pair of wire cutters.

The officer indicated a drawer where Peterson found two pairs. He shoved them into the gaping pockets of Father Lambert's trousers and fled back downstairs.

Father Richard Wojcik struggled to the port side of the roofed-in, glass-enclosed Promenade Deck and sat next to his solemn friend, Father John Dolciamore. Wojcik was thankful that he had worn his rubber-soled walking shoes to the lucky Scrabble game. He was pleased by the traction he felt as he crossed the tilted waxed floor.

Chairs bolted to the deck or wedged against the bulkheads were quickly filled. Some of the female survivors sat with jewel boxes on their laps. Latecomers to the muster station had to find a place on the floor. For some, staying in place on the slanting, highly polished finish now streaked with oil seemed impossible. Many of the women, dressed in party gowns, night-clothes, or other slippery silks and satins, kept sliding on the smooth surface as they sat. First one, then others of the women pulled off their nylon stockings. They hiked up their skirts, oblivious to modesty. Some even carefully removed their panties and threw them aside, squatting down bare-bottomed on the floor. It seemed the only way to stay in place.

Father Wojcik stared out at the night, aware of the difficulty of rescue in the treacherous fog. He prayed for help.

Nearby, an elderly woman, dressed in a nightgown, shivered spasmodically in the warm summer night. The priest wondered why she was so cold. He realized that she must be shivering from fear.

He moved next to her. "Would you like me to hold your hand?" he asked softly.

She looked up at him in the dim light, and when she saw the clerical collar her face softened. "Yes," she replied.

They sat silently in the dark and held hands.

Alfred and Beverly Green at the first-class muster station were worried more about their friend Walter Carlin than their own fate. The old colonel stared unseeingly at the panorama in front of him. Over and over he replayed the scene of his wife's bed floating out to sea as he, toothbrush in hand, stood by unable to help.

"I want to recover Jeanette's body," he moaned. "I'll offer a reward. I'll pay anything." He cried softly. His life meant nothing to him now.

The Greens spoke quietly to each other, so Carlin could not hear. "We must watch over him," Mrs. Green said. "He's in shock."

Father Paul Lambert, unable to move freely around on a now precariously slanted deck because of his bulk, crawled on his hands and knees to groups of nervous passengers. One by one Lambert heard their confessions. Finally exhausted, he sat in a corner of the Promenade Deck while other passengers formed a line in front of him. Each person crawled forward for a moment of privacy with the priest.

It was well after midnight when a man wearing a white officer's uniform with a black rabat around his neck crawled over to Lambert. He was Monsignor Sebastian Natta, the ship's chaplain. In his hand he held his silver ciborium, which contained only a few crumbs of the sacred wafer. Natta had been offering communion to passengers. Now he thrust the last few crumbs of the sacred host at Lambert.

Natta crawled over to the railing, ceremoniously heaving the sacred vessel into the sea, leaving little doubt in Lambert's mind. The chaplain knew the ship was going down.

Young Peter Thieriot sat on the floor of the Promenade Deck next to Max Passante. Peter's eyes searched through the crowd of anxious passengers strung along the high port side of the deck, sure that he would find his parents among them. He had positioned himself near a stairway where he could check each latecomer who straggled up to the muster station. He could not seem to grasp the meaning of the collapsed wall of his parents' suite. Passante was sure that both the boy's parents were dead, but he tried to be encouraging.

"I can't understand where my parents are," Peter said finally. "I'm sure they'd come to find me."

Passante shrugged evasively.

"I'm going to look for them," Peter said, suddenly rising. Passante reached to stop the boy, then decided it would be better for Peter to be occupied.

Peter had explored the ship before and had an intimate knowledge of its geography. Now he searched his mind for areas where his parents might be waiting. *Perhaps,* he thought, *they went back up to the Belvedere Lounge for a drink after I went to bed.* He walked up to the Boat Deck and forward to the lounge, dim now in the amber lighting. A few couples still sat there, clutching life jackets, waiting. Peter's parents were not in the lounge.

Maybe they are down below, helping to rescue people, Peter thought. His father would do all he could to help in an emergency. Peter found a narrow stairwell near the front of the ship and half tumbled downward, his feet slipping on the strange angle of the steps. He moved down past the Promenade Deck, the Upper Deck, and the Foyer Deck, then stopped as he saw that A Deck was covered with two feet of water. It was impossible to descend farther.

Peter's eyes widened as a man dressed only in jockey shorts sloshed past the stairwell, water up over his knees, oily trash swaying back and forth against him. He, too, seemed to be searching for someone.

Peter realized that his parents could not be down here. He turned and climbed back to the Promenade Deck. Forward from the first-class Ballroom was an open area toward the bow of the ship. Peter moved in that direction and came upon crewmen chattering excitedly in Italian. The men had pulled an inflatable raft from its housing on the deck and activated the compressed air cylinder that filled it. Peter watched in astonishment as the crewmen threw the raft overboard, then one by one jumped into the water. One of the men landed directly on the raft and screamed out in pain. Peter wondered why the men seemed so desperate to save themselves. He had been told that the ship could not sink.

Troubled by not finding his mother and father, Peter wandered back to Passante. The older man did not ask him if he had found his parents.

A few minutes later, a priest approached him. The cleric remembered that Peter had helped to serve Mass several times during the voyage, and he suggested that the boy lead the Rosary.

Anxious to help, Peter agreed. He found a quiet spot on a landing between the first-class Ballroom and the deck, where a double bench was divided by a high back. He sat on one side of the bench as people gathered near him.

"Hail, Mary, full of grace! the Lord is with thee. Blessed art thou among women, and blessed is the fruit of thy womb, Jesus," Peter began.

Solemn passengers responded: "Holy Mary, Mother of God, pray for us sinners now and at the hour of our death. Amen."

Peter became conscious of a man who came to sit on the other side of the bench in the darkness, perhaps, thought Peter, to be near the prayers. He glanced across the rear of the bench and saw the head and shoulders of a well-dressed man, his head quietly bowed. After a few minutes the man left silently. As Peter continued the litany he was suddenly aware of a stench. While those around him responded to the prayers, Peter peered over the back of the bench. He realized that the man, unwilling or unable to locate a bathroom amid the confusion, had defecated on the seat.

Peter continued to say the Rosary, only faster.

Dr. Stewart Coleman was now convinced that he had made a fatal mistake. In his rush to reach the muster station he had neglected to bring life jackets for himself and his wife.

"I'm going down for our jackets," he told his wife.

Mrs. Coleman tried to persuade him not to venture below. She worried about his back ailment, the result of a New York taxicab accident years earlier. Coleman was sometimes crippled by a disabling pain when he exerted himself, but he would not be dissuaded. He removed his wire-rimmed glasses, cleaned them of oil and smoke, and perched them back astride his nose. He plunged down a stairway leading to the Upper Deck.

In the semidarkness, he squinted with his weak eyes at the cabin numbers until he found his room. He bundled the orange jackets in his arms and turned to go back upstairs, working his way slowly through the maze of corridors and occasionally stumbling against the list of the ship. As he reached a foyer at the base of a main stairway, his foot suddenly slipped on an oil slick. He tumbled to the floor, life jackets flying out of his arms, his glasses thrown from his nose. His body fell heavily to the floor and he slid down the slope, his head striking sharply on the base of a potted palm.

Dazed, Coleman lay there for a moment, feeling the pains moving up his bad back. He tried to focus his eyes, but without his glasses the foyer was a blur. He slowly pulled himself to his feet, gathered the jackets once more into his arms, and searched desperately for his eyeglasses. Unable to find the spectacles, Coleman decided to abandon them. At least he had the jackets. Again he moved toward the stairway, but as he lifted his foot tentatively toward the first step, the ship heaved toward starboard. Coleman lost his balance and once more tumbled to the floor, sliding back down to the low side of the foyer.

Bruised and now only semiconscious, Coleman knew he was in danger. New pains shot through his spine. He found it difficult to pull himself back to his feet. He grimaced and approached the stairs unsteadily for a third attempt. Again the ship lurched, throwing Coleman to the floor.

He lay there breathing heavily, at the dim edge of reality, convinced that the ship was sinking and taking him under with it. There was nothing more to do. He felt himself slipping slowly, almost gently, into darkness, when a steward suddenly appeared.

Coleman saw the face bending over him. He struggled to retrieve his will. "I need help," he murmured. "My glasses, my glasses."

The steward searched the foyer, found the eyeglasses, and placed them back on Coleman's bleeding nose. He helped Coleman to his feet, slipping his arm around the dazed passenger's waist. Together they moved slowly up the angled stairs, then back out to the Promenade Deck.

As Coleman spotted his wife he suddenly remembered the life jackets. He looked down and smiled when he realized he was still clutching them tightly in his arms.

In the cabin-class Ballroom, amidships on the Promenade Deck, safely above and behind the fifty-foot gash created by the *Stockholm*, Ruby MacKenzie was alert, watching from the high side of the room for any signs of rescue activity. She was determined that her daughter, Ann, would be among the first off the ship, if they were forced to abandon it. Ruby and Ann had come to the high side of the tilted Ballroom by kicking off their shoes and pulling their way along barstools fastened to the floor. Mrs. MacKenzie was surprised that some people remained clustered on the starboard side, apparently lacking the energy or desire to crawl to the top.

Each lurch of the ship loosened additional chairs, bottles, and cocktail glasses. The debris slid down the sharp slope of the floor, sometimes lodging against one of the four proud pillars in the center of the room, but more often crashing into the starboard-side passengers.

Mrs. MacKenzie's attention was diverted. She watched curiously as a man pulled a piece of twine from his pocket and held it against the top of a window frame on the high side of the deck. A few minutes later he repeated the strange ritual.

"What are you doing?" a female voice asked. The man shrugged, apparently not wishing to alarm the woman with his explanation.

"I know what you're doing," Mrs. MacKenzie spoke up, "you're measuring the list. You're making a plumb line."

The man nodded, and once more held the twine up to the window. The bottom of the string hung noticeably farther out from the ledge each time he measured.

Ann MacKenzie stared out through the plate-glass windows at the black water, barely visible in the fog. "Do you think there are any sharks out there?" she asked her mother.

Mrs. MacKenzie thought quickly for a reassuring answer. "Oh, no," she said with too much conviction, "the water's too cold for sharks."

Ann sensed her mother's anxiety at the question and stared once more at the water. She was a good swimmer, but the thought of meeting a shark alone in the night alarmed her. Although religion was never important before, she now began to pray fervently.

It was not hot, but anxiety seemed to stimulate a warm, humid atmosphere. Ann was visibly perspiring in the short tweed coat she wore.

A friend approached. "Take off your coat, Ann. Aren't you hot?" she queried.

"No," Ann said sharply, "I'm all right."

Then the woman realized that the young girl was almost naked under the coat.

Sister Callistus sat next to her friend Sister Marie Raymond, on a chair wedged against a pillar on the high side of the cabin-class Ballroom. Glass-topped tables were sliding in all directions. Broken glass was everywhere.

Sister Callistus watched a man, seemingly drunk, fumble with the clasps of his life jacket. He had it on backwards. Tears of frustration rolled down his face.

"Stand up straight," she commanded the helpless man. "I'll help you." He complied. The nun pulled the jacket off of him, turned it around, and slipped it properly over his shoulders. Cautiously she returned to her chair against the pillar.

Next to her, staring out at the fog, Sister Raymond wondered how death would feel. Would it be a long process? Would the water be cold as it slipped around her? She prayed that if she and others were to die that night, the deaths would be happy and that all would go to heaven. She prayed for forgiveness for her sins.

Suddenly the ship lurched, and the nun's crippled leg cracked into the chair next to her. It pained. Sister Raymond worried that the leg might hinder her if they tried to abandon ship.

Another sudden spasm of the *Doria* increased the angle to starboard. A set of band drums went tumbling chaotically across the room, the cymbals ringing out a piercing protest. "We're going under! We're going under!" a woman shrieked, her face a pale mask. Friends forced her to lie down, and covered her body with a tablecloth.

The bartender, who only an hour before had been serving drinks to these same passengers, realized that he must take charge. He found a thick rope. Half-crawling, half-walking, a cigarette dangling from his lips, he made his way around the four pillars in the center of the room, stringing them together in a rectangular pattern. Then he calmly pushed furniture against the rope to prevent it from sliding into the passengers, whistling as he labored.

Sister Angelita Myerscough crawled over to the bartender. "Is the ship going to sink?" she asked.

"This ship could lie here for two years and never sink," he told her, exhibiting a naive confidence in the ship's now violated watertight compartments.

Sister Angelita was not so sure. The ever-deepening list was proof that more water was flooding the lower decks all the time. She was convinced that somehow the security of the watertight doors had been penetrated. Above her on the high side of the room she could see Sister Raymond and Sister Callistus sitting quietly.

"I'd like to go up there and sit with those two sisters," she said to the bartender. "Do you think I could?"

"Sure." The bartender assisted her to the rope. The nun pulled herself slowly up until she reached the pillar where her two friends sat.

"How are you?" she asked.

"We're all right," Sister Raymond replied. "What do you think will happen?"

"I don't know. The Lord's will be done." Sister Angelita eased herself into an upholstered chair that was wedged against other fallen furniture.

A woman nearby, sitting barefoot on the floor, shivered. "My feet are getting so cold," she complained.

Sister Angelita saw a deck blanket on the floor in front of her and she leaned over to give it to the woman. The sudden shift of weight pulled her chair loose from its place, propelling it wildly down the overpolished floor, the black-robed nun with it, aiming directly at the people on the low side. Sister Angelita squealed helplessly, her arms and legs flying out of control.

A man watching her descent quickly handed his baby to his wife. He jumped up from the Ballroom floor, pulled off his coat, and fashioned an impromptu net to catch the unfortunate woman. Sister Angelita slammed into him, the two of them crashing hard against a shatterproof window.

Sister Angelita moaned in pain, then struggled to a sitting position. Flexing her arms and legs, she realized that she had not been seriously injured. "Thank you so much," she said to her rescuer. "Are you all right?"

"I'm fine," the man assured her. He took the baby from his wife and cradled it in his arms.

"I think I'll just stay down here now," Sister Angelita said. She remembered that July 25 was the feast day of St. Christopher, patron of travelers. "He's going to be a busy saint tonight," she whispered to herself.

Father Tom Kelly watched as the general anxiety grew in the cabin-class Ballroom. The young priest had just completed four years of study in Rome where he was ordained the previous Christmas. He was on his way back to the Chicago archdiocese where he was scheduled to celebrate his first public Mass this Sunday. Kelly never before had a chance to practice the priestly techniques he had learned in Rome. Now, as the *Andrea Doria* lay helpless on its side, Kelly knew that he must minister to the passengers in any way he could.

Many of them sat forlornly in chairs and on the floor, waiting for the unknown. An added fear filled the eyes of those who had no life jackets. Kelly silently listened in on conversations as husbands and fathers discussed the hazards of making the fearsome journey to the darkened areas down below. He saw women stare jealously at others strapped into their bright orange life preservers.

Kelly realized that he could do something. He crawled quietly among the huddled passengers. "I need volunteers who will help me bring life jackets up from below," he said.

"I just can't leave my wife," one man protested. Others shook their heads and turned away in shame. Then Kelly saw one head nod in assent.

"I'll go," the man bravely told the priest. Two others hastily agreed to follow.

The four men carefully moved downward from the Promenade Deck into the ship's crippled innards. The stairwells sloped precariously as they inched lower, their hands braced against the walls, their palms sticky. None knew the extent of the danger; none knew how much time the listing *Andrea Doria* would give them. Kelly was an excellent swimmer and former lifeguard instructor. He felt confident he could survive if the ship went down while he was standing on deck. But no one below could possibly escape if the ship suddenly capsized.

The men reached the Upper Deck and fanned out on individual missions, searching for unlocked cabins with life jackets stowed in their closets. They walked into rooms with money and expensive jewels lying carelessly about, discarded as worried passengers realigned their priorities.

The four men assembled at the base of the stairway, their arms now full of life jackets. They had trouble grasping the handrails and feared that a sudden lurch would send them spinning to the landings far below. They finally reached the Promenade Deck, where they parceled out the jackets to women, children, and older men, several of whom sobbed in gratitude.

The four could not stop now. Moments before they were despairing and confused. Now they were involved in a mission of survival. They turned to go back downstairs, hesitated for only an instant as they contemplated the chasm just above the waterline. Then they plunged ahead, Kelly in the lead.

Four times they went down and four times they returned with the orange life jackets. Each trip was more difficult as the ship angled steeper to starboard, and the men were forced to venture to cabins more distant from the stairwells.

After the fourth trip Kelly sat on the floor of the Ballroom, breathing spasmodically. He could not force himself down below deck again. He was suddenly overcome with exhausting fear, his sense of mission seemingly gone.

An old man crawled next to him and peered into the priest's eye. He did not speak, but Kelly could feel the message. The old passenger did not have a life jacket, and the priest was wearing one that he brought up from his last trip below. Though he felt guilty, at that moment Kelly could not respond. He had no more to offer. He moved away from the old man, silently refusing the unspoken request.

Kelly found himself at a window on the high side. He stared down at the water and was amazed at the degree of the list. His confidence that he could swim away from the sinking ship was faltering: no one could clear the protruding side of the hull. Kelly stared silently out the window and saw his own death reflected in the fog. It seemed such a shame, all those years of religious study destroyed in one night. His silver chalice lay unused in his cabin.

Why had God placed him into such a frustrating situation? Surely there was a purpose to his existence. The realization struck Kelly that perhaps his entire life had been pointed toward this one dismal night.

If I am going to die, Kelly resolved, *I am going to die functioning. I'm going to look death squarely in the eye.*

He turned and called in a loud voice for everyone's attention. The room grew quiet. The desperate passengers hoped that the long-awaited instructions from the ship's silent captain were now forthcoming. Everyone stared at the lean young man in clerical garb, who returned their gazes with a purposeful expression.

"Anyone who wants to should quietly make an act of contrition," Kelly said, "then I will give you absolution."

Each of the ballroom's occupants looked at the priest. For the first time some of them privately faced the thought of violent death at sea.

Kelly's voice bellowed out, "*Ego vos absolvo ab omnibus peccatis vestris in nomine Patris et Filii et Spiritus Sancti.*" It was the plural form of absolution reserved for such moments of impending mass disaster.

A man reached out a hand and tugged at Kelly's black jacket. "I'm a Protestant," he said almost guiltily. "Can you do something for me?"

Surely denominations made no difference at such a time? Kelly thought. "Have you ever done anything wrong in your life that you are sorry for?"

"Yeah."

The priest spoke the Latin words for forgiveness and absolution, then moved on.

On the high side of the Boat Deck, in the open air underneath the lifeboats hanging wedged into their davits, Mike Stoller stood with his wife, Meryl. They were in a darkened alcove near a doorway that led to the first-class section. More than a dozen passengers had gathered at this point, rather than at their muster stations, because the proximity of the lifeboats gave them comfort. But their view of the rest of the ship was blocked. The cabin-class Gymnasium lay between them and the center of the *Andrea Doria*. Ahead, locked doors closed off their passage to the first-class sections.

The list of the ship forced them to clutch at the rail or sit at the base of the outer wall of the Gymnasium. In this isolated spot, their world was restricted to the fog blanket and the useless lifeboats hanging over their heads. Mike Stoller grew impatient. He knew his wife could not swim. "We've got to have our life jackets," he said to Meryl. "I'm going down to get them."

"Please get mine, too," a woman pleaded with Stoller. "Here's my room key."

The Stollers' cabin was on the starboard side of A Deck, near the rear of the ship; the other woman's cabin was on the opposite side of the same deck. Stoller knew he would have to make a second trip to come back up to a high deck and cross over to get down to port. He hesitated momentarily, then said, "OK, I'll get you a jacket."

Stoller's appearance belied his youth. A full beard compensated for early baldness. His rumpled corduroy jacket completed the bohemian image of a newly successful songwriter. At twenty-three, Mike Stoller had good reason to live. With his partner, Jerry Leiber, he had composed the hit "Black Denim Trousers and Motorcycle Boots," and the royalty check had paid for a three-month trip through Europe. But his early success meant little to him as he found his way down the darkened hallways toward his cabin on A Deck.

He found the cabin lit by the amber emergency lighting. To his surprise he saw that the locked door was flung wide open. As he pulled the two life jackets from a closet his eye spotted his 8-mm movie camera. "Leave it here," he said aloud to no one. "Leave everything here. Get the jackets and get out."

Stoller moved back down the corridor, grasping the life jackets in one arm and using the other to brace himself against the wall. His perspective was distorted by the closed-in corridor, and as the *Andrea Doria* rolled in the water Stoller feared she would capsize. He tried to concentrate on moving forward to drive the fear out of his head. He had promised to fetch a third jacket for the woman, but he knew he could not climb up, cross over to port, and go back down again for the extra preserver. The only solution was to give the woman his own life jacket. *After all,* he thought, *I can swim.*

He had reached the landing, and was hurrying to the base of the stairs leading back up to his wife when he suddenly felt something jerk at his arm. One of the life jackets began to slip from his grasp. Stoller turned to see a heavyset teenage boy, his face wet and florid, tugging at his life jackets. Behind the boy were a man, a woman, and a teenage girl. Stoller recognized them as other cabin class passengers.

Stoller tugged back at the life jackets. The boy lost his grip and Stoller stumbled back against a wall from the force of his efforts.

"Please! We need a life jacket for our father," the boy shouted. The family circled him menacingly.

"They're not for me!" Stoller yelled. He gathered the jackets in his arm like a fullback cradling a football, lowered his head, and powered his way between the boy and his father. He pulled himself free and rushed upward.

Up in her alcove on the Boat Deck, Meryl Stoller was convinced that she was abandoned. "Mike!" she screamed, but no one answered or offered solace. "Mike! Mike! M-i-i-ke!" she called out in a continuous wail.

Measured by the clock, Stoller had been gone for perhaps fifteen minutes. To Meryl it seemed like hours. When Stoller finally made his way back, he found Meryl facing in toward the center of the ship, her arms behind her, hooked around the open railing for support, her face as gray as the fog. Meryl's breath came in protracted heaves as she loosened her grip on the rail and clutched for her husband's arm. She thrust her fingernails beneath his skin, babbling nonsensically.

Mike grasped her shoulders and swung her in front of him.

With one hand he cuffed her on the cheek. Her vacant eyes suddenly cleared. Anger crossed her face until she realized why he had struck her.

Nothing could force Stoller to go back down below for the third jacket. He gave one of the two jackets he carried to his wife and the other to the woman.

The small group that had gathered with the Stollers animatedly discussed their fate. "They can pump fuel and water over to the port side," someone said knowingly. "They'll right the ship. Everything will be OK."

Stoller watched a young man shake his head quietly in response to the argument. He knew the dissenter was an engineer.

This is it, Stoller said to himself. He was suddenly seized with the thought of being sucked into the swirling water as the *Andrea Doria* went under.

"I wish I had been on one of those planes over the Grand Canyon," Meryl said to Mike, thinking of the crash of a TWA Super-Constellation and a United Airlines DC-7 just twenty-five days earlier, which claimed 128 lives.

"Why?"

"Because then I would have died quickly. I wouldn't have to stand here waiting."

Robert Young, the American Bureau of Shipping inspector, was lying flat on the high side of the Promenade Deck, holding on to the side rail and looking out over the water.

Perhaps the most knowledgeable passenger on board, Young wanted data. His professional eye tried to assess the chances. He and his family were all superb swimmers, but a sinking ship creates a whirlpool of sucking tides too powerful for even the strongest athlete.

He saw the port lifeboats still fixed to their davits and guessed the reason. If the lifeboats remained unused, Young wanted to instruct his family to jump several minutes before the ship went under.

He saw that the ship had rolled over far enough to expose

the bilge keel, a stabilizing fin on the side of the hull that normally rides deep in the water. To Young that meant that the ship was going to sink; the only question was when. He could only hope that ships were speeding to the rescue. But he knew the peril of both the *Doria*'s list and the unyielding fog outside.

Young craned his neck upward. He saw Captain Calamai struggling to climb to the port wing of the bridge, which now stuck out at a sharp angle approaching the vertical. Even in the dimming light Young could see that the captain was having difficulty crawling up the slope. When Calamai reached the rail, he carefully scanned the port side of the ship.

Young knew that the captain was searching out the same information. He, too, was trying to estimate how much longer the *Andrea Doria* would remain afloat.

Throughout the ship, desperate passengers gave themselves over to the inevitable as it appeared that no help would come to them in the dense fog. Where was the crew? Why were there no announcements?

A well-dressed man in the first-class muster station anxiously exchanged addresses with the couple sitting next to him. "If you make it, tell my family that my last thoughts were of them," he said.

Nearby, two men made an inheritance pact, scrawling their last wills on scraps of paper and giving them to each other in case only one survived.

Suddenly, the ship's dormant loudspeaker crackled to life. An expectant hush settled over the passengers throughout the boat. Here at last was the long-awaited announcement, the instructions on how to abandon ship. Finally, there was some guidance.

The loudspeaker uttered only one word, in Italian: "*Calme.*" Then it became silent again.

The word had the opposite effect, for the voice that had uttered it was quivering in fear.

10

THE VISION

ON THE DECKS OF THE *Andrea Doria*, passengers were lost in a fog of ignorance. Captain Calamai's decision to withhold information deliberately was contrary to the accepted practices of ship captains and airline pilots. In command of a stricken craft, most captains would share at least some of the details with their passengers. But not once did Calamai take the ship's microphone to reassure the seventeen hundred people who waited in darkness.

Badano had at least twice ordered the passengers in both Italian and English to gather their life jackets and assemble at their muster stations. But at no time did Calamai inform the passengers over the loudspeaker that the ship was in danger of sinking, that half the lifeboats were useless, or that the passengers would have to abandon the ship. As a result, a pervasive feeling of helplessness spread throughout the ship.

Paradoxically, there was more reason for hope than the despairing passengers realized.

The *Andrea Doria*'s SOS was picked up at 11:22 P.M. at the East Moriches, Long Island, Coast Guard radio station, which notified its New York Rescue Coordination Center at 80 Lafayette Street. The Coast Guard was unable to dispatch rescue planes or helicopters because visibility was reported as "nil." But within minutes Coast Guard cutters were dispatched from various ports on the eastern seaboard. They included the *Yakutet* from Portland, Maine, the *Acushnet* from Portsmouth, New Hampshire, the *Evergreen* from Boston, the *Hornbeam* from Woods Hole, Massachusetts, the *Lagare* from New Bedford, Massachusetts, the *Yeaton* and the *Owasco* from New London, Connecticut, and the *Tamaroa* from New York. The *Campbell* was diverted to the area from an Atlantic training cruise. All the cutters, however, were small and would have difficulty holding many survivors.

Only fifteen miles from the crash site, Captain Joseph A. Boyd, of the 6600-ton United Fruit Company freighter *Cape Ann*, en route from Bremerhaven, Germany, to New York, steered his ship toward the distress signal. Boyd would do his best, but he had only two small lifeboats.

Other ships reported in. The *Robert E. Hopkins*, 16,000-ton tanker of the Tidewater Oil Company, was on its way. So were the Danish freighter *Laura Maersk*, the Honduran tanker *Manaqui*, and the U.S. Navy destroyer escort *Edward H. Allen*.

A Navy transport, *Pvt. William H. Thomas*, bound for New York from Leghorn, Italy, with 214 passengers, was maneuvering toward the site when a wireless message came in from the Navy. The master, Captain John S. Shea, a fifty-year-old Brooklynite, read that he had been placed in charge of the rescue operation. He was worried. The *Andrea Doria* dwarfed his ship and the assorted small freighters and military vessels on their way. He needed help. He stared into the fog and prayed for a miracle.

Two hours to the east of the crash site, fifty-three-year-old Baron Raoul de Beaudéan, the vacation replacement master of the great French luxury liner the *Ile de France*, puzzled over the distress call he had received shortly after 11:20 P.M. It was inconceivable to him that the beautiful, seaworthy *Andrea Doria* could be in danger, yet no captain issues an SOS without good reason. The *Doria* was a large vessel, and de Beaudéan knew that giant ships rarely encounter an emergency so seri-

THE DEATH
OF THE
ANDREA
DORIA

Top: The Andrea Doria, which was considered by many
to be the most beautiful ocean liner of its day. (UPI)
Bottom: The Stockholm. (UPI)

A lifeboat flees the dying ship.
(Loomis Dean/Life Magazine)

The port side of the crippled Andrea Doria
shows the useless lifeboats still in position.
At the stern is the swimming pool net used by many
disembarking passengers.   (National Archives)

Andrea Doria survivors board the Ile de France.
(Loomis Dean/Life Magazine)

Opposite, top: In this Pulitzer-prize winning series of photographs by Boston Traveler photographer Harry Trask, the Andrea Doria first plunges bow first into the water... (Wide World)
Opposite, bottom: ... displays the name Andrea and one of her giant twin screws... (Wide World)
Above: ... and leaves behind a whirlpool of churning debris. (Wide World)

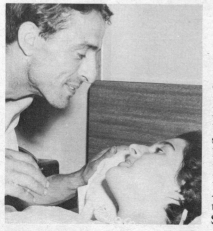

Fourteen-year-old Linda Morgan with Bernabe Polanco Garcia, the Stockholm sailor who found her after she was thrown from her bunk on the Andrea Doria to the bow of the Swedish ship. (UPI)

The Stockholm, its bow shattered from the impact, is shown in dry dock awaiting repairs. Its reinforced steel bow cut sharply into the side of the Andrea Doria. (UPI)

ous that they sink quickly. He could barely imagine her sinking, and even then, probably only after days of foundering. Surely there would be ample time to rescue the passengers and crew.

The *Andrea Doria*, he realized, must have been the large ship he had seen on the radar as the *Ile de France* had passed about ten miles south of the Nantucket lightship. Peering through his monocle at the radar screen, de Beaudéan had seen the *Doria*'s pip merge with that of the lightship. "He is sinking the lightship!" the French captain jokingly said to an officer. The baron was aware that radar at that distance could give only an approximate reading of the true position of another ship.

The *Ile de France* was far away from the collision site, at the edge of responsibility. The decision to answer or ignore the call was entirely within the baron's discretion. He had more than nine hundred passengers on board who expected to arrive at Le Havre, France, on schedule. If he turned his ship completely around and sailed back toward New York for a needless response to an emergency that could well be handled by others, he would be reprimanded. He was only a substitute captain. It was his first voyage in command of the flagship of the French Line.

The tall aristocrat lit a cigarette and peered at the intense fog as he weighed his choices. If he turned back unnecessarily, others might criticize him. "Other ships are probably close to the collision site," he commented to one of his officers. But if he did not respond he risked living with a pained conscience the rest of his life. At 11:54 the baron made his decision. He would go to the *Andrea Doria*. As the great French liner moved into a sweeping turn that headed it back to the west, Captain de Beaudéan ordered his engine crew to increase speed from the cruising velocity of 22 knots to the maximum 24. He doubled the watch, and asked for volunteers to man eleven of the ship's thirty-two lifeboats.

On the *Andrea Doria*, Captain Calamai was aware of some of the activity. During the first hour after the collision messages poured into the radio room:

From the *Pvt. William H. Thomas:*

> TEN MILES AWAY: HAVE EIGHT BOATS.

From the *Cape Ann:*

> WE HAVE TWO BOATS FOR ANDREA.

From the *Laura Maersk:*

> WE WILL BE THERE IN TWO HOURS.

But the Italian captain did not share these messages with his passengers. He knew the rescue ships were small and he was afraid to raise the passengers' hopes falsely. He also knew that the ships would have difficulty approaching the crash site in the fog.

The closest ship was not ready to help. Calamai pleaded with the *Stockholm* to send lifeboats, but there was no immediate response. He knew the other ship must also be in danger and had to be concerned about its own passengers.

Calamai ordered flares shot from the bridge to guide the rescue ships in, but the dark fog blanket quickly absorbed the sizzling red lights. The captain was concerned that soon he would be unable to communicate by wireless with other ships. The *Andrea Doria*'s electrical power was dangerously weak. If he was forced to rely on signal lights the fog would nullify them as well.

It was now approaching 12:30 A.M. More than an hour had passed since the collision. Though many ships were reportedly on their way, none had yet arrived. The fog was still so dense that Second Officer Guido Badano could not see the bow of the *Andrea Doria* from the bridge. He worried that he might have measured the position inaccurately and sent out misinformation with the SOS. Badano went into the chartroom with Cadet Mario Maracci and took another loran fix. Maracci wrote the position down on an envelope that lay nearby. He checked the distances to known objects and found his reading to be accurate. The *Andrea Doria* was nineteen miles west of the Nantucket lightship and sixty miles south of the coast.

Badano stepped into the wireless room. "Which is the position you transmitted?" he asked the wireless operator.

"The position was 40°30', 69°53'," the radioman replied.

Badano was satisfied that the correct position had been sent with the original SOS.

But where were the rescue ships?

Once Captain Nordenson was confident that the *Stockholm* would survive, he concentrated on helping the other ship. He sent a wireless message to the *Andrea Doria:*

LOWER YOUR LIFEBOATS, WE CAN PICK YOU UP.

Calamai replied:

WE ARE TOO BENDING. IMPOSSIBLE TO PUT BOATS OVER SIDE. PLEASE SEND LIFEBOATS IMMEDIATELY.

Nordenson quickly ordered his officers to ready the lifeboats. He put Second Officers Lars Enestrom and Sven Abenius in charge of two of the three motor-powered craft. Other crews prepared the larger, slower boats that were hand-propelled.

Enestrom moved down to the Sun Deck and ordered sailors to remove the lifeboat covers. A steward stepped over to the young officer. "Take these," he suggested, thrusting several blankets into Enestrom's arms.

A scream suddenly shattered the relative peace of the ship. "There go our lifeboats," a frightened passenger called out. A group of *Stockholm* passengers clustered on the deck had seen the hurried lifeboat preparations. They had thought they were safe, until now.

Nordenson grabbed the ship's microphone. "Now we are going to put lifeboats over the side," he announced. "They are not for you. Don't get worried now because everything is under control. The lifeboats are for putting on survivors from the other ship, the *Andrea Doria.*"

From the *Stockholm* radio room another message flashed across the dark sea:

WE ARE LAUNCHING ALL AVAILABLE LIFEBOATS.

It was 1:08 A.M. Two hours had passed since the collision. Two of the motor-powered lifeboats, dwarfed by the ghostly white *Stockholm,* settled into the water on a night mission to rescue an unknown number of people from a sinking ship obscured by an impenetrable fog.

To a sailor there is no greater glory than a rescue at sea. As their ships raced to aid the stricken *Andrea Doria,* silent men with dry lips awaited the moment when they would gamble their lives to save others. The men had a full night's work ahead of them. Nearly seventeen hundred people were trapped on the dying ship. They knew they would probably have to contend with panic. They knew the sinking *Andrea Doria* would create dangerous tides and that at any moment she might capsize and crush the hovering lifeboats. They knew, too, that the waters would be crowded with maneuvering rescue ships, hidden in the fog.

As the *Ile de France* approached the collision site, Baron Raoul de Beaudéan navigated with a soft touch through the fog that sometimes obscured the view of his own bow. His eyes constantly fastened on the radar, he ordered the small course changes that would guide his 44,500-ton ship into the midst of other rescue ships that were homing in on the coordinates given in the SOS. He chain-smoked nervously. The fog now drifted in patches. He offered an intense prayer that the fog would lift.

At a distance of seventeen miles, de Beaudéan spotted four pips on his radar screen, but it was impossible to identify the *Doria.* He would have to maneuver from one ship to the next in the treacherous fog until he found the wounded liner. He worried about the lifeboat crews who would have to move back and forth in the blinding haze.

De Beaudéan radioed a terse message to the Coast Guard:

THE SITUATION IS CRITICAL. VISIBILITY IS NIL.

Then without warning the *Ile de France* seemed to burst through a wall of fog into a clear Atlantic night.

Through his binoculars, the baron finally picked out the canted Italian ship. Her extreme list surprised him. He was afraid the *Andrea Doria* would capsize, or that his lifeboats would be sucked into the gaping hole on the starboard side.

The *Ile de France* drifted in slowly, its master maneuvering to the starboard side of the *Andrea Doria*, where his own ship would provide a shelter from the slight swell. A cool breeze seemed to be rising. The rescue ship slid into position four hundred yards away, her engines backing slowly to brake her forward motion. Of the liner's 827 crewmen, 160 stood ready to man eleven large lifeboats.

Across the water Captain de Beaudéan could hear the screams and prayers of the trapped passengers. Hoping to make his presence known to the *Andrea Doria*, the baron ordered his powerful outside lights switched on.

After hearing confessions in the cabin-class Ballroom and on the enclosed Promenade Deck of the *Andrea Doria*, Father Tom Kelly made his way to an outside area of the deck farther aft. He came upon a group of Italian emigrants who were near hysteria. Kelly wondered what he could say to calm them. He remembered that it was Thursday now, for two and one-half hours had passed since the crash. It was 1:40 A.M. This meant that today was the Feast of St. Anne. Speaking in Italian, Father Kelly addressed the emigrants: "Let us pray to St. Anne, the mother of Mary, who is going to save us."

The Italians suddenly calmed as they joined the young priest in prayer.

Who can say why the vile, humid mist, so much a part of the tragic circumstances that had compounded disastrously, lingered so long over the waters west of Nantucket? Was it the unpredictable anger of the sea, or merely the unknowing meanderings of the warm, moisture-saturated southwestern breeze as it blew over the cool Labrador current?

Each man and woman stranded on the *Andrea Doria* had his or her own rationale for the plight. But there were common threads of fear, resignation, pain, and panic. So encompassing was the gloom, so numbing the heavy air, that the vision caught its witnesses unaware.

It was a cold front, swinging down from the northwest, that pushed aside the warmer mass in its path. Dry, clear air moved suddenly into the area designated geographically as 40°30' north, 69°53' west. Wispy patches of mist skimmed across the waves. The damnable cloak that isolated the *Andrea Doria* from the world broke into pieces. The curtain hung over the surface for a moment. Then, as if ready for the final act of a great drama, it rose quickly, revealing a black night sky and a round glowing moon.

Just as inexplicably as it had settled on the two ocean behemoths, the fog lifted gracefully from the scene of the wounded *Andrea Doria*.

To the passengers, sitting like an expectant audience awaiting the chilling conclusion of the play, the rising curtain revealed a surprising heroine at center stage. No one had seen her moving in. Rather, she was suddenly, inexplicably *there*. A dazzling aurora of white lights, strung in Christmas-tree fashion, sketched the unmistakable outline of a great ship. Floodlights illuminated her twin red funnels. Light from the portholes shimmered in her wake. She was larger even than the *Andrea Doria*, sailing, it seemed to the disoriented perceptions caused by the sloping decks, sharply uphill.

Near the stern of the ship on the open Promenade Deck, a crowd of Italian emigrants suddenly looked up and across the water. They could see, as if in a vision, in blazing bright letters so huge there could be no mistake, the name that would remain in their souls forever:

ILE DE FRANCE.

11

THE LIFEBOATS

ONCE CAPTAIN CALAMAI ORDERED the lifeboats lowered, crew members of the *Andrea Doria* swarmed alongside the boats hanging low on the starboard side. Many of them had abandoned their assigned stations in order to be near the few available boats.

Frantic crewmen ripped off the canvas covers and climbed inside. Others released the winches, lowered the boats, and jumped after them. The water filled with white-jacketed stewards thrashing out to the safety of the lifeboats. Few passengers were aware of the crazed activity, for most were clustered on the opposite high side of the ship. Their view was blocked by the ballrooms and lounges that spanned the length of two main public decks, and by a fog which still isolated them.

Frank Clifton, an alderman from Toronto, saw several crewmen climbing into a lifeboat. Instinctively he joined them in the boat. As the craft pulled away, he counted forty crewmen in the boat. There were only four passengers, including himself, yet there were dozens of empty seats.

Calamai had ordered his officers, with Staff Captain Magagnini in charge, to lower the starboard-side lifeboats. Magagnini, Kirn and Franchini supervised the activity. The original plan was to lower the boats to the Promenade Deck where passengers would step into them and then be brought down to ocean level.

But the list of the ship made the plan impossible. As the boats were lowered, they swung too far out beyond the deck for passengers to enter from the Promenade Deck. Magagnini ordered the boats lowered directly into the water instead. Passengers would have to be brought into the boats by ladders or ropes.

The crewmen of lifeboat 13 were unable to cast off one of the ropes that secured them to the *Andrea Doria*. They struggled in vain with the tether as the boat rode the ocean swells and additional crewmen scrambled down from above.

"Franchini," Magagnini commanded, "go help."

Second Officer Curzio Franchini climbed into the lifeboat, joining the men grappling with the rope. He instructed the sailors to pull on the rope to create slack. The line came loose. Freed from its mooring, the half-filled lifeboat washed away from the looming side of the *Andrea Doria*.

Franchini looked back up at Magagnini. "Go around and gather the other boats," the staff captain called down. "Go to work along the side, near the stern."

Now in command of lifeboat 13, Franchini called out across the water to the other boats, ordering them to pull up close to him. "Go back around the stern," he commanded. As lifeboat 13 steered toward the rescue ropes dangling from the starboard side near the stern, Franchini could see two of the other boats following.

Ruby MacKenzie stood at a window on the high side of the Promenade Deck, cheered by the sight of the nearly full moon overhead. Movement caught her eye. A lifeboat drew away from the stern of the *Andrea Doria*, heading toward the *Stockholm*, which lay silently off to port. Mrs. MacKenzie was overjoyed by this first indication of rescue, but then her spirits sank. It was not a boatload of passengers on their way to safety. The lifeboat was filled with white-jacketed stewards abandoning their own ship. Mrs. MacKenzie decided that she had better not tell anyone what she had seen.

George P. Kerr, the European manager of Proctor & Gamble, Inc., stood with his wife Matheson and his thirteen-year-old daughter, Kyrie, on the high side of the Boat Deck. They had watched the efforts of crewmen as they tried unsuccessfully to launch the port side lifeboats.

"There's no hope of getting these lifeboats down," someone muttered.

Kerr, a Scotsman by birth, waited for a time for the captain to take command of the desperate situation. But when no instructions were forthcoming, he moved his family down a canted stairwell to the Promenade Deck and to the low rail at the starboard side. They were among the first passengers to witness the lifeboat activity.

Below them, riding unsteadily in the water, was a boat filled with Italian crewmen, mainly elevator operators, kitchen helpers, and stewards. Kerr steered his daughter, Kyrie, toward a rope ladder. "Go down into the boat," he said.

Kyrie stared at the boat and its cargo of crewmen. The dark expanse of water between the stricken ship and its hovering lifeboat frightened her. "No," she balked. "I'm not going down into the boat. I would rather stay here with you."

Kerr turned to his wife. "You go first then. She'll follow."

Mrs. Kerr leaned over the rail and clutched at the swinging rope ladder. Suddenly someone grabbed it from above. It swung inward, one of its heavy wooden slats crashing into Matheson Kerr's face. She spun back into her husband's arms, her left eye beginning to swell and blacken.

Despite her pain, she grabbed the rope ladder determinedly, but the lifeboat had already pulled clear of the ship. Kerr saw a second lifeboat, off to one side, and beckoned. "Come here!" As the boat pulled into position at the base of the rope ladder, Mrs. Kerr quickly moved down to safety.

As thirteen-year-old Kyrie climbed over the rail to join her mother in the lifeboat, the listing *Andrea Doria* lurched. Fearful that the huge liner would topple over onto them, the Italian crewmen pulled at their oars. Mrs. Kerr fought their outward motion by holding fast to the bottom of the rope ladder until it stretched out almost horizontal, like an umbilical cord securing the lifeboat to the mother ship. Kyrie quickly climbed down into the boat.

Despite the many empty seats, the panicked crewmen still tried to row away from the shadow of the *Andrea Doria*. Kyrie now joined her mother, and the two of them gripped the bottom of the rope ladder tautly as an older woman above them moved onto it and started her descent into the lifeboat.

"Hold on," an angry George Kerr called down to the sailors. "Let more people come down." But the frightened crewmen now worked their paddles in concert, and with a sudden lunge of power, the lifeboat pulled away. Mrs. Kerr and Kyrie lost their grip on the rope ladder. It flew from their hands, swinging wildly inward, smashing against the black hull of the *Doria*, with the screaming woman clinging to it desperately.

"For heaven's sake, stop!" Mrs. Kerr called out, but the crewmen continued to row and the boat moved out toward the darkness. Frustrated, George Kerr hurled a shoe at the fleeing crewmen as other men quickly scrambled down to pull the abandoned woman passenger back aboard the *Andrea Doria*.

From her vantage point next to a pillar on the high side of the cabin-class Ballroom, Sister Callistus saw something flash past the Promenade Deck windows. She was stunned. She had seen a lifeboat, jammed with men wearing the gray life jackets of crew members. She realized she must keep secret what she had seen, for it might set off panic.

But others had seen it, too. "People are getting off!" someone shouted. "Why aren't we?"

The Ballroom erupted in panic. Passengers scrambled to their feet, looking for the best path toward a doorway to the open deck. Some on the high side lost their grips and plunged down the slippery, sloping floor.

"Wait!" the bartender yelled quickly. Everyone stood still.

"I'll go and see what's happening," he said. "Stay right here. Don't move."

About a mile to the south, Bertil Norderlander, wine steward on the *Stockholm*, waited with others for the *Andrea Doria* lifeboats which would bring the first passengers to safety on the Swedish ship. He could see the first boat approaching hesitantly, for the occupants could see that the front of the ship was badly damaged.

Swedish sailors leaned over the side. One by one survivors grabbed for waiting hands and were dragged aboard. In the rush of activity the realization came upon Norderlander slowly. The Swedish sailors registered shock. They were not helping terrified passengers on board. This boat, the very first, was loaded with Italian crewmen, most of them stewards and waiters. The first man to board wore officer's epaulets.

In rapid succession, two more *Andrea Doria* lifeboats tied up at the *Stockholm*. Angry Swedish sailors helped *Andrea Doria* crew members aboard. Not until the third boat, also filled mainly with crew, were ten children lifted to safety.

High above on the starboard wing of the bridge, Peder Larsen, relieved of his duties as helmsman, trained a spotlight on the gangway where the lifeboats tied up. He, too, was surprised at the sight of a lifeboat full of gray-jacketed Italian crewmen.

Lars Enestrom, second officer of the *Stockholm*, guided motor lifeboat number 7, the first to be launched from his ship, around the stern of the *Andrea Doria*. He moved to the rear of the starboard side where most of the Italian emigrants and tourist-class passengers had gathered. He positioned the craft beneath two ropes hanging from the rail. There was a slight rising swell. Enestrom feared that his boat might be smashed against the side of the sinking ship. "Throw down an extra rope," he shouted in English. There was no answer to his request. Apparently, no one realized that a lifeboat waited below.

A face peered over the rail, some thirty feet above. Voices

chattered quietly in Italian. Then, quickly, men in white cloth jackets topped by the gray life preservers of the crew scurried down the waiting ropes, expertly hand over hand, and took seats in the boat. Enestrom saw that some of them had sailors' tattoos on their arms.

Up above, a shout pierced the expectant atmosphere. "A lifeboat is waiting. Hurry!" Two and one-half hours of pressurized emotions broke free in an instant. Frantic men, women, and children leaped forward, crushing one another against the rail. An Italian officer stood near one of the ropes, his cry of "Women and children first!" drowned by the onslaught. One at a time, a handful of passengers awkwardly slid down the ropes, clinched tightly between their hands. Many burned the flesh of their palms as they descended.

"Jesus Christ!" Enestrom exclaimed. "So many people."

The *Stockholm*'s lifeboat soon had fifty survivors aboard, mostly male crewmen and a handful of female passengers. Above him Enestrom could see a man balancing a child on the rail. The Swedish officer feared that the man would drop the helpless child down. "Wait!" he shouted. Quickly Enestrom and three other sailors grabbed the corners of a large blanket stowed in the bottom of the boat and fashioned an impromptu safety net.

The child's body hurtled down in the darkness, angling for the net. The sailors steadied themselves against the roll of the waves and felt the satisfying weight of the child tug at the center of the blanket. Crying but unhurt, the child scrambled to his feet. A *Stockholm* steward wrapped him in a blanket and helped him to the small radio cabin in the front of the lifeboat. One at a time, three other children were thrown safely into the blanket.

Giovanni Morrone made his way to the rail, concerned not for himself but for his wife, Vincenza, and his nine-year-old son, Mario. He was ready to help Vincenza over the rail when two Italian nuns grabbed his arm. "Let us down," they pleaded.

Although not a religious man, Morrone decided it was an appropriate time to defer to the Church. "All right, go ahead," he said. "But hurry."

The first nun slipped over the rail and slid quickly down to the lifeboat. But the second woman panicked. She froze at the rail, the rope in her hand. "You don't want to go down?" Morrone said. "Then step aside." The nun said nothing, but still clutched the rope fiercely. Morrone was mad now. "Look, you either go down or I'm going to throw you over!" he raged. Spurred on by Morrone's anger, she climbed over the rail and slid gingerly down to the boat.

Enestrom now saw another lifeboat from the *Stockholm* ready to pull into position, and he turned his own boat around to return with his passengers.

At that moment, Giovanni Morrone was helping Vincenza over the rail, and down the rope. He saw her slide down toward the water. Suddenly, he realized that the *Stockholm* lifeboat had pulled away, and watched horrified as his wife reached the end of the rope. The screaming woman lost her grip and fell heavily into the ocean. Her life jacket kept her afloat, but wailing in fear, she quickly floated away into the darkness just beyond the stern.

"We'll have to hurry," a sailor yelled as the second lifeboat from the *Stockholm*, number 8, commanded by Second Officer Sven Abenius, slid around the stern of the *Andrea Doria*. "The ship looks like she might go under fast." Abenius was shocked by the severity of its list.

As lifeboat number 8 approached, the scene at the stern had become chaotic. Hundreds of passengers were crushed against the rail, shouting at the approaching lifeboat. Per Hinnerson, a nineteen-year-old deck apprentice assigned to work in the lifeboat, could hear passengers above booing the Swedish sailors. "This is not the time to place blame," Hinnerson shouted back. "It's better if you come down to the lifeboats."

Abenius steered the craft to the position vacated by Enestrom's boat and began to take on passengers. At the same time, the water grew noisy and white as passengers who could not reach the ropes jumped overboard and took their chances in the sludge-filled sea. Sailors pulled some of the passengers, their bodies now slippery with oil, out of the ocean.

Some sputtered in the sea, unable to reach the craft. Hinnerson and a swimming teacher from the *Stockholm* leaped into the ocean and dragged the soaked survivors to the safety of number 8. One unconscious woman was pulled through the water by her hair, then over into the boat, her leg badly scraped by the friction from the sideboard.

The heaving *Doria* kept swaying to starboard. Hinnerson feared she would actually topple over. Abenius watched the black hull carefully, ready to back the lifeboat away from the danger.

"Only women and children," crewmen shouted angrily, but some men as well slid down the ropes.

Tullio di Sandro, emigrating from Naples, had become maddened with fear. It was not his own life that mattered. But his wife, Filomena, and his four-year-old daughter, Norma, must be saved. He lifted Norma over the railing. "Catch her. Catch the child," he called down. The Swedish crew, however, could not understand the plea spoken in Italian. They were busy trying to maintain the lifeboat in place without catching a swell broadside and smashing into the *Andrea Doria*.

Without waiting for a response, di Sandro launched little Norma's body overboard, throwing her out in an arc to reach the lifeboat. Abenius looked up at the sound of a hard thud, in time to see the child's body hit the iron casing directly in front of him. Gentle arms pulled the girl to shelter. She lay unconscious. A patch of discoloration immediately appeared around her eye, bulging threateningly. "How could they throw a child right down into the boat?" shouted a dismayed passenger.

As the boat pulled away for its return trip to the *Stockholm*, the cries of Tullio and Filomena di Sandro submerged into the noisy confusion that had engulfed the stern of the *Andrea Doria*.

Number 1 motor lifeboat, the *Stockholm*'s smallest, with a crew of four and a capacity of only twenty persons, reached the Italian liner under the command of Third Mate Carstens, now somewhat recovered from the shock of having been in charge of the bridge at the moment of the collision. He had no time for reflection as he maneuvered toward a group of anxious people waiting at the starboard rail near the stern. There seemed to be confusion above. The lifeboat waited for a time until people discovered its presence and began descending the rope.

To Carsten's surprise, the first person who slid into the lifeboat was not a passenger, but an able-bodied Italian in a waiter's uniform. He was followed by an elderly woman so petrified that sailors had to pry her fingers loose from the rope once she was safely into the boat.

From above, a young woman was lowered by a rope tied to the back of her life jacket. As her kicking feet touched the floor of the boat, a swell suddenly pushed the craft away. The screaming woman was left dangling in the water. Carstens maneuvered his tiny boat back to her, and sailors dragged the frightened woman aboard.

As the small boat quickly filled, Carstens felt another swell lift him, this time toward the hull of the *Doria*. The boat smashed hard against the ship, breaking the connection between its steering pin and the rudder.

Steering with an oar used as a makeshift rudder, Carstens pulled his battered lifeboat away. He saw lifeboats from the *Andrea Doria* hovering nearby, partially filled with crewmen. He shouted at them to pull close to the ship and rescue their passengers.

Realizing that he could do little at his own disabled lifeboat station on the port side, Third Officer Eugenio Giannini worked his way down to the Promenade Deck. A small group of passengers in the forward part of the deck looked anxiously to him for guidance.

"Follow me. There are plenty of lifeboats on the other side of the ship," he said. He then heard commotion above him and realized that some passengers had gathered on the Boat Deck on the open balcony in front of the Belvedere Lounge. "There are many, many lifeboats," Giannini leaned out and called up to them. "Come with me."

Giannini organized the passengers into a single file and ordered them to follow him. The calm assurance in his voice quieted the group. Giannini led his charges down a stairway one level to the Upper Deck and through the interior corridor back toward the stern.

It was a solemn but hopeful procession which followed the young Italian officer. Quietly they passed through the amber-lit corridor, not far from the cabins where Jeanette Carlin had been washed out to sea, where Linda Morgan and Joan Cianfarra had disappeared, where Camille Cianfarra had met a painful death, and where, at this very moment, Thure Peterson and Giovanni Rovelli worked in desperation to save two trapped women.

Indian file they moved back into the cabin-class section. Giannini stopped outside the tourist-class lounge, where a group of passengers joined his entourage. He turned left at the stern of the boat and led them to the starboard side, where the tilted deck was low to the water.

Giannini calmly addressed his charges. "There is no reason to be scared or frightened because now there are plenty of boats. You must keep quiet and calm. Everybody will be rescued."

Other crewmen responded to the activity and joined Giannini at the rail. The Italian officer decided that his priority was to get ropes or a substitute. He remembered an old American war movie in which Marines had slung cargo nets over the side so men could climb down rapidly.

"Get the cargo nets," he said to the boatswain.

"They are in the holds. We can't get them," the sailor replied.

"What about the swimming pool nets?" Giannini suggested.

Several sailors gathered the protective net that covered the tourist-class swimming pool. Giannini lashed it to the rail on the starboard side. Four or five men could climb down it at the same time, but Giannini cautioned the passengers that it was only advisable for the young and agile. The others would need assistance.

Using the three-inch line normally attached to the cargo

booms, Giannini and the sailors working with him fashioned slings to lower women, children, and old people to a growing flotilla of lifeboats now approaching from the various rescue ships.

Here, because of Giannini's calm directions, the procedure moved smoothly.

If only he had a knife, Rovelli reasoned, perhaps he could slice through the wreckage that still trapped Jane Cianfarra and Martha Peterson in cabin 56. He remembered the knives in the kitchen, where he worked.

He made his way quickly aft, and plunged down a stairwell to the Foyer Deck. Stumbling through the maze of corridors he moved into the deserted galley where he walked through a clutter of pots and pans. Grabbing a large butcher knife, he retraced his steps.

The steward arrived back at cabin 56 just as Thure Peterson returned with the wire cutters he had found in the radio shack. Frantically they attacked the bedspring that held Jane Cianfarra captive. One by one the coils sprang open, freeing the woman. Rovelli draped her left arm over his shoulder and gently eased her under the partition into cabin 58.

While Rovelli comforted the woman, Peterson ran up to the Promenade Deck for help. Three passengers and a crewman quickly volunteered and hurried down to cabin 58. Rovelli had laid Mrs. Cianfarra onto a blanket. Four men each grabbed a corner and carried the shocked woman up to the Promenade Deck.

Peterson crawled back into cabin 56 to comfort his wife. Suspecting that her fate was necessarily the same as that of the ship, Martha Peterson begged her husband to leave her and save himself. Thure refused, once more vowing to get her out.

On the Promenade Deck, Rovelli knew that he must find heavier equipment if they were to free Martha Peterson. It was now obvious that they needed a sophisticated tool, an automobile jack, to lift the wreckage.

Without instructions to the contrary, most of the passengers on the port side of the enclosed Promenade Deck still waited patiently, but futilely, for rescue from the high side of the ship. They could not see the *Ile de France* from there, but news of its arrival had reached them as people filtered in from elsewhere on the ship. Unaware that lifeboats already hovered on the other side of the *Andrea Doria*, they waited for directions from the crew.

A steward approached Marion and Malcolm Boyer. "Mr. Boyer, I think you should go to the opposite side of the ship," he suggested. "They are starting to take off passengers, but they are going to take them off from that side only." He gestured down to starboard. With the steward's help the Boyers moved forward from the first-class muster station to a slim corridor that transversed the width of the ship. Safety lay some seventy-five feet below them at the starboard side.

The Boyers held to a side rail as they inched downward. Oil brought up from the lower decks by fleeing passengers made the floor slippery. The couple moved slowly. If they fell they might slide the entire way down to starboard, where glass doors blocked the path to the rail. A few other passengers were crawling on their hands and knees, but the Boyers kept their feet.

The careful journey completed, the Boyers, hand in hand, made their way aft along the enclosed Promenade Deck, toward a small group of people gathered near a rope ladder. They could see a woman lying on the deck next to the bottom rail, illuminated by spotlights from the *Ile de France*. It was Jane Cianfarra, her face contorted in pain. Another older woman lay on a blanket comforted by a young woman whom Boyer guessed was her granddaughter. A French couple stood nearby, looking anxiously out toward the water for a lifeboat. Four Roman Catholic novitiates completed the small party.

The Frenchman spotted a small lifeboat approaching. "Come here!" he yelled in French, leaning over the rail and gesturing. But the lifeboat seemed intent on reaching the stern.

"Let me yell to them in English," Boyer suggested. He

leaned over the rail. "Over here!" he cried out. "We have an injured woman." It was an American lifeboat from the Navy transport *Pvt. William H. Thomas*, but someone yelled back that they were fully loaded.

The group waited anxiously until someone shouted that a lifeboat from the *Ile de France* was approaching. It carried a load of passengers taken off near the stern, but there were still a few empty seats. The boat tied up beneath the rope ladder as the French passengers explained to the sailors that an injured woman and an elderly lady were in need of urgent care.

A husky Italian sailor knelt over Jane Cianfarra. "Lady," he said, "the only thing I can do is put you on my shoulder and carry you down." The sailor lifted her onto his wide back. With one arm braced around her and the other grasping the thick side rope of a Jacob's ladder, the steward gingerly backed down to the waiting lifeboat. French sailors reached up for his burden, then gently laid Jane Cianfarra in the bottom of the boat.

The Italian sailor climbed back to the deck. "She must go next," he said, pointing to the elderly woman who lay on a blanket. Hearing that, the woman screamed in fear. The sailor gestured to the four novitiates. "Pick up the corners," he commanded. The young men each grabbed a corner of the blanket, and lifted the woman onto the sailor's back. Carrying the blanket like a sack, he again climbed down to the lifeboat.

He returned to the deck a second time and helped the granddaughter onto the rope ladder. Then the French couple descended.

Mrs. Boyer took her turn at the ladder, and lowered herself to safety. Marion Boyer thought he should remain aboard until the remainder of the women and children were taken off. "There's no one else here to get on," the Italian sailor reasoned with him. "Why don't you just go ahead?" Boyer climbed down to the boat, followed by the four novitiates. The lifeboat cast off for the *Ile de France*.

Italian sailors moved slowly through the enclosed Promenade Deck, gathering passengers for evacuation in small groups. One of them approached an elderly couple. "We are taking off the women first," he explained. "Come." He held out a hand to the wife.

The old woman clasped her husband's arm, gently but determinedly. She smiled. "We're both very old," she said. "I don't intend to save myself without him. If we are going into a boat, we are going together. If we're going to end, we're going to end together."

Clinging desperately to the rail of the deck promenade, Jean Ruth noticed that passengers nearer the front of the ship had disappeared. "Let's move up that way," she suggested. The Greens and Ruths moved forward where they encountered a steward.

"The lifeboats are ready," the steward said. "Women and children first."

Beverly Green felt a pang of fear, her first touch of terror that night. "I don't want to leave you, Alfred," she said.

"I know," Alfred answered, "but maybe it's better if we do what we're told. Don't worry. We're going up to the Boat Deck. We'll try to get off from up there."

Grasping handrails, Beverly Green and Jean Ruth pulled themselves to the point indicated by the sailor, one of the corridors that connected the starboard and port sides of the ship. They could see a clear path to the lower side. They stumbled down the oily, slanted deck the width of the sloping ship to the open rail below. Jean Ruth marveled at the sight of the shining *Ile de France*.

Leaning over the rail, Mrs. Green looked with annoyance at a couple sitting together in a waiting boat, angry that the sailors had forced her and Alfred to part. Then she caught sight of the woman's stomach and realized that she was pregnant. Of course her husband should stay with her.

The wait was short at this station. Soon Beverly Green slipped down a rope to the lifeboat. Jean Ruth felt a numbness in her arms from holding onto the topside rail for so long. She did not know if she could climb down unaided. Sailors quickly trussed her with a rope and lowered her over the side. While others scrambled down into the lifeboat, Mrs. Green and Mrs.

Ruth looked up toward the Boat Deck for their husbands. They saw them standing at the rail with Colonel Carlin.

Suddenly Mrs. Green saw another lifeboat approach, searching for a mooring position alongside the *Andrea Doria*. "Over there!" she yelled, pointing to the rope where the three men waited. As the boat moved to the designated spot, the women relaxed. They knew the men would be saved.

Robert Young, the American Bureau of Shipping inspector, helped his wife and two children onto ropes and down into a boat. As it pulled away he was dismayed to see how slowly the paddle-operated lifeboat moved. Young remained at the rail to help others into the boats. As he worked feverishly a crewman approached him. His face signaled desperation.

"See if you can get me a jack," the crewman pleaded with Young. "There is a woman trapped down below. Maybe there's a jack on one of these other ships."

Young leaned over the rail and called to a sailor in the boat beneath him. "Can you get a jack?"

An uncomprehending French face peered up.

"We need a jack. An automobile jack."

Soon the boat pulled away, and another quickly took its place. Again Young was unable to communicate his request. He continued to work at the rescue effort, his experienced hands tying sure knots as he helped fasten safety ropes to the life jackets of women and children. A young *Andrea Doria* stewardess worked at his side, guiding passengers off the ship, impressing Young with her sureness.

A small boat pulled into position near Young at the base of the rope ladder. "Do you think you can get us an automobile jack?" Young called down. "A woman is trapped below."

"We'll try, sir," replied a courteous American sailor.

Ruth Roman waited her turn in the slow-moving line at the starboard rail, illuminated by spotlights from the *Ile de France*. The irony of the night was apparent. On the screen, the beautiful actress had portrayed terror many times. But this was no movie; it was real. She clutched her son, Dickie, tightly and repeated her earlier promise to take him on a picnic.

A young Italian naval cadet volunteered to bring Dickie down to the lifeboat. Miss Roman held the excited child on his back as others secured the boy to the man with ropes. The cadet backed down the rope ladder into a boat already packed with survivors. A woman passenger reached for the boy and sat him on her lap. As the cadet climbed back up the rope ladder, sailors prepared to cast off for the trip to the *Stockholm*. "Wait for his mother," the woman pleaded.

"No time, no time."

Ruth Roman lifted one leg over the rail of the *Andrea Doria* only to see the lifeboat moving slowly away.

Dickie looked up from the woman's lap and waved to his mother. "Picnic," he called to her happily.

The corridor that connected the port and starboard side of the ship near the first-class section of the Promenade Deck became a busy thoroughfare as passengers moved from muster stations on the high port side toward the rescue scene on the low starboard deck.

Earlier, several of the passengers navigated the slanted corridor on foot, holding tightly to the side railings to keep from falling onto the slippery deck. But by the time Mayor Dilworth and his wife, Ann, made their descent, the ship's list had turned the corridor into a chute angled sharply at over thirty-five degrees. The best possible passage was now to slide precariously down the waxed, oil-slicked deck to the opposite side, the target being a set of double doors which entered onto the starboard Promenade, then to the lifeboats.

Mayor Dilworth and Ann got to a sitting position, and side by side, hurtled down the chute. As they neared the bottom of their slide, the mayor reached out for Ann's shoulder to help break her fall. He caught her foot by mistake, twisting her body around. She crashed headfirst into the door, shattering its tempered glass. Ann cried out, clutching at her right eye. The mayor inspected the injury in the dim light. The eye had begun to swell and blacken, but Ann had escaped serious injury.

Together they moved toward the rail, where a solemn line of passengers waited.

"I don't want to leave without my husband," Ann said to a steward.

"You must," the crewman replied. "You will hold up the entire rescue operation. Women and children must go first."

Ann stood silently by her husband for a moment, her eye throbbing. When her turn came, she hesitated only a moment. She wanted to throw her arms around Dilworth, but she felt it was inappropriate. Quickly she climbed over the rail and down a rope into a lifeboat.

Dilworth remained above at the rail, helping others into the boats. He braced his foot against the top railing, now dipping so low to the ocean that it could not be used as a handhold. One by one the passengers filed up to the rope. The mayor, along with crewmen, tied ropes to their waists as added protection until they reached the safety of the lifeboats.

The three Scrabble-playing priests were among the last to leave the false security of the high side of the Promenade Deck. Father Wojcik and Father Dolciamore worried that Father Lambert's bulk and his inordinate fear of water would make it difficult for him to abandon the ship. They felt he should go first.

When their turn came to make the slide down to starboard, the two younger priests helped Lambert ease into position on the deck. As they released his arms, the huge man tumbled chaotically, his black priestly cape flapping. A group of men gathered at the low side broke his fall. Wojcik and Dolciamore followed down the deck.

Lambert was helped to his feet and directed out a doorway. As Wojcik and Dolciamore rose to follow, they could see their fears realized. Lambert had frozen in place and was blocking the path of other passengers behind him out onto the deck. The heavy priest's hands were stretched out over his head and planted firmly on the door frame, presenting a large, black-robed obstruction on the avenue to rescue.

"Come on! Hurry!" sailors outside on the open deck pleaded. But Lambert stood fixed. They nudged him, gently at first, then more vigorously. But to no avail. Father Lambert refused to move out of the doorway. He was immobilized by his fear of water, and each step toward the lifeboats heightened, rather than relieved, his anxiety.

A crewman turned to the younger priests. "You people better get down into the boat and we'll try to get him out another way," he said, pointing a way to bypass the doorway through an open window nearby.

Wojcik and Dolciamore crawled carefully through the window, and out onto the deck, where crewmen assisted them to a rope. They slid down to a waiting lifeboat.

"My God! It looks like a Hollywood movie set," Wojcik exclaimed. Floodlights from the *Ile de France* and other ships illuminated the tottering side of the *Andrea Doria*. The priests shuddered at the sight of the open sore about a third of the way back from the bow, its edge tearing into their cabin.

Above them, crewmen had finally succeeded in prying Lambert loose. They led him to the rail, but the immense priest balked again, this time at the sight of the rope ladder. Crewmen in the lifeboat held it at the bottom to keep it steady, but it still swayed rhythmically with the wave action.

"Just get one foot on it," a sailor told Lambert. "If you get one foot on it your system will take over. You'll get down."

Lambert gingerly swung one foot over the rail, then another. But as he moved his hands from the rail to the rope, his enormous weight pulled the ladder suddenly taut. It flew from the grasp of the sailors below and spun dizzily above the lifeboat, carrying the screaming priest in its wild arc. The sailors grabbed again for the bottom of the ladder and managed to hold it tight. Lambert, still heaving, clambered down to safety.

When the lifeboat was ready to pull away, word came from above. "The captain wants a doctor and two crewmen to come back on board," someone said. Unhesitatingly a doctor grabbed his black bag and went back up the rope ladder. Two crewmen scrambled after him. Father Wojcik thought it was the most courageous act he had witnessed.

Liliana Dooner had waited for what seemed like hours on the high port side of the Promenade Deck near the stern. It was increasingly evident that no lifeboat activity was taking place on this side of the ship. Desperate to save her daughter, Maria, Mrs. Dooner contemplated the frightening journey down to the low side of the stricken liner where there might be a better chance of rescue. An Italian crewman struggled past, trying to calm the passengers. "Hold on," he said. "The captain is going to straighten out the ship."

At that moment the *Andrea Doria* lurched further over on her right side. *That's it. I'm going down there,* Mrs. Dooner said to herself.

Her torn party dress hanging on her hips, the upper half of her body covered only by the thin purple half-slip she had pulled over herself, Liliana eased her way to the sloping wall outside the tourist-class Pool Veranda. She sat down on the deck. With Maria on her lap she inched her way toward the starboard side. As she moved, her torn dress slid off and her half-slip crawled up above her waist. With the single-mindedness of a concerned mother, Mrs. Dooner moved slowly down past the swimming pool where she had spent most of her free time during the week to the starboard rail at the low side of the ship.

At the rail, she found a rising tide of panic. The first wave of lifeboats there had filled quickly, but there was now a disquieting lack of rescue activity at this position. Other boats had moved to stations farther forward on the starboard rail. Mrs. Dooner tried to work her way forward, but the doors to cabin class were locked from the other side. The crazed mother pounded at the door but this escape route was closed.

Elbowing her way back to the rail, Liliana prayed for a miracle. She fought to keep her sanity until Maria was safe.

A man standing next to her noticed that she was clad only in the flimsy half-slip and he offered his jacket. "If you get to

New York," he said, "give it back to me. All my possessions are in there."

Mrs. Dooner thanked him and scanned the gloomy ocean for signs of rescue. The *Ile de France* and the smaller *Cape Ann* were clearly visible, but the large French lifeboats all seemed to be concentrating on the forward areas of the ship. Suddenly she spotted a small lifeboat nearing the *Andrea Doria*. A desperate plan came to her mind. She grabbed a rope that was tied to the rail. "Help me," she pleaded with the man next to her.

What are you doing?"

"I'm going to lower my daughter over the rail. If they see a child hanging down there, they'll come."

Together they knotted the rope under Maria's arms. The uncomprehending child, who until now been secure in her mother's embrace, started to cry. Liliana tried to keep her voice from shaking as she explained to Maria how to hold tight to the rope with her hands. But as the man lowered Maria over the side, the child let out a terrified, plaintive scream.

The human lure was effective. A crewman on the lifeboat saw the child and changed course toward the stern.

Halfway down, little Maria raised her arms pitifully toward the deck of the *Andrea Doria,* screaming "Mommy! Mommy!" As she did, she released her grip on the rope.

"Hold on!" several passengers called out.

Mrs. Dooner gasped as she saw her child begin to slip from the rope harness toward the cold sea. She reacted instantly. She threw off the borrowed jacket and leaped to the starboard rail. Hands reached out to hold her back, but Liliana struggled free and jumped over the side into the darkness.

Her body fell what seemed to be an interminable distance, even for this accomplished swimmer. Liliana hit the water feet first and seemed to descend forever. Kicking desperately upward, holding her breath, she felt something brush against her arm just as she surfaced. It was Maria. Quickly, Liliana pulled the child onto her back.

Shouting at Maria to cling to her, Mrs. Dooner floated in the ocean for several minutes, waiting for the lifeboat, which was forced to sit off the *Doria*'s side because of rising swells. Liliana realized that she would have to swim out to the boat. Clasping her right hand around Maria's arm, she swam with her free left arm, checking regularly that the child's face was safely above the water.

As she approached the lifeboat, the water around Liliana suddenly began to churn with other passengers who had jumped from the *Andrea Doria*'s deck in desperation. As Liliana came alongside the lifeboat, American sailors from the *Cape Ann* reached out and pulled the frightened child in.

Just as Liliana was about to crawl into the boat herself, she heard a piercing scream behind her. "Help!" Still in the water, Liliana turned toward the *Doria* and saw a thirteen-year-old-girl, Cecilia, whom she had met aboard, dangling helplessly a few feet above the ocean from the end of the same rope she had used to lower Maria.

"Hold on! Hold on!" Liliana screamed across the water.

Pushing away from the security of the *Cape Ann* lifeboat, Liliana swam back toward the *Andrea Doria*. A few minutes later, now beneath the black hovering hull, Liliana grasped the frightened teenager. Mrs. Dooner held onto the rope herself for a few moments to regain her strength. The *Cape Ann* lifeboat edged in as close as it dared to the *Doria*. Holding onto Cecilia with one hand, Liliana then swam out into the ocean for the second time toward the waiting lifeboat.

After crewmen pulled Liliana and Cecilia aboard, Mrs. Dooner sat in the bottom of the lifeboat, little Maria crying softly in her lap. Liliana's purple half-slip was soaked and now barely covered her body. She did not care. She had experienced a sudden feeling of energy and elation. When all had seemed lost, she had saved her daughter and a young friend. A black American sailor sat nearby, smoking. "Please," Liliana said, reaching for the cigarette. It was the best she had ever tasted.

The young Canadian tourist-class passenger, John Vali, found a few pieces of rope lying near the swimming pool. He tied them together and fastened them to the rail. More lifeboats hovered nearby now, but they were unable to pull in directly under the stern. The swell had picked up, increasing the danger of collision with the hull. "Climb down," Vali ordered Melania Ansuini, the nineteen-year-old Italian he had met that night in the Social Hall. "They'll pick you up."

When Vali realized that Melania was afraid, he decided to go first to aid her descent. He plunged into the water, almost hitting the side of a lifeboat as it maneuvered close by. Two men pulled him in. "Come down," he called to Melania.

The young woman slid down the rope toward the waiting boat. As she approached, she released her grip, but missed the bobbing rescue craft. Melania fell hard into the water, the force of the drop knocking her unconscious.

Vali saw her floating on her back in the water. Quickly he scrambled over the side of the boat into the ocean, and thrashed toward Melania. Grasping her hand, he paddled back to the boat, where sailors pulled them in. In a few minutes Melania opened her eyes, crying and thankful.

Giovanni Morrone fought to remain functional. Earlier, he had watched horrified as his wife, Vincenza, had floated away from the stern into the ocean darkness. There was nothing he could do for her now. He had to save his son. "Mario," he yelled, "climb onto my back!"

He grabbed his briefcase containing the family's passports and his business papers. Clutching the case with his teeth, Mario clinging to his back, Morrone slipped down the rope. Nine-year-old Mario heard his father begin to sob. "What are you crying about?" he asked.

"There's no boat down there," his father replied.

"Well, let's just go down anyway," Mario said innocently.

Morrone believed that the *Andrea Doria* might capsize at any moment. He decided that his boy was right: they must take their chances in the water. Together they plunged into the cold sea.

They surfaced, choking on the seawater. Morrone paddled as best he could, keeping both of their heads above water, conscious that Mario could not swim. Debris from the crash and globs of coagulated oil fouled the water. It was dark at this point of the stern. All the rescue searchlights seemed trained farther up toward the bow.

Morrone swam toward the bow for several minutes until a lifeboat saw them bobbing in the water. It approached cautiously. Morrone felt his strength giving out just as a sailor. threw a preserver into the water, jumped on top of it, and paddled toward him. The sailor grabbed young Mario by the arm. He held the boy's head above water as others pulled them aboard.

Giovanni Morrone looked around the boat, and once more peered desperately out into the ocean. There was no sign of his wife, Vincenza.

Three-year-old Rose Marie Wells grasped at her torn left hand and whimpered. It still throbbed from the pressure of the steel bunk that had trapped her in her cabin after the crash. Now on the open Promenade Deck at the stern, she kept her good arm tightly around the neck of her mother. Her sister, Shirley, eyes glazed in shock, tore at her mother's skirt. Such a night was difficult for the children to comprehend.

Alba Wells was still worried about her nine-year-old son, Henry. Her daughters were alongside, but she had not seen Henry since before the collision. She waited in the crazed atmosphere of the stern, watching for a lifeboat and searching for Henry.

A steward approached. He was the same man who had come down to A Deck to help her free Rosie. "Where's Henry?" Mrs. Wells asked. "Have you seen Henry?"

"I talked with the others," the steward replied. "Someone saw Henry on the far side of the ship. They said he got into one of the first lifeboats. You must go now with the girls."

Alba Wells, sure that the steward was lying, felt a numbing despair. She knew that Henry was dead. Rosie cried in her ear. The mother would have to grieve for Henry later; now she must save her girls. She followed the steward to a position near the rail. The congestion at the stern was clearing as more and more lifeboats appeared from the rescue fleet.

Sailors tied a rope around Rose Marie's waist and lowered her over the rail. Sympathetic hands drew her close into a boat. Shirley followed mutely.

Before Mrs. Wells could grasp a rope, the packed lifeboat moved away. The frightened mother was all alone. "Well," she muttered in resignation, "at least they're safe."

Another lifeboat drew close. Mrs. Wells grabbed the rope and climbed over the rail. The ship swayed heavily in the increasing breeze. As she slid toward safety, Mrs. Wells felt the rope swing well out over the water, then back toward the ship. As she struck the side of the *Andrea Doria*, pain coursed through her left arm. She lost her grip and slipped down the rope, burning the flesh of her palms. She dropped heavily into the lifeboat and collapsed. Someone covered her with a blanket.

All around her, passengers cried. Some whimpered softly in gratitude for their rescue. Others wailed the names of missing loved ones. As the boat pulled away, Alba Wells looked back up for Henry. He was not there.

Margaret Sergio was determined to remain aboard the *Andrea Doria* until she found her sister. "Come to a lifeboat," a sailor urged; "we are taking off the women and children."

"No."

"You must go now," Paul Sergio urged.

"No." Margaret clung to the railing. She sobbed for Maria and the children. Other women and children from the touristclass area were being evacuated, but Margaret held fast. Paul saw a group of sailors talking among themselves. Suddenly the sailors grabbed Margaret, pulling her hands free. She reached out for Paul, but he moved back.

"Go down," he cried. "Save yourself. At least one of us has got to be alive for the family. I'll stay here and wait."

Margaret wailed, kicking at the sailors as they tied a rope around her waist and forced her over the railing. She was still crying when she dropped into the lifeboat which was headed for the safety of the *Ile de France*.

From her vantage point on the low side of the cabin-class Ballroom, Sister Angelita Myerscough could see lifeboats arriving at the side of the *Andrea Doria*. Once the *Ile de France* had appeared, a sense of hope pulsed through the room. But the rescue operation had been going on outside for more than an hour and still there was no activity to move the passengers out to the rail. Sister Angelita decided to find out what was happening.

The nun crawled over toppled furniture toward a door. Outside there was a stairwell that she knew led to the open Boat Deck above. A square table and a set of band drums blocked the doorway. She worked carefully to clear a path through the obstructions.

"What are you doing?" a woman asked nervously.

"I'm just going out to see what's going on," Sister Angelita replied. Her answer seemed to calm the woman. Finally someone was taking action.

Sister Angelita squeezed through a narrow opening in the cluttered doorway, and crawled into the stairwell. She pulled herself up to a standing position by grabbing the handrail. As she was about to step upward she heard a muffled grunt. A man, trying to crawl up from below, kept slipping back on the oily, tilting stairway. The nun braced herself against the doorjamb and held out her free arm. The man grabbed her hand. With a desperate heave he pulled himself up to the landing.

Sister Angelita continued up to the Boat Deck, where she saw a few people gathered near a rope ladder.

"Hey, Sister, come on. Come on!" a crewman yelled.

"I just came out to find out what's going on."

"We're putting people in the lifeboats right here. We're waiting. Come on. No time to lose."

"There are a lot of people back there," the nun protested. "Let me go back and tell the other people so they can all start coming out."

"No, Sister, don't do that. Come on. We don't have much time to lose. We'll take care of them."

Sister Angelita realized that she should trust the crewmen to do the job. She could help best by following orders. She took off her shoes and tied the laces together. She sat on the deck, slid over to the rail, where she stood up and grabbed the top of the rope ladder.

"Come on," the sailors urged gently, "hurry."

The nun fingered her rosary. "Holy Mary, mother of God," she said, lifting her leg over the railing, "pray for us at the hour of our death."

She suddenly became tranquil as her feet touched the swaying rope ladder. Sister Angelita grabbed onto one of the slats.

"Sister, hold onto the rope, not the slats," a sailor yelled from above. She did as told, and slithered down the rope ladder as easily as she had climbed down from the hayloft as a child in Illinois.

She was the first passenger to reach that lifeboat. A crewman helped her to a seat, while others worked vigorously at the paddles to keep the boat in position against the sucking action created by the wound. Soon other passengers climbed down. Sister Angelita was pleasantly surprised when her roommate, Giovanna, sat next to her. The two women had not seen each other since Giovanna worked so hard to wake the nun from her sleep.

The lifeboat rocked in the choppy water as the slow boarding process continued. Suddenly Sister Angelita glanced up fearfully to see the huge black hull of the *Andrea Doria* seem to come crashing down onto her. She screamed.

"Take it easy, Sister," a sailor cried out, "we're just riding the waves."

The bartender returned from his exploratory journey to find an expectant audience in the cabin-class Ballroom. "There are boats coming to our rescue," he announced. "If you will just be quiet and come in an orderly manner, I will lead you out." From their position, there was no clear pathway to slide down to the low side; the bartender organized a different escape plan. Forming the passengers into a single file, he would lead them, hand in hand, up a staircase and around the back of the ship. By clinging to the top rail they could move all the way around the stern to the low side. Sister Marie Raymond listened to his plan and worried about the ache in her leg.

"Stay with me," she said to her friend Sister Callistus. "I might have trouble getting off."

"I'll stay with you," Sister Callistus reassured her. "I'll be right here. But when you get to that railing you forget you're crippled. You just get over it."

In the dark night the two nuns slowly made their way up a staircase that lay almost on its side, then around the port deck toward the promise of a lifeboat. Once outside of the ballroom they caught their first full sight of the magnificent *Ile de France*, standing brightly lit in the water only four hundred yards off.

"Thank you, Lord," Sister Raymond whispered.

A lifeboat waited near the stern. In front of the two nuns was a family with several children, including twin baby boys. Sailors strapped one baby to the back of the father, the other to the mother's back. Carefully, the parents climbed down to the boat. Their other children were tied to ropes and lowered down.

Then Sister Raymond moved to the rail. She was directed by a familiar sailor with deep blue eyes, who had greeted her daily on the voyage with a prayer he now repeated. "Praise be Jesus Christ," he said softly.

"Now and forever more, amen," the sister replied.

She was over the rail and climbing down the rope ladder before she remembered her crippled leg.

"*Piano. Piano*," the sailor called from above. "Go slowly. Go slowly."

She reached the boat and waited while sailors untied a safety rope from her waist. She could not remember anyone fastening it onto her.

Then it was Sister Callistus' turn. She stared for an instant down at the lifeboat and the rope ladder that swayed wildly over a wide expanse of threatening water. She took a deep breath. As she hopped over the rail her long black habit swirled about. She slid down to the small wooden boat that, to her, was so clearly an answer to her prayers.

Ruby MacKenzie pushed her daughter Ann close to the rail. There, a small Italian sailor helped the girl over the side and onto a Jacob's ladder. Mrs. MacKenzie looked down. She saw Ann drop safely into a lifeboat, then she prepared to follow.

Suddenly a man shoved his way to the rail, pushed Ruby aside and started to climb over.

"Women first!" a crewman screamed at him.

"It doesn't matter," the man grunted as he scrambled down.

Mrs. MacKenzie took the rope ladder. But a sailor called up from the lifeboat. "We're full. We're shoving off."

Mrs. MacKenzie relaxed her grip on the rope. She turned to see that only she and two other men were left at this lifeboat station. *Ann's off*, she said to herself. *My life isn't that important.*

Then a small motorboat pulled close. "We'll take the rest of them," a voice yelled.

Mrs. MacKenzie again stepped to the rail, struggling to hang onto her large pocketbook, crammed with nickels she had won earlier that evening playing cards. "My God, woman, Think of your life!" a crewman bellowed as he angrily grabbed the pocketbook and heaved it overboard. Mrs. MacKenzie made her way slowly down the swinging rope ladder, reaching tentatively for each rung.

"Hurry! Hurry!" came shouts from above and below.

In the boat she stumbled to a seat and sat quietly for a moment to catch her breath. Her eyes fixed on an object in the bottom of the boat. She leaned over toward it. It was her pocketbook, drenched, and still full of nickels.

A frantic voice called down to the *Stockholm*'s lifeboat number 8 on its second trip to the *Andrea Doria*. "People are trapped in the hole. See if you can pull them out." Second Officer Junior Sven Abenius guided his boat forward to a point underneath the starboard bridge wing. The gaping hole in the hull was a tangle of jagged steel and shattered wood. Pillows, blankets, and pieces of clothing slipped into the sea with each spasm of the ship.

Swedish apprentice Per Hinnerson peered into the black wound. He could see no one. In any case, he realized, it would be impossible to remove anyone from this precarious spot. Hinnerson looked above to the bridge where the *Doria*'s captain was conferring with several of his officers. He wondered why they were not organizing the evacuation more efficiently. Abenius turned his lifeboat back toward the stern to rescue more passengers.

Down in cabin 56 on the Upper Deck, Thure Peterson and Giovanni Rovelli were stymied. Without heavy equipment they could not free Martha Peterson from the wreckage. Peterson decided to see the captain once more, for the promised help had not materialized. He desperately needed a jack. He moved back up toward the bridge on the Sun Deck, a journey of incredible agony now as the ship moved closer to her death. He paused only briefly on the Promenade Deck for a gulp of brandy offered by sympathetic friends.

On the bridge, Peterson anxiously confronted Calamai. The promised help had not arrived, he told the captain, and his wife was still trapped under wreckage in their cabin.

"I need an automobile jack," Peterson told the surprised captain. "You must radio the Coast Guard and tell them to bring one to the ship."

Calamai listened sympathetically, but the troubled master gave Peterson's request a low priority. "It would be a hard thing to get," the captain answered. "It would take too much time."

The captain looked at Peterson's dejected face. "Could we substitute something for it? Could we free her with a flame?" he asked. When Peterson looked at him doubtfully, Calamai assured the distraught husband that he would order a search for another heavy tool. He turned to a crewman. "See what you can do to help Dr. Peterson," he ordered. The crewman grabbed a fire ax and followed Peterson back down to the Upper Deck.

By the time the two men reached cabin 58 Rovelli had gone up to the Promenade Deck to check on the jack. After Peterson quickly explained the problem, the crewman hacked repeatedly at the wall between the two rooms, trying to open a hole into cabin 56. But with each swing more debris fell on Martha, who cried out in agony.

The crewman moved back into the corridor and through the door of cabin 56, where he wielded the fire ax again in the hope of freeing Martha. Each swing only showered the trapped woman with more wreckage. His will failing in the darkened, sinking ship, the crewman dropped the ax and left.

Once again the Petersons were alone. Martha pleaded with Thure to put her to sleep. Just as desperately, Thure begged her to maintain her courage. He told her he was going to see if Rovelli had located a jack.

He found Rovelli on the Promenade Deck standing next to the rail at one of the open glass windows. The ship was nearly deserted now. Peterson moved next to him, but there seemed to be nothing to say. There seemed to be no way to pull Martha from the wreckage, yet Peterson could not give up.

From the darkness below them an American voice from a lifeboat called out. "Hey! We got the jack."

On his third trip to the *Andrea Doria*, Second Officer Lars Enestrom guided his *Stockholm* motor lifeboat once more to the stern of the stricken ship. Crewmen on the lifeboat tautly held down the two ropes slung over the *Andrea Doria*'s decks in order to make the descent easier. But the young Swedish officer grew concerned at the length of time it took many passengers, particularly women, to climb down. The *Andrea Doria* was shuddering and listing precariously. Enestrom worried that she might suddenly capsize.

Enestrom signaled them to hurry, but still the passengers

came down slowly. One woman lost her grip on the rope, and fell the last ten feet into the lifeboat, clutching at her leg in pain.

An old man was helped over the rail. He grasped at the rope fearfully, and allowed his feet to push off from the side of the ship. But he refused to slide down to the lifeboat. He swung out over the water, dangling helplessly, while sailors in the lifeboat and angry passengers waiting their turn for the rope grew frustrated.

"Grab a blanket!" Enestrom shouted. "Be ready to catch him if he falls."

After perhaps a full minute, a passenger climbed over the railing, grabbed the older man around the waist and pulled him back toward the deck. The frightened passenger stood petrified on the outside of the ship's railing, his feet on the edge of the deck. Others grabbed the rope, and slid past him into the lifeboat.

When the lifeboat was nearly full, Enestrom saw an *Ile de France* boat pull up next to him on the right, sandwiching his boat between it and the *Andrea Doria*. Since the *Ile de France* was closer than the *Stockholm*, Enestrom suggested to his passengers that they move to the French boat. They scrambled from one lifeboat to the other, except for the woman who had injured her leg.

The French boat cast off to return. As more passengers climbed down to Enestrom's boat, he saw that someone had helped the frightened old man over the rail and back onto the deck of the *Andrea Doria*.

Finally, with a load of forty-five passengers, mostly women, Enestrom cast off to return to the *Stockholm*.

Father Tom Kelly stood in the enclosed Promenade on the high side adjacent to the cabin-class Ballroom with a group of passengers who had been waiting futilely in the Ballroom. It was now obvious that they were isolated; there was no exit from this point. They would have to go to the back of the ship and over toward starboard to reach the lifeboats.

Kelly directed the passengers into an orderly line and began a human shuttle along the topside rail toward the stern. Deck chairs cluttered the lower side of the Promenade, and passengers were forced to cling to the rail at the high edge to work their way aft. The passengers removed their shoes and ran rapidly along the inclined deck to keep from sliding down. The young priest raced back and forth, assisting women to the open area near the stern.

As Father Kelly was about to take his own place near the end of the line, a sailor thrust his head into a stairwell from the Boat Deck. "Some of you can come back up here," he called.

Kelly and a few others near the end of the line turned back and climbed up a nearby stairway. Kelly leaned down and called out. "Is anyone left?" His voice echoed through the emptying ship.

Once up on the Boat Deck, the young priest worked his way around to the starboard side. He saw a rope tied to the rail. Below it, a lifeboat waited close to the hull. Kelly grabbed the rope and hopped over the rail, suddenly encountering the strange fear that his own weight on the rope would pull the *Andrea Doria* over. As he slid into the lifeboat he was greeted by a Swedish sailor who saluted smartly and said, "Good evening, sir. We're the ones who sank you."

The lifeboat filled quickly. The *Stockholm* sailor instructed his new passengers on the use of the sticks placed in front of each seat. By pushing and pulling on them, the passengers powered the boat's propeller. As they were ready to cast off, a motor launch drew alongside and threw a line to the lifeboat.

"We'll tow you," someone yelled from the motorboat. Sailors tied the boats together. Kelly could see a man in the rear of the motorboat pulling at a cord. The engine would not fire. Both boats rocked heavily in the whirlpool suction from the nearby hole in the *Doria*.

"Let's get the hell out of here!" someone yelled.

Sailors cast off the rope holding the lifeboat to the motor launch. The passengers set to work laboriously paddling to pull the boat away from the sinking ship.

Passengers pulled in unison. Slowly the boat moved free of the suction. Steadily it eased around the bow of the *Andrea Doria*, heading toward the *Stockholm*, which sat placidly in the water about a mile away. The paddling was hard work, but Kelly was filled with a euphoric sense of peace. There was nothing but black, almost tranquil sea between the lifeboat and the *Stockholm*. The blazing spotlights were all trained on the starboard side of the *Doria*. Here, to port, the disaster seemed forgotten.

"Look!" someone shouted. All eyes in the lifeboat suddenly turned toward a late-arriving merchant ship that had suddenly maneuvered into the void seeking to help. It seemed to be running directly toward their lifeboat.

Passengers worked desperately at their paddles to clear the path of the onrushing ship. There was no time to think of the irony now. They had been saved from a sinking ship only to be crushed by another. The huge ship bore down on them fast. With no radio and no running lights, the lifeboat was helpless.

"Light a match!" somebody yelled.

Passengers searched for matches in drenched pockets and purses. A few were found and lit quickly by shaking hands. But the weak, desperate signal was of no use. The huge ship continued on its path directly toward them.

In the back of the lifeboat one of the Swedish crewmen suddenly lit an entire pack of matches. The flame sizzled throughout the silent lifeboat. The approaching ship saw the signal and threw a spotlight forward of its path, brilliantly framing the helpless lifeboat. Quickly, the ship swerved safely off to port. Grateful passengers pumped at their paddles. As the ship approached, they could see sailors lowering a boarding ramp near the bow. The ship was an oil tanker.

"Over here!" sailors yelled down at them from the tanker. They, too, wanted to share the honor of rescue.

From a distance, the *Stockholm* appeared to be a sleek racing liner with no visible damage. The lifeboat passengers took a straw vote and decided to proceed on to the larger vessel. They bent their backs to the paddles. Only when they drew close could they see the battered nose of their attacker.

The group of about twenty people clustered between the open port rail of the Boat Deck and the cabin-class Gymnasium had seen none of the rescue activity. Isolated from the rest of the ship, away from their muster station, they sat wedged against the bulkhead for support. For a while they busied themselves singing "Shine On, Harvest Moon," and other old sing-alongs. More than three hours had passed since the collision, with no direction from the crew. Above them the starboard side lifeboats hung untouched. Death seemed very close.

"Maybe one of us ought to go down to the low side to see what's happening," someone said.

"If you go down there, you're not going to get back up."

"Maybe we should all go."

"If we do that, maybe our weight would sink the ship."

"We're going to die anyway, so what's the difference?"

There was a brief silence. Then someone said, "I think we should go. Maybe they're lowering lifeboats down there. They sure can't lower them from up here."

The group decided to form a human chain to stretch as far as possible down the width of the ship, past a transverse bulkhead that would offer a grip. There was an emigrant family clustered with these mainly American cabin-class passengers. The Italian mother was frantic with fear as the passengers formed into a line. "My children! My children!" she screamed, looking wildly about for them, though they were holding her hands and tugging at her skirt.

Young songwriter Mike Stoller took one of the children by the hand. His wife, Meryl, took another. Slowly they moved aft from their position to the side of the bulkhead. They worked their way down, leaning against the smooth metal wall, stumbling the last few steps and crashing into the starboard rail.

Their bruises were quickly forgotten. Before them was the sight of an impressive rescue armada, with the *Ile de France* on center stage. The Stollers left the Italian children to the care of their parents. Quickly they moved toward a rope ladder where a crewman in blue denim was helping passengers down to a boat. The ladder looked precarious, swinging well out over the water.

"There is a net at the back of the ship," the crewman suggested.

The Stollers looked aft. They could see a horde of people near the stern. Their chances were better here. The crewman tied a rope around Meryl Stoller's waist, then helped her climb over the rail onto the rope ladder. She looked down and her body tightened. "I can't move," she moaned.

"Get going!" Mike yelled at her.

"If I'm going to die, I'd rather die where I am," his wife cried.

"Leave them!" someone shouted from the boat.

Mike pushed Meryl down the first few rungs, then climbed over the rail himself, stepping on his wife's hands to force her along.

"Leave them! Leave them!" the voice yelled from below.

Finally they dropped into the boat, which was nearly full. As a few others climbed down to safety the same voice kept yelling, "Leave them! Leave them!" Mike Stoller recognized the man as a passenger he had met earlier in the voyage.

The crewmen showed the passengers how to operate the paddles. With a full load, the passengers set to work to escape the suction of the *Andrea Doria*. The boat swayed wildly out of control for a time, but then pulled away. In front of them the passengers could see the warm glow of the *Ile de France*. But the lifeboat unaccountably swung off to the side, away from the gleaming target.

"That way, that way!" the same passenger screamed, pointing toward the French liner. Still the lifeboat veered away.

The angry passenger jumped up in the boat and glared at the crewman who struggled at the tiller. "That way!" he screamed again. When there was no response he rushed toward the sailor, stepping on angry passengers. "I'm going to kill you!" he yelled. Other passengers wrestled him to the floor of the boat. He lay there crying.

"The rudder is broken," the crewman explained. "I can't steer. We must keep paddling to get away. One of the ships will pick us up."

Forcibly held down, the passenger finally caught the impact of the words. After a few minutes he was persuaded to man one of the paddles. The others watched him suspiciously.

Bouncing along at the whim of the sea, the lifeboat finally veered toward the freighter *Cape Ann*. Passengers watched hopefully as they approached, then fearfully as the tiny craft swung toward the sharp prow of the freighter.

"What the fuck are you people doing?" a sailor's voice yelled from above.

"Gee, it's good to hear a nice foul American voice," Meryl Stoller said, pleased.

The lifeboat drifted past the bow toward an iron staircase on the starboard side. As men reached out to grab the staircase, a bilge pump discharged, nearly swamping the boat and drenching several passengers, the Stollers among them.

Strong arms held the lifeboat to the ship. Passengers inched up the stairs, assisted by friendly faced sailors. When Mike Stoller reached the deck of the *Cape Ann*, he let the air out of his lungs for what seemed like the first time in four hours. Then all at once he burst into tears.

Senior Chief Officer Luigi Oneto and Junior Second Officer Guido Badano leaned far out over the starboard bridge wing to view the rescue activity. Oneto was amazed by the severe list of the ship. He had been frantically busy during these early morning hours, but now he had a moment to weigh the probabilities. He finally realized that the beautiful *Andrea Doria* would go under. "I don't think we can sail with her anymore," he said softly, out of Calamai's hearing.

"I don't think so either," Badano replied.

It was close to 3:00 A.M. Thirteen-year-old Peter Thieriot stood as one link in a human chain that stretched from the port side of the Promenade Deck through a hallway adjacent to the first-class Ballroom down to the low starboard rail. The men in the line assisted the last few older passengers and women down the sloping floor toward the safety of the lifeboats. When the port side muster station was clear, the man at the top of the line descended and the chain lowered itself, link by link. When

Peter reached the starboard rail, he found himself at a point near the middle of the ship, close to his own cabin. By now the list was so great that he could almost step directly from the deck into a waiting lifeboat from the *Ile de France*.

As the boat pulled slowly away from the dying *Andrea Doria*, Peter looked back, hoping that he would see his parents scrambling into a boat. What he saw instead was a cavernous black hole, located just in front of the ramp where he and his family had boarded at Gibraltar. Peter remembered his father telling him that the porthole forward of the ramp was the location of his parents' suite. That porthole was missing now, swallowed by the ugly black sore. Peter stared at the hole all the way over to the *Ile de France*.

Thure Peterson and Giovanni Rovelli, one a giant of a man and the other a diminutive but determined waiter, strained at the ropes tied to a 150-pound jack that sat in a lifeboat from one of the rescue ships. With a heave they pulled it over the rail, where it crashed against Rovelli's wrist, then thudded heavily to the deck. Rovelli winced in pain. Alternately pushing and pulling the heavy iron tool, oblivious to the chaos about them and intent only on saving Martha, they called on reserves few people ever tap. They covered the distance across the deck and down the stairway to cabin 56 slowly, pausing to rest only when collapse was the only alternative. The ship felt nearly on her side by now. The two men worried that time was running out.

Hurriedly they pulled the jack into the confined space. They tried to set it in place under the heavier debris, but the jack handle was too long. While Rovelli placed cushions protectively across Martha's body, Peterson raced back around and into cabin 56 through the doorway, and found the ax left there earlier. He furiously chopped through a towel rack in the bathroom. Now he had a jack handle.

Scurrying back into cabin 58 and under the wall to 56 he inserted the towel rack into the jack.

Martha moaned softly.

Rovelli worked to pump up the jack. As it finally began to lift the heavy debris off Martha, Rovelli's hand touched the woman's face. The skin was icy.

The chiropractor knelt over his wife. He listened for a heartbeat, felt in vain for a pulse, lifted a limp eyelid. At 4:10 A.M., exactly five hours after the collision, Martha Peterson was dead.

Thure Peterson's face paled. Tenderly he kissed his wife good-bye, then removed a ring from her hand. Together with the waiter he crawled back into cabin 58, stunned as water lapped at his feet.

Once more Thure Peterson decided to return to the bridge. He had to tell someone. The bridge was desolate, with officers gathering ship's papers. Calamai turned toward Peterson.

"She is gone," Peterson said quietly.

The man who had lost his ship stared silently at the man who had lost his wife. A bond of despair united them. "If you would like," Calamai stammered in unfamiliar English, "perhaps we could send your wife's body off in a lifeboat."

"No. She is gone."

Calamai ordered an officer to take Peterson back to the Promenade Deck, where Rovelli guided the dazed husband into a lifeboat. Rovelli followed.

As the rescue craft pulled away from the *Andrea Doria*, Thure Peterson looked back at the black hole in the Upper Deck where cabin 56 had once been.

He wept.

Captain Calamai stood silently on the starboard bridge wing, observing the rescue effort below. He spoke softly to Junior Second Officer Guido Badano. "If you go back to Genoa and see my family, you will be my witness," he said. "You can say that I am at peace with myself. I did what I had to do."

Confused by the comment, Badano replied, "What are you saying? The *Ile de France* is close by." He gestured at the blazing lights of the French liner. "We will be saved. If I go back to Genoa, you will go back to Genoa."

Calamai looked at his young officer but did not reply. It was then that Badano realized his captain's intent to go down with his ship.

Third Officer Eugenio Giannini had been out on the stern of the Upper Deck for hours, lowering passengers to the lifeboats. At first there had been only a few, but word had spread to groups of people waiting in the tourist-class Social Hall and other areas nearby. The passengers had filtered down to the small area, where they disembarked.

Giannini stayed in telephone communication with Calamai on the bridge. Now the last passenger at this station had been saved. Giannini picked up the telephone to ask Calamai for further orders, but the line was dead. Staff Captain Osvaldo Magagnini, who had also finished his rescue duties, went forward to return to the bridge.

About fifteen crewmen, including an engineering officer, stood with Giannini, waiting for instructions from the young officer. Now isolated from his superiors, Giannini needed new orders. Below him, in a waiting lifeboat staffed by a few crew members, he saw the ship's first purser.

"Comici," he yelled, "go over near the bridge. Ask what I should do."

Comici directed the lifeboat forward, up toward the dangerous currents near the hole. Giannini waited anxiously, for the *Andrea Doria* was now listing at least thirty-five degrees. The men could simply step off this platform into a boat. Giannini hoped they would soon receive orders to abandon ship.

The scene in front of him was unbelievable. Rescue ships, led by the lights of the *Ile de France*, crisscrossed their spotlights along the starboard side of the stricken liner. The *Andrea Doria* lay helpless in the glare, the heroine of an epic tragedy.

"Giannini!" a voice called from below. It was Comici. "The captain says to come back near the bridge with your crew and wait for further orders."

"Wait," Giannini said. Several of the crew members with him were older men. The young officer knew they would have difficulty making the trek back to the bridge. He ordered the older ones into the boat with Comici, then led the handful of other men up a flight of stairs to the Promenade Deck, past a smashed window, and forward. The ship's own power supply was nearly gone, supplemented only by a gasoline-powered emergency generator near the bridge. Light from the rescue vessels cast eerie shadows on the desolate ballrooms and lounges. The *Andrea Doria* resembled a ghost town.

The procession headed by Giannini neared the front of the Boat Deck on the starboard side, underneath the bridge wing. The men sat and lay down on the floor, awaiting further orders.

On the bridge, Staff Captain Magagnini reported to a weary Captain Calamai: "We have checked all parts of the ship to which we have access. All passengers have been disembarked in the lifeboats."

"Order the crew to abandon ship," Calamai said. "Ask for volunteers to remain behind."

Magagnini relayed the orders. Grateful crewmen, their rescue mission completed, slipped into waiting boats. The officers and a few sailors, about twenty in all, remained on the bridge. Three lifeboats stood ready at the starboard side, not far from the *Andrea Doria*'s mortal wound.

Calamai turned his attention back to the remote possibility of saving his once magnificent ship. Perhaps she would remain afloat long enough to be towed to shallow water. "Send a message to the Coast Guard," he ordered Second Officer Badano. "Ask for tugboats." Badano went to the wireless room and relayed the instructions.

The weak message flashed out:

WE NEED TUGBOATS FOR ASSISTANCE.

Calamai turned to his officers. "Save the books," he ordered. Officer Cadet Mario Maracci crawled across the chartroom floor, gathering some of the ship's logbooks from a jumble of papers and maps.

"Give the course recorder graph to Maracci," Calamai said to Badano a few minutes later. "He has the other papers." Working with difficulty against the severe list, Badano prepared to remove the recording paper that provided a continuous record of the ship's heading throughout the voyage. Badano scrutinized the graph and tore off the twelve-hour portion that detailed the ship's movements before and after the collision. He folded it and handed it to Maracci, who put the graph inside his tunic with the logbooks.

Preparing for the dark journey back toward the lifeboats at the stern, Badano slipped into his cabin for a flashlight. As he moved through the corridor, he encountered Maracci. The cadet's uniform jacket bulged.

"Did you take everything?" Badano asked.

"I am full of papers," Maracci said, pointing to his chest. "I am in trouble. If I fall into the water I will sink."

Badano returned to the bridge. "Did you save the logbooks?" Calamai asked.

"Maracci said he had them," Badano confirmed. Neither of them looked underneath the pile of papers on the chartroom floor, where several of the logbooks had been overlooked.

The remaining officers and men assembled to abandon ship. Single file they moved down from the bridge. Working their way to the starboard side of the Boat Deck they could see evidence of the dramatic carnage. Suitcases, ripped open, littered the low side. Bits of wood and clumps of oily sludge cluttered the water where the lifeboats waited. Ropes hung everywhere.

Balancing with one foot on the deck and one foot on the rail, Staff Captain Magagnini could feel salt water bite into the broken blisters on the soles of his bare feet.

Third Officer Giannini dropped into lifeboat number 11, his long ordeal ended. The others followed in reverse order of rank. Halfway down the rope ladder, Staff Captain Magagnini looked up to see Captain Calamai on the deck, his arms folded in resignation. On his head was his jaunty blue beret.

"Come on, Captain. Come down," Magagnini urged.

"Go down," Calamai replied. "I'll stay here and wait for the tugboats. If I have to, I will swim out to you."

Magagnini listened, then quickly began his ascent up the ladder, back toward the deck of the *Andrea Doria*. He was determined not to leave Calamai behind. "If you remain here,

I will stay with you," he vowed to the captain. From the lifeboat below, Oneto, Giannini and others made the same pledge.

Calamai looked at his officers, then finally said, "I will come." He followed Magagnini to the lifeboat.

"Giannini," Calamai said, "tell the *Ile de France* she can go." Giannini grabbed an Aldes signal lamp and flashed the captain's message to the French liner.

"Giannini," Calamai added quickly, "also tell them thank you."

At 5:30 in the morning of July 26, 1956, the last three lifeboats pulled away from the *Andrea Doria*, taking with them a defeated crew and a sunken captain. Piero Calamai knew that he would never again go to sea.

What the captain did not know as his lifeboat headed for one of the nearby Navy ships was that not everyone had left the *Andrea Doria*. One passenger, very much alive, had been left behind.

12

THE SLEEPER

ROBERT HUDSON SHIFTED UNEASILY in his bunk in the tourist-class section of the *Andrea Doria*. He had slept soundly for the first time in weeks under the influence of a narcotic prescribed for the back he had injured while working on the freighter *Ocean Victory*. Now the pains had returned. His bed felt strangely hard. Still groggy, he struggled to a sitting position. He felt behind himself with his good left hand. His right hand was heavily bandaged where he had cut himself. His fingers encountered the hard metal of a bulkhead, not the soft mattress he expected. He seemed to have moved somehow from his top bunk and was huddled against the cabin wall near the ceiling.

Instinctively Hudson reached out for the light switch, but the cabin remained dark. He fumbled through his personal belongings in a netting slung from the side of the bunk. Finding his cigarette lighter, he lit it and held the small flame over his watch crystal. It was 5:10 A.M.

When he flipped the lighter shut the room again went dark. Still fighting drowsiness, Hudson tried to reason out the situation. As he pondered, his pupils dilated in reaction to the darkness. Staring out over the top of his strangely angled bunk he could see that his cabin door was flung wide open. From somewhere in the corridor came a vague amber glow.

An able-bodied seaman for eighteen of his thirty-five years, Robert Hudson knew what emergency lighting was. He scrambled down from his bunk, scarcely noticing the pains that shot from his lower back through his left leg. Reaching forward with his left hand, holding the bandaged right hand protectively in front of him, he grabbed the doorjamb. He braced his foot against the bunk and lunged forward, upward to the corridor. Oil and water covered the waxed floor of the hallway. A puddle several inches deep gathered on the starboard side. Until now, Hudson had not noticed the water in his room.

"Is anybody there?" Hudson screamed. There was no reply. "Is anyone there? Please!" There was no way for the plea to carry from the deserted, enclosed hallway on the portside of A Deck, just about midships, up to the open Boat Deck, where, at this very moment, Captain Calamai and the last of the crew were beginning to disembark.

"Ghost ship," Hudson muttered. "My God! She's going down."

Having spent most of the voyage in the ship's infirmary, Hudson knew little of the *Andrea Doria*'s geography. His only trip to the upper decks was the previous afternoon when he had wandered back toward the stern on A Deck and had then climbed upward to the Promenade Deck, where he had watched a trapshooting contest. Quickly he decided to retrace that route now, rather than risk becoming lost in an unfamiliar maze of passageways and stairwells.

Though the corridor ran the full length of the ship, it was obstructed by numerous doorways and offset passageways. Clad only in a pair of boxer shorts, in all but total darkness, in a sinking ship listing forty degrees, on slick, wet, waxed floors, with a numb left leg, two herniated discs in his back, and a torn, useless right hand, Robert Hudson fought to survive.

He no longer bothered to scream. There was no one to hear him. The slim hallway seemed to close in. He forced himself to move slowly. One slip might incapacitate him completely, yet he knew he had little time left.

His good left arm braced against the down slope of the wall, his bare feet searching for traction, he moved aft. He passed by the rooms that comprised the ship's hospital, where he had slept for all but this last night of the voyage. Had he been sleeping there, doctors would have roused him, and he would now be safe on a rescue ship. He pushed through a door that led back toward the rows of empty cabins in the rear quarter of A Deck. Staggering along, he forced the panic from his mind. Only the stamina he had developed in his years at sea could save him.

The corridor seemed to stretch endlessly before him. *I'll never make it*, he thought. *She's going under. She can't possibly stay afloat. She's leaning too much.* He forced himself to stare at the next offset in the corridor, a darkened target in the dim tunnel of his vision. He slipped in a puddle of oily water, but caught himself against the wall. If he fell, he feared he would not be able to rise back to his feet.

Slowly his goal approached. He remembered this doorway. It led to the wide stairway near the tourist-class Foyer. He had climbed the stairs the previous afternoon. He knew if he could make his way up two levels he would reach an open deck. He shoved his way through the door and looked at the stairs.

Slowly, one step at a time, he struggled up, approaching the Foyer Deck. He was near the huge kitchens, which only a few hours earlier were serving elegant dinners to hundreds of unsuspecting guests. They were empty and silent now.

Hudson moved on, up another flight. He was now at the Upper Deck, adjacent to the tourist-class Lounge, with access to the ocean. Now he knew he would have a chance.

With a desperate gasp, he pulled himself out to the tourist-class Promenade. It was 6:00 A.M. It had taken him nearly an hour to reach this point.

The ship was still. Deck chairs littered the low side. Debris was everywhere. Hudson grabbed broken furniture for support as he limped to the edge. He could see better now, for sunlight was edging over the horizon. A thick rope had been lashed from the doorway entrance to the deck railing all the way back to the stern. Grasping the rope for support, he pulled his way back. Water slithered across the deck. Waves splashed over from the starboard side. The low rail was now completely submerged. Hudson moved with care, lest he fall and slide off into the sea. Oily sludge clogged his bare toes. Dressed only in his undershorts, he shivered in the morning air.

Hudson neared the stern, and raised his eyes to the sea, searching for any sign of life. Suddenly a wave rushed across the rear of the deck. It lifted him off his feet, and quickly threw him overboard into the ocean.

The suction is so great it will pull me completely under the ship and I'll surface on the other side, Hudson thought. Then he remembered how huge the *Andrea Doria* was. She lay deep in the water. He would never be able to hold his breath long enough. His lungs had not been ready for the quick plunge. He fought fiercely against an impulse to draw in the salt water. He thrashed wildly, struggling to surface against the commanding suction. Suddenly his arm struck a rope. He reached out and grabbed the swimming pool net, slung out across the stern to help in the evacuation. Hudson pulled mightily and found his head above water. He breathed deeply, then coughed the bitter water from his throat. He cocked his left arm around the net. Half in the water, riding the swell of the current, he looked about.

He saw a lifeboat sitting about three hundred yards off. It was a small craft, manned by half a dozen sailors. They were scanning the ship carefully.

"Help!" Hudson cried out. "Help me. Over here."

A flashlight winked. Its beam played along the stern of the *Andrea Doria*. Guided by Hudson's screams, the light focused on the desperate sailor clinging to the net.

"Help me!" Hudson yelled again. "Quickly. Hurry."

Hudson waited for the men to clasp their oars. He fought against the swift current, energized now by the sight of his rescuers.

But the lifeboat did not move.

"Help!" Hudson called once more. "Hurry. Please!"

Still the lifeboat lay quietly in the water. The flashlight again blinked in Hudson's eyes. They saw him. They heard him. Why would they not come? *My God!* Hudson realized, *the ship is going down . . . now!* In his merchant marine training

Hudson had been taught that a lifeboat must sit off at least three hundred yards to avoid being pulled under by a sinking ship. That was where the lifeboat lay.

As he pondered his fate, Hudson felt himself pulled free from the net by a sudden wave. Again he struggled back to the net and climbed to his uncertain position of safety. His already injured body was battered repeatedly against the ship by the rhythmic current. All that remained of his shorts was the waistband.

Robert Hudson sent forth a string of curses as vile as any seaman ever uttered. They rang loudly and clearly across the waters. The sailors in the safety of their lifeboat heard their parentage, courage, and manhood questioned in bitter epithets. But they would not move in.

If only they would have come five minutes ago, they would have made it, Hudson thought. Now he was going to die, with help only three hundred yards off. Another heavy wave thrust him away from his perch. The undercurrent pulled him down, but he was thrown against the side of the ship, where he again grasped for the net and climbed back to the surface. Hudson was an excellent swimmer, yet he knew he could never escape from the terrible suction even if he was uninjured. His only hope was the reticent lifeboat crew.

At this moment of death, Hudson's Baptist upbringing returned. He prayed out loud. "Lord, save me," he pleaded. "Or save my soul." Images of his rough life flashed past. "Forgive me for my sins," he implored.

He lay silent for a time, riding the swells, waiting for the end. An orange globe of sun rose behind him, the fresh beginning of the day mocking the tragedy it revealed. The *Andrea Doria* lay more horizontal than vertical. Deck chairs, suitcases, random bits of clothing, and splintered wood swayed in the waves. Hudson climbed one notch higher on the net as it slowly sank lower into the sea.

His will returned. "Help!" he screamed. "Please come get me. You can't let me die."

He could see the men watching him from the lifeboat. But they did not reach for their oars.

The desperate man resorted to cursing once more. Then he

prayed, not to God but to the men in the lifeboat. He cried. He begged.

The morning sun rose higher as Robert Hudson lay still. *I'm dead*, he thought. *There's nothing I can do.* Tears blended with the salt water that splashed across his face. He was near delirium now, ready to slip under the surface and let the sea take him. His eyes were frosted with salt. The glare of the sun on the water was blinding. He almost did not see the men in the lifeboat grab their oars and suddenly rush toward him. With the skill of veteran sailors they pulled in unison. The small boat shot forward. In five minutes the men covered the three hundred yards to where Hudson lay.

"Hurry!" he shouted. "Come fast."

"Take it easy. We're coming, we're coming."

"Hurry, hurry, hurry," Hudson intoned.

When the boat reached the stern, two sailors leaned out and hauled Hudson aboard. It was 7:30 A.M. Hudson had been hanging in the net for one and one-half hours. The rescuers dropped him in the bottom of the boat and manned the oars. There was no time to lose. They must clear the suction of the ship quickly, or they would all be lost. The lifeboat fought against the current, broke free, and shot back out to safety.

Once clear of the *Andrea Doria*, two of the sailors attended to Hudson while the others rowed the boat toward their ship, the tanker *Robert E. Hopkins*. Arriving late at the collision site, the *Hopkins* had sent out a single boat to search the waters around the *Andrea Doria*. Hudson was the only survivor they found.

"How do you feel?" an officer asked.

"I'm cold." The officer gave him his coat. Hudson thanked the man. For the moment, all his anger was gone. He was only grateful that they had come for him at last.

"Is that better?" the officer asked as Hudson wrapped the coat around him.

Hudson suddenly remembered his previous injuries. Hot pains climbed up and down his spine. The bandages on his right hand were soaked. Salt water burned in the wounds. "I'd feel better," he gasped, "if I had that bottle of Scotch I left under my bed."

The officer smiled. "I don't have any Scotch," he said, "but I've got some mighty good bourbon in my room."

The lifeboat tied up at the *Robert E. Hopkins*. Hudson was helped on board. As the only survivor on the tanker, he was a celebrity. Crewmen outfitted him with clothes. As Hudson sat on the deck, staring at the hulk of the *Andrea Doria*, he told his story over and over. The officer from the lifeboat produced a fifth of bourbon.

Robert Hudson drank every drop.

13

THE WHIRLPOOL

NEAR DAWN, THE *Ile de France* left the vicinity, steaming back to New York with 753 survivors. Some of the other rescue ships lingered, circling the dying liner at a respectable distance.

The staccato beat of helicopter rotors broke the morning silence. Two of the craft arrived from the north. The first, a small, yellow Coast Guard copter, hovered over the stern of the *Stockholm* as sailors readied the two most serious casualties for evacuation. They strapped a small, unconscious child into a basket. Pinned to her nightgown was a cryptic note written by a Swedish doctor: "Italian child born—is recommended treatment at nearest surgical clinic—consequence of fractured cranium." No one knew the girl's name, only that her condition was critical.

Stockholm crewman Alf Johansson, suffering from a fractured skull, was raised on a stretcher into the copter, which took off for Boston. A larger Air Force craft moved into position. It evacuated *Stockholm* crewmen Wilhelm Gustavsson, Lars Falk, and Arne Smedberg, all of whom were in serious condition. Shortly after the two aircraft landed in Boston, Alf Johansson died, the forty-eighth fatality of the night.

At 9:45 A.M. a solemn hush overtook those who watched as the *Andrea Doria* suddenly lurched helplessly and fell over on her right side. The giant white wake created by the impact obscured the scene for an instant. As it subsided, the *Andrea Doria*'s huge stack could be seen probing the ocean surface. The decks of the once-proud liner were almost perpendicular to the water.

Nearby a thousand survivors gathered at the rails of the *Stockholm, Cape Ann, Pvt. William H. Thomas*, and other ships to watch the writhing vessel. Captain Calamai watched unbelievingly from a late-arriving tugboat. He tried to disguise his grief, but Third Officer Giannini could see that the captain seemed to be dying with his proud *Andrea Doria*. Senior Chief Officer Oneto cried. Small airplanes filled with reporters, news photographers, and curious laymen circled overhead amid a clear blue sky, decorated only with a few puffs of clouds. The *Andrea Doria* was a media event now.

The fallen Italian liner was three miles distant from the *Stockholm.* A murky oil slick extended between the two antagonists, littered with wreckage. Waves surged outward from the dying *Doria.* Portholes that now lay in the water under the ship apparently burst, causing a sudden upward pressure. Geysers of seawater erupted from the portside.

By 10:00 A.M. the bow had slipped underwater. She had held on for eleven hours after the collision. But, like a feisty prizefighter overpowered by a superior foe, the *Andrea Doria* finally acquiesced to an inevitable fate. Settling rapidly, she dragged her red, white, and green funnel beneath the surface. The sea moved in quickly, engulfing the forward portion of the ship. The stern rose out of the water, revealing the giant rudder and the twin nineteen-foot screws. Several of the port side lifeboats finally tore loose from their moorings, spinning wildly within the ever-growing whirlpool created by the ship's descent.

High above, a news photographer snapped a final aerial photo of the black hull. One screw and the name *Andrea* were all that remained visible. It was 10:09 A.M.

As in slow motion, the *Andrea Doria* slipped below the

waves. She settled to the ocean floor 225 feet below. The whirl-pool remained behind for a full fifteen minutes, spinning additional bits of wreckage to the surface. The water glowed as sunlight reflected off the prism of churning oil.

Father Raymond Goedert watched, unable to forget the glorious chapel where he had celebrated Mass every morning of the voyage. Now, as he stood at the stern of the *Stockholm* after his night of terror, he felt confused. He needed to be alone to inventory his feelings about life and death, about the frailties of man, about God's will. He climbed blindly up the stairway of the Swedish rescuer. Soon he found himself alone on an open deck on the starboard side. The array of wreckage stretched in front of him. Below, he could hear the rumble of the *Stockholm*'s engines. She was preparing to return to New York with 545 survivors from the *Andrea Doria*, flanked by an escort of Coast Guard ships.

The wounded *Stockholm* shuddered, seemed to groan, as she moved slowly forward. Goedert heard the grinding noise of metal sliding against metal and turned toward the bow. A chunk of wreckage, some of it the remnants of the *Stockholm*'s nose, some of it the vitals of the *Andrea Doria,* suddenly fell off. It crashed into the ocean, sending waves out from the starboard side.

As Goedert watched, the body of a woman passenger from the *Andrea Doria*, imbedded in the crushed steel on the starboard forecastle, suddenly freed itself from the wreckage of the bow. The body fell into the water, floated past Father Goedert, and quickly disappeared into the open sea.

14

THE DOCK

SHOCK WAVES FROM the collision surged out from the Nantucket coast. By Thursday morning the entire world was aware of the tragedy, though few were cognizant of its scope. And none, not even the principals, had an adequate explanation. Expressions of sympathy and concern were quickly issued.

U.S. Customs and Immigration officials announced they would "simplify the plight of these poor people" as they filtered back into New York, most without passports and possessions. Blank customs forms were provided as normal immigration procedures were waived. Arriving passengers would merely need to supply a name and address.

President Dwight D. Eisenhower issued a statement:

To all of those, of whatever nationality, who participated in the rescue operations following the tragic collision between the *Andrea Doria* and the *Stockholm*, I extend personal congratulations and admiration. The speed with which rescue craft arrived on the scene and the efficient manner in which rescue operations were placed under way saved the lives of many of the passengers and crew of the *Andrea Doria*. Without such assistance, the tragic toll of life from the accident would have been much higher. The rescue work was conducted in the finest tradition of maritime service.

Representative Herbert C. Bonner (D-NC), chairman of the House Merchant Marine and Fisheries Committee, struck a more discordant note. He called for a Congressional inquiry and flew to New York to inspect the damaged *Stockholm* when it arrived.

From the Vatican, Pope Pius XII sent a message to Italian prime minister, Antonio Segni: "The great marine disaster which has stricken Italy and so many of God's creatures raises a deep and painful echo with our earth. We share the suffering of all."

But no distant politician or pontiff could participate in the dramas still being played out on the flotilla of rescue ships making their way back to New York Harbor. There were six ships on their way. In addition to the *Ile de France* with 753 survivors and the *Stockholm* with 545, the *Pvt. William H. Thomas* carried 158, the *Cape Ann*, 129, and the *Edward H. Allen*, 77. The tanker *Robert E. Hopkins* steamed along with its lone prize, Robert Hudson.

For many of the rescued passengers, Thursday, July 26, was a time of celebration and thanksgiving. For others, there was yet more anguish to encounter.

Captain de Beaudéan visited the *Ile de France*'s hospital early in the morning. Doctors were still operating, setting broken ribs, arms, and legs in place. The more than fifty injured survivors filled every available bed. As the nurse took the captain from one patient to another, the French nobleman assured them that the ordeal was over. They would soon be reunited with their families in New York.

De Beaudéan then approached an *Andrea Doria* survivor, much of whose body was encased in plaster. Her bruised face was badly swollen.

"I have lost my two daughters," Jane Cianfarra sobbed.

The baron could think of nothing to say.

Elsewhere aboard the *Ile de France*, there was almost a party atmosphere. Long tables were set out on the upper decks and covered with clean linen. Chefs brought vats of coffee and soup up from the kitchens. A flow of sandwiches followed. Survivors queued at the tables, then lined up again outside the wireless room to send assurances to anxious relatives. The decks were crowded with half-dressed people, some grieving over missing friends, but most felt freshly alive. The *Ile de France* passengers received them with courtesy and charity.

Sister Marie Raymond and Sister Callistus solicited shoes and stockings from the *Ile de France* passengers. One woman gave them ten pairs of shoes. "How can you do this?" Sister Raymond asked.

"I kept one pair for walking and one pair for dancing," the woman said. "If I need more when I get to Paris, I'm sure there's someplace I can buy them."

The two nuns moved among the survivors. They offered each person the choice of a pair of shoes or a pair of stockings. Someone gave the sisters cigarettes to distribute, which they rationed out at the rate of three per person. The sight of cigarettes brought giggles from some of the survivors. The tension was breaking.

Marion and Malcolm Boyer were drinking coffee on the *Ile de France* with a group of survivors when a well-dressed woman in her sixties approached them. "I want you all to come into my stateroom and have some champagne," she invited. "My son threw a party for me last night in New York. He gave me a whole case of champagne. I really don't know what to do with it."

The group happily followed her to her first-class suite, where the woman reached under her bunk and drew out an expensive bottle of French champagne. Then she stepped out into the hallway. "Steward," she called, "would you please cool this for me?"

Malcolm Boyer talked with her hostess, describing the shipwreck. Her back was turned to the doorway when the steward returned with the champagne, now in an ice bucket, and several glasses.

Suddenly there was a loud, explosive noise. "My God," Mrs. Boyer screamed, "the *Ile de France* has been hit!" She turned to see the steward, grinning awkwardly as warm champagne trickled down the front of his uniform.

On the *Stockholm,* however, hostility surfaced quickly. It became evident early Thursday morning as survivors stood in a food line. "Perhaps the *Andrea Doria* crew members should be served first," a disgruntled passenger-survivor commented, "since so many of them got here before us." A burly Italian crewman glared. Both men shook their fists menacingly, but friends held the antagonists back. After the incident, the *Andrea Doria* crewmen kept more to themselves.

Even without such enmity the *Stockholm*'s crippled condition produced an air of solemnity and sorrow. Most of these survivors were among the first off the Italian liner, but they were to be the last to return to New York. Limping along with her Coast Guard escort, the *Stockholm* would not arrive for at least twenty-four hours. No one relished a whole day and night on the crowded, crippled ship.

Carl Watres, fifty-four, of Manasquan, New Jersey, was one of the most exhausted of the survivors. He had worked to help other passengers off the *Andrea Doria,* despite a sickening feeling of nausea. He retched repeatedly on the lifeboat trip to the *Stockholm.* When he finally reached the safety of the Swedish ship, he slumped heavily into a deck chair, still nauseous. He lay there to rest while his wife, Lillian, went to get some food.

Father Tom Kelly was resting on a deck chair when he heard a groan nearby. He looked up to see Watres, half-tumbled from his deck chair, clutching at his chest. Kelly rushed over, and with others helped place Watres back onto his deck chair. The young priest felt for a pulse. There was none.

"*Ego te absolvo . . .*" Kelly droned as someone shouted for a doctor.

Carl Watres was the forty-ninth fatality.

Fourteen-year-old Linda Morgan woke on Thursday morning from a drugged sleep to discover that she could not move her legs. She called out from her bed in the *Stockholm*'s infirmary. A doctor diagnosed two broken kneecaps, injuries sustained when Linda was flung from her bed on the *Andrea Doria* to the bow of the *Stockholm*. The fractures were overlooked the night before in the rush of casualties.

As doctors treated her, Linda asked, "Have you contacted my mother? Does she know I am all right?"

"Everything has been taken care of," she was assured.

In fact, Linda's name had somehow been excluded from the list of *Andrea Doria* passengers rescued by the *Stockholm*. The girl did not even realize that the *Andrea Doria* had sunk, or that she had suffered less than the rest of her family.

Bernabé Polance García, the Spanish sailor who had found Linda on the bow, stopped in with a present. He had searched the forward area once more and discovered Linda's Camp Fire Girl's autograph book, which he returned to her. Later, he approached Captain Nordenson to discuss the possibility of adopting the girl who, he was sure, was now orphaned.

Still under sedation, Linda drifted back into sleep. Later that day her name would appear in hundreds of newspapers as one of those killed in the collision.

Once his rescue mission was over Captain de Beaudéan of the *Ile de France* was anxious to resume his schedule. Moving rapidly, he brought the French liner into New York Harbor early Thursday evening. His plan was to transfer the survivors to tugboats and turn back toward Europe without docking. De Beaudéan called the French Line office in New York to request the tugs. "Have you fallen on your head?" the line official replied. "You have to come in. Everyone is waiting for you."

The first ship encountered by the *Ile de France* as it entered New York Harbor greeted her with three whistle blasts, the traditional salute normally reserved for ships of the same line. Soon there was a friendly armada of tugboats, ferries, and pleasure craft, all saluting the French liner and receiving the *Ile de France*'s resounding salute in return. More tugboats approached, showering the side of the *Ile de France* with a welcoming spray from their fire hoses.

Thousands waited for a glimpse of the majestic ship and the haggard survivors who gathered at her rails.

"*Sto bene. Sto bene*," Italian emigrants cried to waiting relatives. "I'm all right. I'm all right." The dock erupted with tears of joy. Onlookers applauded and cheered the heroic French sailors.

ABC radio newscaster Edward P. Morgan rushed on board the *Ile de France* and quickly sought out the purser. "Where is Mrs. Cianfarra?" he asked.

The purser checked his list. "She is in the infirmary."

Morgan followed the officer's directions to the ship's hospital. He found his ex-wife sedated but conscious, and in great pain. She blurted out the story. Her husband was dead. Their daughter, Linda Morgan, and her daughter, Joan, were both missing.

The broadcaster hurried back to the ABC studios on West Sixty-seventh Street. He arrived at 6:45 P.M., only fifteen minutes before his regularly scheduled nationwide newscast. The news director already had a substitute ready with a prepared script, but Morgan argued strongly that he could do the show extemporaneously. Reluctantly the news director agreed, but he kept the substitute standing by in the event Morgan faltered.

Minutes before air time, a reporter from *The New York Times* reached the studio by telephone. He wanted a photo of Morgan's daughter, Linda.

"Why?" Morgan demanded.

"You know she's dead."

"No! I don't know," Morgan raged.

Realizing the mistake in his approach, the reporter gently explained that a Dr. Thure Peterson had reported seeing the bodies of both Joan Cianfarra and Morgan's daughter, Linda.

Morgan listened and steadied himself as the second hand of the studio clock approached the vertical.

"Good evening. Here is the shape of the news," he began in his accustomed style. "Tonight it is the shape of disaster. There are other headlines: Stassen meets with Republican Chairman

Hall . . . Mr. Nasser of Egypt announces the intention of nationalizing the Suez Canal.

"But the main story—the story around the world tonight—is the story of the sinking of the Italian liner, the *Andrea Doria* . . .

"This reporter has just returned from a trip down New York Harbor to board the liner *Ile de France*, and has come back after interviewing a number of the first survivors to reach New York City. This is a jumbled story—a story told in the faces of the persons that you see on the ship. Perhaps the best way to tell it—from notes—and from memory, is just to jog down through the notes as I go.

"Take, for instance, a particular case. The case of a person who had . . . relatives . . . aboard the *Andrea Doria* and was notified this morning about five o'clock that the two ships . . . had collided in fog last night. There is the numbing, the wait, the confusion, the conflicting reports. And then, in the afternoon, the news that correspondents would be picked up by the Coast Guard and taken down the harbor to board the . . . *Ile de France* . . .

"A lump comes in one's throat as one sees this vessel . . . as we push under the starboard side of the *Ile de France*, one looks up and sees a line—a necklace of faces—looking down from the rail. Somebody wants to know who are the passengers and who are the survivors. Soon one is able to tell. Here a shirt tail is sticking out. Here a nightshirt. Here a bandaged head. . . . You get aboard and then the story comes—told in little fragments. . . .

"There was Camille Cianfarra, the Madrid correspondent of *The New York Times*, his wife, his stepchild, and another child. Where were they? one asked.

"One was told that Mrs. Cianfarra was badly hurt and was in sick bay of the *Ile de France*. One finds her. She is badly hurt but she is not on the critical list. She has multiple fractures and cuts. She asks about her husband. It is reported, but it is not confirmed, that Camille Cianfarra of *The New York Times* is among the dead. The children may be aboard another ship. It is not proved. It is not certain. . . .

"She and her husband were in the stateroom—perhaps—

which suffered the direct hit of the prow, the bow of the *Stock-holm*. She was trapped. Her husband was trapped in another part of the room. She tried to call to him. She tried to get to him and could not. And he did not answer. She thought that the door to the children's stateroom was open. She did not know. She was not sure. She did not hear their cries. . . .

"Slowly, little by little, torturously for the persons who don't know—happily for the persons who do—the whole pieces of the disaster will be fitted together. It is a horrible thing—but an inspiring thing—to see the way people react under duress. . . .

"This is Edward P. Morgan, saying good night from New York."

Morgan did not tell his nationwide radio audience that Mrs. Cianfarra was his ex-wife, nor that one of the missing girls was his own daughter, Linda.

The moment he was off the air, Morgan called Dr. Thure Peterson at the number given him by *The Times* reporter. He identified himself. "I know this is a difficult time to talk with you," he said, "but I must know. Did you actually see the bodies of Mrs. Cianfarra's two girls?"

Peterson choked back his personal anguish. "Yes," he said quietly, "I did see the bodies."

On board the freighter *Cape Ann*, two hours behind the *Ile de France*, Meryl Stoller listened to indignant American sailors tell how, when their lifeboats reached the *Andrea Doria*, Italian crewmen had tried to descend ahead of passengers. Despite the danger in prolonging the rescue, the *Cape Ann* sailors had threatened to beat back the Italian crew with their oars. The cowering crew retreated. Passengers boarded the boat.

"We should do something," said another survivor. "We should tell everyone about the crew."

"Let's write a petition," suggested Mrs. Stoller.

With Arthur Fischer, a garment manufacturer from New York, Meryl Stoller composed a document detailing what they perceived to be the failures and abuses of the *Andrea Doria* crew:

It is our intent to show that there existed a state of complete negligence on the part of the crew and the officers toward its obligations and responsibilities to the safety of the passengers of the ship.

No instructions were received by public address system (which was in operating condition) or by word of mouth from the crew that danger was imminent and life belts should be donned.

As a result passengers acted on their own initiative. . . . Crew members assumed no posts or took any organized action at any time during the entire period of the emergency. . . .

The statement carried one disclaimer:

. . . a small number of crew members .   . carrying out a private sense of responsibility . . . worked alongside the passengers . . . in aiding the abandoning of the ship.

The document concluded:

It is our firm belief that the above-mentioned facts constitute abhorrent disregard for the fundamental responsibilities of the officers and crew of the ship for the safety of the passengers in their care. We believe this to be the direct cause of the large number of casualties.

Fischer and Mrs. Stoller circulated the petition among the 129 survivors aboard the *Cape Ann*. Ninety agreed with the charges and signed willingly. When the *Cape Ann* reached New York, Fischer tied the petition to a rope and lowered it to waiting newsmen, who soon published the charges throughout the world.

When they had cleared customs, Mike and Meryl Stoller received news that drew their minds away from the disaster. Jerry Leiber was waiting for them. Leiber was Stoller's song-writing partner, the cocomposer of "Black Denim Trousers and

Motorcycle Boots," the hit song that had financed the Stollers' three-month European vacation.

"Do you know who Elvis Presley is?" Leiber asked.

"I remember hearing 'Heartbreak Hotel' before I left for Europe. He sounded real good," Stoller replied.

"Well, since you've been gone, he's become the biggest star ever," Leiber explained. A few years earlier Leiber and Stoller had composed a song that was a hit in the rhythm-and-blues field but never reached the popular market. Now, Leiber said, Presley had recorded it. The song was called "Hound Dog."

Thursday night was an anxious one for many of the survivors who arrived on the early rescue ships.

One of them, Paul Sergio, was now convinced that his sister-in-law, Maria, and her four children were dead. When he reached the *Ile de France* in a lifeboat, he had found his wife, Margaret, aboard, but in shock. Although partially relieved by the sight of Paul, she remained distraught throughout the trip to New York. Their sons, Tony and Joe, met them at the Clinton Hotel after a nonstop drive from South Bend, Indiana. There was still no word about Margaret's sister, Maria, and her four children.

Margaret lay on a hotel bed sobbing hysterically. Paul was worried about her. "She should be home," he said to his sons, "with the other children. We must get her mind off Maria."

Joe, the younger son, was delegated to drive Margaret home. Paul and Tony would remain behind, hoping for good news from the *Stockholm*.

Alba Wells had spent Thursday dragging her daughters, Shirley and Rose Marie, about the decks of the *Ile de France*, searching for her son, Henry. She was oblivious to the rising pain in her spine and shoulder from the injuries she received while leaving the *Andrea Doria*. By the time the *Ile de France* pulled into New York she had given herself over to grief. She knew Henry must be dead. As she stepped onto the dock, she felt her legs crumple. She dimly perceived a policeman rushing up and covering her with a blanket.

She woke in St. Vincent's Hospital, with Rosie in the bed

next to her. Her husband, Charles, hurried to see her, and was greeted by tears streaming from Alba's dark eyes.

"Where's Henry?" she cried.

Charles Wells brightened. "He's all right! He's just fine. Now you get some rest."

Mrs. Wells smiled and sank back to the pillow. A nurse, in the white robes of a nun, administered a sedative.

Charles Wells walked slowly back to the waiting room, the optimism drained from his face. Henry's name was not on any of the survivors' lists radioed in from the rescue ships.

Giovanni Morrone and his son, Mario, arrived Thursday night on the *Pvt. William H. Thomas*. They were met by Giovanni's brother Joe. Out of young Mario's presence, Joe informed his brother sadly that his wife Vincenza's name was not on the survivors' lists. Giovanni fought back the tears. He remembered seeing his wife slip from the end of a rope and float off into the dark water. "Don't worry," he told his son, "Mother will be found somewhere on one of the other ships."

They went with Joe to buy shoes.

Tullio and Filomena di Sandro were distraught. They had no word of their only child, their four-year-old daughter, Norma. They had last seen her unconscious body pulled into a lifeboat after Tullio tried to throw her to safety from the deck. As soon as they had arrived on the *Ile de France* they had checked with the authorities. But there was no record of the child. The di Sandros remained at the dock, asking everyone for news of their girl. They described a tiny gold ram's horn bracelet that Norma wore on her left wrist.

"There's a four-year-old girl in the hospital in Boston," a woman told them. A Red Cross worker phoned Brighton Marine Hospital in Boston and confirmed that the unidentified child wore a bracelet similar to the one described by the di Sandros. The girl was still unconscious. Her condition was critical.

A news photographer hurried the di Sandros into a car. At 10:00 P.M. on Thursday night they sped off on a wild drive to Boston, picking up police escorts in Rhode Island and Massachusetts. The convoy arrived in Boston at 3:15 A.M.

At Brighton Marine Hospital doctors led the di Sandros into

the intensive care unit, where a small child lay in a deep coma, the right side of her face puffed grotesquely.

"My baby daughter!" Mrs. di Sandro screamed. She rushed to pick up Norma, but a nurse restrained her. "She's mine! She's mine!" the distraught mother cried. She collapsed to the floor.

The mother was revived. Doctors explained gently that they had operated to relieve internal skull pressure from a cranial fracture. "We've done everything we can," a physician said. "All we can do now is wait and hope she wakes up." They listed her condition as "very poor."

After a restless night, Giovanni Morrone was at the dock early Friday, rechecking the lists of survivors. Only the *Stockholm* remained at sea. He ran his finger down the alphabetical list of names radioed to shore by the Swedish liner. There was no Vincenza Morrone. Suddenly he found the name Postiglione. Vincenza's maiden name! Perhaps in her confusion Vincenza had omitted her married name. Expectantly, Morrone asked officials to check the identity of Vincenza Postiglione. Radio messages flashed back and forth. The woman had been located. Yes, she was Mrs. Morrone. After dropping from a rescue rope and floating out of her husband's sight, she had been picked up by a *Stockholm* lifeboat.

An ecstatic husband rushed off to Mario with the news.

The *Stockholm* drifted slowly toward pier 97 at the foot of West Fifty-seventh Street at noon on Friday, July 27. Thousands waited for her. Two days earlier, as a sleek, white super-yacht, she had pulled proudly away from the same pier. Now she slinked back, her bow annihilated. On her starboard side she bore the cryptic legend STOCKHO . . . On her portside she was merely the . . . HOLM. Raw edges of torn metal thrust out and forward from her broken nose. No one cheered her arrival, as they had greeted the other rescuers. She was a solemn, awful sight.

Most of the survivors aboard the *Stockholm* had managed to send radio messages to their relatives. A few had not. Small clusters of expectant families gathered near the gangway to peer intently at each survivor. For men and women like Paul and Margaret Sergio, Charles and Alba Wells, and Edward P. Morgan and Jane Cianfarra, the arrival of the last rescue ship could mean a glorious reunion or the end of hope.

A group of photographers waited with the relatives, hoping to capture the emotions of these desperate moments on film. Suddenly they looked up.

"Mommy!" a small voice cried out.

Ruth Roman broke into tears. Dickie was safe. The beautiful actress stumbled toward her child. "Everything's all right now. It's all right," she sobbed happily, while, all about her, cameras whirred.

Edward P. Morgan was confused. A late radio report from the *Stockholm* identified a Linda Morgan as a survivor. Was Dr. Peterson mistaken? Amid his own sorrow had he erred in his perceptions? The newscaster did not want to raise his hopes.

He rushed to the *Stockholm*. Police would not let him on board immediately, for he carried only Washington press credentials. After a delay, he finally boarded and found Purser Curt Dawe.

Dawe smiled. "I want you to know that your daughter behaved admirably in the sick bay," he said. "She did not think about herself. She was concerned about her mother."

Morgan stood dumbfounded. "You mean . . . she's alive!" he stammered.

"Yes. She is alive. She's been taken to the hospital."

Soon after Morgan arrived at St. Vincent's Hospital, where he found Linda being prepared for X rays prior to surgery. They embraced joyously. Morgan could not comprehend the implications of it all. He could only weep in gratitude.

Linda, groggy from morphine, mumbled, "Where's Mother?"

Morgan placed a hand on his daughter's brow. "Your mother is all right. She's in another hospital. You can talk to her on the phone soon." Then he halted. Though he had seen Linda frequently over the years, he had not lived with her since she was two years old. Now it was time for him to be a full-time father again. "They haven't found Cian," he said gently. "Joan is missing, too."

Father and daughter cried together.

After Linda was taken in for X rays, then surgery, the broadcaster placed a call to his ex-wife. "Jane, brace yourself," he said. "Linda is alive. I just talked with her."

From the other end of the line came a loud, deep cry of happiness.

Thursday night and all day Friday, Alba Wells hovered between drug-induced sleep and brief periods of semiconsciousness. Her husband slipped away from her hospital bed to await the *Stockholm*'s arrival. Henry's name had not been reported on the *Stockholm*'s survivors' list. But the ship was the last rescue vessel and their only hope that the boy was alive.

Late Friday afternoon, as the sedative wore off, Alba Wells talked with Rosie. The girl's hand was bandaged, and might require surgery, but she was not in pain. She seemed to understand that she had gone through an extraordinary experience. Mrs. Wells did not burden her daughter with fears about her missing brother.

A nurse entered. "We have good news for you, Mrs. Wells," she beamed.

"Henry?"

The nurse nodded. "Yes. Henry's alive." She helped Mrs. Wells into a wheelchair. The smiling mother quickly pushed down the corridor to the waiting room, where Henry leaped into her arms. Through her tears, Alba Wells listened to the story of Henry's adventure. A Methodist minister had lowered the boy off the *Andrea Doria* into one of the first lifeboats. Henry had been taken to the *Stockholm*, where he had fun playing with the sailors. No one had explained to him about sending a radiogram. No one had asked him for his name.

Paul Sergio and his son Tony had spent Thursday evening and Friday at the dock, waiting for the rescue vessels. When the *Stockholm* arrived, they elbowed their way through the crowd and watched anxiously as survivors moved onto the pier. They tried to will Maria and the children off the ship. But there was no sign of their relatives.

The wounded *Stockholm* was the last ship. "We'll wait one more day," Paul said anyway. "Perhaps there is a ship we don't know about." But they both knew there was no hope.

The elder Sergio had lived in New York for several years after emigrating from southern Italy. That night, to keep their minds busy, the cobbler took his firstborn son back to the Italian neighborhood. They found Mulberry Street, dark and grimy, its pavement steaming in the July night. Paul searched out his favorite restaurant. There was a new owner. The food was not as good as it used to be.

Back out on the street squealing Italian children ran through the narrow alleys. They reminded Paul Sergio of his nephews and nieces. "They're gone," he sobbed. "I know it. I knew it all along. I just couldn't admit it."

Arm in arm, father and son walked the streets of New York late into the night.

"Good evening. This is the shape of the news," said Edward P. Morgan as he began his radio broadcast on Friday night. "Tonight it is still the twisted lines of tragedy interspliced with the thread of happiness and even maybe miracle spiraling from the collision at sea between the Italian liner *Andrea Doria* and the Swedish liner *Stockholm*. . . .

"The Coast Guard in its latest figures says that of the 1,706 aboard the *Andrea Doria*, 1,660 have been accounted for as safely ashore, injured, or dead.

"The known death toll is 10, although a late report indicates three more injured have died. That leaves, unofficially, 36 persons missing. . . .

"The daughter of this reporter, Linda Morgan, accounted for one of the incidents of the tragedy which some would classify as a miracle. Sleeping in a stateroom on the starboard side of the *Andrea Doria* which bore the full brunt of the *Stockholm*'s crash, she was officially reported as killed. Instead, she was catapulted apparently onto the bow of the *Stockholm* where a crewman found her alive in the wreckage. She was among the litter cases brought to New York today, not in critical condition. . . .

"Within the space of 24 hours this reporter has been pushed down the elevator shaft to the sub-basement of despair and raised again to the heights of incredible joy, washed, one suspects, with slightly extravagant rivulets of some heavenly champagne.

"Last night, as far as the world at large was concerned, a girl, age 14, nationality American, named Linda Morgan, was dead. She happens to be this reporter's daughter. She had been killed, by the incontrovertible evidence of an eyewitness. . . . But Linda is *not* dead. She was hurled, one can only deduce, by the impact, from her bunk into the wreckage of the bow of the *Stockholm* where she was found, alive, painfully but not critically hurt. . . .

"There is something sacred, I feel, about the mystery of life which, in the alchemy of the unknown, enables people as they face the supposed tragedy of death, their own or that of another. It makes other things seem so petty and unimportant. . . .

"Through all this incredible blackness and sunshine I kept remembering what a wonderful human being from Philadelphia named C. Jared Ingersoll once told me in recounting how he kept right on going after the death of his wife and then his son. 'I try to live fully,' he said, 'so that when my luck changes there will be little room for regret or recrimination over time lost or misspent.' This reporter hopes tonight he has learned that lesson well enough to teach it with tenderness to a girl young enough to grow with it into a full blossom that will give joy to others for her very living. Perhaps, perhaps, she has learned it already herself.

"This is Edward Morgan, saying good-night from New York."

SAVED!

At 9:15 Friday night, four-year-old Norma di Sandro died at the Brighton Marine Hospital in Boston without regaining consciousness.

Fifty-one people had died as a result of the collision of the two great ships: forty-six passengers from the *Andrea Doria* and five crewmen from the *Stockholm*.

It is a tragic statistic. But perhaps a more significant, and often overlooked, fact is that 1660 men, women, and children, many of whom never expected to survive, were taken safely off a ship that threatened to slide into the ocean at any moment.

15

THE HEARINGS

On Friday afternoon, after the *Stockholm*'s arrival, Captain Nordenson met reporters on the bridge. He was flanked by Charles S. Haight, an attorney from the law firm of Haight, Gardner, Poor & Havens, counsel for the Swedish-American Line. On the advice of Haight, Captain Nordenson carefully sidestepped all questions concerning responsibility for the crash.

"Do you think you are to blame for the collision?" a newsman asked.

"I don't think I should answer that question," Nordenson hedged. "I don't want to hurt anybody."

"Are you worried about the repercussions?"

"I won't answer that. I don't want to appear as if I were bragging about myself."

"Does that mean there might have been mechanical trouble?"

"No."

Haight, a tall, cultured attorney, cut short the interview, explaining that the full story would be revealed at the appropriate legal proceedings.

On Saturday, Captain Calamai presented a statement to reporters assembled at the Italian Line office at 24 State Street in Manhattan. He stated clearly that the *Andrea Doria* was "struck by the *Stockholm*." Dressed in gray slacks, blue blazer, and white shirt, his face gaunt and solemn, Calamai answered questions carefully. At his side was attorney Eugene Underwood of the firm of Burlingham, Hupper & Kennedy.

"Why was there no announcement about the lifeboats?" a reporter asked.

Calamai answered with assurance. "I call all my deck officers to the bridge. I give orders to prepare all lifeboats. But I did not make any address personally to the passengers because we could not use the lifeboats on the port side because the list to starboard was too high. Then I advised all passengers in Italian to be calm. At the emergency stations other officers told the passengers in English to be calm. When the starboard boats were prepared I gave orders to embark women and children first."

"Is it true that the first three lifeboats to reach the *Stockholm* carried only *Andrea Doria* crew members?" another reporter asked.

"I deny it! I deny it!" the captain responded.

No accusation stung more than this one. Yet some observers, including Robert Young of the American Bureau of Shipping, pointed out that many of the crewmen had given their life jackets to passengers. Because their life jackets were gray and the passengers' were orange, witnesses might have drawn the wrong conclusion when they saw gray jackets in the boats. In addition, the sense of isolation and panic among passengers may also have fostered hysterical stories.

These mitigating points may have had some substance. Stories of desertion probably were distorted. Yet there is hard evidence that many crewmen did flee. Most of the survivors who were interviewed twenty-two years after the fact still claim that many crew members abandoned their stations and fled. These are among the survivors' most vivid memories. Statistics are also revealing. The first lifeboats ferried their occupants to the *Stockholm*. As the *Doria* drifted farther away from the Swedish ship, the lifeboats then went to the *Ile de France* and other nearby rescue ships. "The *Stockholm*'s rescue statistics were bad for us," Staff Captain Magagnini later observed. "Our boats took 229 passengers to the *Stockholm* and 222 of our own crewmen. Some of the crew did go with the first boats. Not all men are the same."

Another individual testimony is perhaps the most damning. When he arrived back in New York, Richardson Dilworth was asked about the crew's behavior. "It was one of the finest things I have ever seen done," he declared. "The tireless and courageous work of the crew in getting all those people safely down the ladders and cargo nets to the lifeboats without apparent thought for themselves."

As mayor of Philadelphia, Dilworth could not say otherwise. He was concerned about his popularity among his Italian constituents in South Philadelphia. But privately, years later, Dilworth characterized the crew's behavior as "atrocious." There seems little doubt that a significant percentage of crew members deserted.

Such an unfortunate conclusion must be tempered. No matter how many crew members fled, many others remained behind, working in peril. Most of the fatalities occurred at or near the collision point. The vast majority of passengers who survived the collision were evacuated safely. This is incontestable proof that many crew members performed their duty. That their bravery should be undermined by the cowardice of their comrades is a tragedy within a tragedy.

The first lawsuit was filed by Nancy Leo of Miami, who suffered a broken leg and internal injuries while fleeing the *Andrea Doria*. She charged that the collision was the result of "negligence and recklessness." She asked for $100,000 in damages from each shipping line.

Within weeks there were more than a thousand individual suits filed against the Italian Line and the Swedish-American Line. The Italian Line sued the Swedish-American Line for $30 million, the appraised value of the *Andrea Doria*. The Swedish-American Line countered with a $2 million suit, for repairs of the *Stockholm*'s bow and for loss of business.

Though the collision occurred outside territorial waters, the litigants decided to pursue their cases in a U.S. court, since the majority of plaintiffs were living in America.

Amid the morass of suits and countersuits, the objectives of the shipping lines were clear. Both wished to prove the other ship at fault and thus avoid any liability. The lawsuits were consolidated into a single class action filed in the U.S. District Court, Southern District of New York. Judge Lawrence E. Walsh first required that the companies post bond. For the *Stockholm* it was set at the value of the damaged ship, $3,904,233.30. Since the *Doria,* at the bottom of the sea, was worthless, Walsh ordered the substitute bond of $1.8 million for the cargo value. The total of $5.7 million would be held in trust by the court pending the outcome of the case. With unprecedented speed, the discovery depositions were scheduled to begin September 19, 1956, less than two months after the collision.

On August 4, a Saturday, Italian Line attorney Eugene Underwood met with his assistants and with representatives from the shipping company. They outlined the case.

The *Andrea Doria* had these problems:

* She was speeding in the fog.
* She was riding high in the water with empty fuel tanks.
* Calamai's left turn moments before impact violated the rule of the road that a ship should turn toward danger to minimize impact.
* The rough logbook, which records all the navigational orders issued on the bridge, had not been saved. Cadet Maracci had apparently not seen it amid the papers lying on the chartroom floor.

The *Stockholm* had these problems:

* She was twenty miles north of the recommended course.
* If she was in fog, she was speeding and her captain was not on the bridge; if she was not in fog, she should have

been aware that she was approaching an area of poor visibility.
* She turned directly into the *Andrea Doria*.

Clearly, both ships had to assume a portion of the blame. To explore these issues in open court raised the possibility that liability would not be limited to the posted bond. The senior partner of the Italian Line's law firm, Harold Kennedy, penned a note to *Stockholm* attorney Charles Haight and dispatched it by messenger:

Dear Charlie,

This is a mutual fault case. For the good of the industry, let us settle it now 50-50 and worry about the details some other time.

Regards,
Harold

An hour later the reply arrived:

Dear Harold,

Your offer is refused. You are solely at fault.

Regards,
Charlie

On September 19, 1956, at the Federal Courthouse on Foley Square, New York, the discovery depositions began. These preliminary hearings were intended primarily so that each side could hear the other's evidence prior to trial. But few expected the case to go that far. Once the stories were in the open, a settlement would probably be negotiated.

The depositions were expected to last six weeks. Judge Walsh's presence was not required. Instead, he appointed a series of special masters to preside in his absence. The room was crowded with newsmen and curious spectators, and with some sixty attorneys who were present to represent their clients, those who had been injured or the families of those who died as a result of the collision. As lawyers for the shipping companies, Haight and Underwood would ask most of the questions. But every interested lawyer had a right to cross-examine each witness.

Shortly after 10:00 A.M., Johan-Ernst Bogislaus August Carstens-Johannsen, still the third mate of the *Stockholm*, was sworn in as the first witness.

Carstens clearly did not relish the spotlight. His boyish-round face flushed. At Haight's gentlemanly urging, Carstens repeated the story he had told many times. He first spotted an unknown radar pip at a distance of twelve miles. He began to plot the advance of the pip and estimated from its course that it would pass to the port side, or left, of the eastbound *Stockholm*. When the *Andrea Doria* was finally sighted visually, at a distance of less than two miles, she was clearly to port. Suddenly, for no apparent reason, Carstens said, she turned directly across the path of the *Stockholm*.

It was a straightforward story, told calmly with few interruptions from Carstens' attorney. But when Italian Line attorney Underwood rose to his feet for cross-examination, the spectators leaned forward in anticipation. Underwood was a courtroom lawyer who would probe every detail of the simple narrative. Underwood stood in front of Carstens and, in the manner of a careful detective, he elicited more details from the witness. But very shortly Haight was on his feet with an objection. Almost with every question Haight would interject a comment, an objection, or a query about the validity of the Swedish interpretation.

Sometimes bristling over the interruptions, Underwood continued to pursue his witness. Carstens' story held up well until Underwood asked a seemingly innocuous question about Peder Larsen, who had been helmsman at the time of the collision:

Q: How often did you check him by looking at the steering compass?
A: I have to check him very often. . . .

Surprised by the admission, Underwood pressed for more:

Q: Why did you have to check him often? Please, speak up.
A: He is more interested of the surrounding things than the compass.
Q: You mean, he is not a good wheelsman, don't you?
A: He is when he wants to.
Q: Well, he didn't want to be that night, did he?
A: Well, I don't know why.
Q: You checked up on him quite often because he was not steering a good course, did you not?
A: The night the collision occurred I didn't check him so often, because I had much to do.
Q: You didn't check him as often as you should, hey?
A: Nobody said I should check him often.
Q: I understood from your answer to my question that you felt the necessity of checking him often because he was inclined to allow his attention to wander and not steer a good course, is that correct?
A: Yes.

Underwood produced the course recorder from the *Stockholm*, the permanent record of a ship's headings at every moment of a voyage. He asked Carstens to examine it. The young third mate acknowledged that in the minutes before the crash the *Stockholm* was yawing as much as two and one-half degrees to either side of the assigned course. Underwood sought the significance of the wavering helm:

Q: Inasmuch as your ship was yawing 3 or 4 or 5 degrees and the bearing was a very fine bearing, it was of the utmost importance to be certain about your observations, was it not?
A: Yes.
Q: But you did not look at the compass, you asked the helmsman what the heading was, is that right?
A: If I had left the radar, he may have gone away from 91, so I had to rely upon the helmsman in a case like this.

213

Q: With your ship equipped as it was, that is, having no gyro repeater, you had no alternative but to rely on the wheelsman, did you?

A: Yes.

Q: And if the helmsman is in error by one degree, that may throw off your bearing by as much as 50 percent, may it not?

A: Yes.

Later Carstens testified that the course recorder showed Larsen's steering to vary by as much as seven degrees.

In the succeeding days of his cross-examination of Carstens, though continually challenged by Haight, Underwood laid the groundwork for a later confrontation with the *Stockholm* captain. He carefully went over key points with Carstens. The third mate had estimated the ships to be ten miles apart at 11:00 P.M. By his own testimony, the collision occurred at 11:09:

Q: At your speed of about 18 knots, how far would the *Stockholm* advance in nine minutes?

A: Let us see now . . . 2.7 miles.

Q: If the *Doria* was 10 miles away, nine minutes before the collision, and if the *Stockholm* advanced 2.7 miles in the same time, then the *Doria* had to cover 7.3 miles, did she not?

A: Yes, but what I understand from this question, you mean 2300 (11:00 P.M.) as a fixed time, but I have said it was about 2300.

Q: If the *Doria* covered 7.3 miles in those nine minutes, what would her rate of speed have been, could you figure that out?

A: 7.3 miles?

Q: Yes. That is the difference between your advance and the 10 miles that you observed.

A: It would be something over 40 miles (knots) anyway.

Q: I get it at 47 miles (knots).

A: Yes.

The conclusion was absurd. The *United States*, fastest passenger liner in the world, had a top speed of thirty-three knots. Clearly Carstens had erred in his calculations or in his notation of the time.

Carstens remained on the stand until October 3. His testimony covered more than twelve hundred pages of court transcript. Exhausted by his ordeal, Carstens was finally excused. Anticipation rose in the hearing room as the next witness, *Andrea Doria* Captain Piero Calamai, walked forward.

Shortly after the collision, Captain Calamai had been hospitalized. The official diagnosis was phlebitis, or inflammation of the veins in his legs. In reality, the captain was confined as a precautionary measure. Despondent and withdrawn, his friends feared that he might end his own life. He spent nine days in the hospital, then returned to Genoa to visit his family. By October 3, recovered from the worst of his depression but still sullen and humorless, Calamai shuffled to the witness chair. He spoke in a low tone, haltingly, sometimes narrowing his eyes as he concentrated on his answers.

Now it was Italian Line attorney Underwood's turn to be gentle and understanding. He led Calamai quietly through a recital that was as innocent as Carstens'. They had spotted a ship on the radar. They could clearly see it would pass them to the right, so they turned left. Just after making visual contact, they saw the other ship suddenly veer directly at them.

Haight, the *Stockholm* attorney, stood up to cross-examine Calamai. He forced the admission from the *Andrea Doria* captain that his staff did not plot the continuing course of the radar pip. Because the bearing was increasing, the *Stockholm* seemed to be on a parallel course that would take her to starboard, or right, of the *Andrea Doria*. Haight produced Calamai's official report to the Italian Line, a *Doria* exhibit. In the report, Calamai had detailed the radar bearings and distances of the pip prior to the collision. Haight asked the captain to chart the course represented by that data, as his staff could have done the night of July 25.

After more than a day of objections and judicial wrangling, the court instructed Calamai to do so. Sitting in the witness chair he carefully laid out the course. His face grew white. Then Haight demanded: ". . . is it not correct that the radar observations, distance and bearing, as set forth in your report to the Italian Line, Exhibit D-28, show that in fact the *Stockholm* was not on a course parallel to the course of the *Doria*?"

While Underwood objected, Calamai studied his own drawing. It showed the *Stockholm* not passing to the right, but bearing down directly on the *Andrea Doria*. Calamai was directed to answer. "I can see it now from the maneuvering board," he said almost in a whisper.

After nearly two weeks on the stand, Calamai finally saw Haight sit down. But his ordeal was not over. Leonard J. Matteson, who represented several companies that had lost freight on the *Doria*, continued the cross-examination. He asked Calamai to examine photographs of the *Andrea Doria* as she lay sinking into the ocean. Like a grieving husband brought to the morgue to identify his wife, Calamai quivered with anguish.

A succession of other attorneys representing claimants in wrongful death, personal injury, and property loss followed, taking Calamai over the very same testimony. On October 22, what Underwood called Calamai's "trial by ordeal" finally ended. The two and one-half weeks of inquiry, the formal public stripping of the captain's already embarrassed pride, took a sad toll. When Calamai left the witness stand he was a sad, bent man. He would never again enjoy life.

Attention shifted abruptly back to the *Stockholm.* Captain Harry Gunnar Nordenson marched to the witness chair. He was tired, having spent his days supervising repairs of the *Stockholm* and his nights preparing his testimony with Attorney Haight. Lately he had been experiencing pains in his legs, which a doctor had diagnosed as phlebitis. Bandages were now tightly wrapped around the captain's limbs. Nordenson tried to forget his physical problems as he began to testify.

Haight drew from him the explanation of what many thought was the *Stockholm*'s greatest error. Why was the Swedish ship traveling east in a westbound lane, twenty miles north of the recommended course?

Nordenson explained that the area around the Nantucket lightship is a busy intersection of shipping lanes. By embracing the coast he could clear that congested area more quickly. He risked meeting traffic head-on, but that was safer than the cross traffic encountered near Nantucket.

Nordenson had little to tell of the events leading to the collision, for he had been in his cabin writing in his diary. His direct testimony was short.

Italian Line attorney Eugene Underwood began his cross-examination:

Q: Captain, your third mate was Mr. Carstens-Johannsen on the day of the collision. Is that correct?
A: Yes.
Q: Did you have confidence in him?
A: Full confidence.

Underwood proceeded to other matters, allowing the spectators to digest Nordenson's confidence in his mate. The lawyer presented a variety of directives that advised the proper eastbound course from New York. In all instances the recommended course was twenty miles south of the *Stockholm*'s position. Nordenson was unshaken. He continued to affirm that he had been taking the same course for years, his course was safer, though not recommended, and was perfectly legal. He also pointed out that by keeping close to the Nantucket lightship he avoided dangerous cross traffic.

At times Underwood became so frustrated by the witness that he shook his finger in Nordenson's face. He claimed that Nordenson took the *Stockholm* nearly two hundred miles in a lane of head-on traffic in order to avoid fifteen miles of cross traffic:

Q: Captain, wasn't it sort of like jay-walking across an intersection where you have two-way traffic on both streets? Wasn't it like that?
A: No, I considered it safer.

Underwood suddenly shifted subjects. The captain had affirmed his "full confidence" in Carstens. But, asked Underwood, was there not a glaring error in Carstens' calculations?

Q: If the vessels were 10 miles apart, nine minutes before the collision, what was their combined speeds?

A: 66.

Q: Now, Captain, inasmuch as your speed was 18 knots, that attributes the speed of about 40 knots to the *Doria*, does it not?

A: Yes.

Q: So that is it not a fact, Captain, that that 10-mile, nine-minute calculation is not true?

Nordenson saw the bind. He was being asked to acknowledge an error in Carstens' testimony, a man in whom he had full confidence. If 11:00 P.M. was the time when Carstens noted the pip to be ten miles off, he had misread the radar or the time.

A: Well, I could not—I don't know that because—I don't know what the analyst says of this.

Q: Well, now, Captain, isn't it true?

A: Yes, it is true, of course, the *Andrea Doria* can't make that speed.

Q: Isn't it true, Captain, therefore, that it is quite impossible that the *Doria* was 10 miles away nine minutes before the collision?

"Yes," Nordenson answered.

Q: Now, Captain, if the 10-mile distance is right, and the *Stockholm* was making 18 knots and the *Doria* 22 knots, that is, their combined speed was 40 knots as you mention, how long before the collision was the *Doria* 10 miles away? Can you figure that?

Simple mathematics would show that the ships were ten miles apart fifteen minutes before the collision. But the captain seemed unable to respond to the question. For several minutes, the attorneys argued the point. One of the attorneys then stood up with a watch, announcing that five minutes had passed with Nordenson unable to make the simple calculation.

Suddenly the room spun in front of the Swedish captain. He could no longer hear the lawyers. "I don't feel well. May I be excused?" Nordenson murmured.

"What is that, Captain?" the presiding officer asked.

"I don't feel well," he answered.

The hearings were hastily adjourned. Nordenson was rushed to St. Luke's hospital with Underwood's challenging question still unanswered.

The next morning Nordenson was absent from the hearing room. "I would like to state on the record," Haight announced, "that we are suspending at this time temporarily the continuance of the testimony of Captain Nordenson, who was taken ill here yesterday under circumstances, for which I think it is a fair statement, all of us here should have recognized sooner than we did that he was taken ill. I hope he will be able to be with us next week and finish then."

Underwood managed a reply: "Mr. Haight, of course, speaks for himself, and I am aware of the master's absence this morning. Beyond that I do not concur."

Haight called a number of minor witnesses, other officers and seamen from the *Stockholm.* During the next few days Haight explained that Nordenson was still ill. Underwood demanded a doctor's affidavit.

On November 7, two weeks after Nordenson's last courtroom appearance, Haight produced an affidavit from two physicians certifying that the captain had suffered a small cerebral thrombosis. Nordenson, they said, should be able to leave the hospital shortly. After three more weeks of convalescence, he would be able to testify.

While Nordenson recovered, the procession of minor witnesses continued, adding little knowledge to the critical concerns. But on November 14 the courtroom testimony took a dramatic turn. A twenty-six-year-old Dane strode to the witness chair and took the oath. His name was Peder Larsen. He was at the helm of the *Stockholm* at the moment of the collision. Haight led him through a brief description of the interplay

between himself and Third Mate Carstens. Larsen's story cor-
roborated Carstens'.

Underwood began his cross-examination.

Q: Your job is to watch the compass, is it not?
A: Yes.
Q: Did you say that while you were at the wheel the ship
   was yawing?
A: Yes, a little, one to two degrees . . .
Q: Is that because your attention was wandering?
A: Yes, maybe.
Q: Do you know what Mr. Carstens-Johannsen testified
   about your attentiveness?
A: No . . .
Q: Did you see the newspaper accounts about his testi-
   mony concerning you?
A: Yes, but I didn't understand all of it.
Q: Did you understand that he said that you were more
   interested in surroundings than in your steering?
A: Yes.
Q: Is that true?
A: Yes, but I kept the course within one or two degrees.
Q: If your attention was wandering, how do you know that?
A: Well, I was also looking at the compass.
Q: Occasionally? Why do you smile, Mr. Larsen?

Haight interrupted, objecting to the personal question. But
Underwood pressed the point:

Q: Now, Mr. Larsen, why did you smile?
A: I was thinking a funny question was put to me and I am
   allowed to smile.
Q: Do you consider my questions funny?
A: Yes, I do.
Q: What do you find funny or humorous in my questions?
A: Well, that is private, what I am thinking about it.
Q: I want to know, Mr. Larsen, what you think is funny
   about my questions. What causes you to smile?

Haight was on his feet once more, and this time exercised his right to adjourn the hearings and ask for a procedural session before the presiding judge.

Judge I. R. Kaufman listened to the contending lawyers in his chambers and admonished both of them to restrict themselves to business. The hearings, he pointed out, were dragging on.

When Larsen resumed the stand, the question of his laughter was dropped.

Captain Nordenson returned to the witness stand on December 3, five weeks after becoming ill during Underwood's cross-examination. He was to testify only in the mornings.

Underwood moved quickly to resume his challenge:

Q: Now, Captain, if the *Doria* was 10 miles away and was making about 22 knots, and the *Stockholm* about 18 knots . . . how many minutes would it take for them to come together? Can you figure that?
A: With a combined speed of 40?
Q: Of 40 knots.

This time Nordenson answered promptly.

A: Fifteen minutes.

Underwood produced a paper from the voluminous pile of physical evidence. It was a copy of Nordenson's report to the Swedish Board of Trade.

Q: In view of the fact, Captain, that it is impossible for the *Doria* to have been ten miles away nine minutes before the collision, why did you write up your log book that way and why did you write up your report to the Swedish Board of Trade that way?
A: Well, that was in the log book. I couldn't change that. I am here to tell exactly the truth. Even if there was a mistake, I mean I couldn't change it. It was there.

Underwood had made his point. The testimony had shown that Carstens had either erred in recording the time or the distance of the fateful radar pip.

Just as Underwood was building his argument against the *Stockholm,* Haight continued to search for weaknesses in the testimony of *Andrea Doria* witnesses. Haight cross-examined Second Officer Curzio Franchini about his ship's movements during the minutes before the crash.

> Q: If the captain had not been on the bridge and you had altered *Doria*'s course to the left 4 degrees at 3½ miles from the *Stockholm*'s echo, and then at 2½ miles you saw from the radar by plotting that the passing distance was decreasing, not withstanding your change to port, what would you have done?

> A: I would not like to answer because it takes me in a position to criticize eventually the maneuver of the commander. Whatever I would have done, I would not want to answer because the captain did his maneuver.

> Q: Mr. Franchini, I respect your not wanting to in any way criticize the captain's maneuver, but each one is in this court to answer questions as best he can, and I do, please want an answer to my question . . .

> A: Do I have to answer?

> Mr. Underwood: . . . Captain Franchini, if you understand the question, you should answer it.

> A: Thank you. Academically speaking, most probably I would have inverted the motion of the engines and I would have turned to one side.

> Q: To which side would you have turned?

> A: Probably to the right.

Later, Haight brought up the question of Calamai's final maneuver, his desperate left turn to outrun the *Stockholm.* Third Officer Eugenio Giannini was on the stand.

> Q: What do you believe would have happened if the *Doria,* instead of going hard left, had made no rudder movement at the time hard left was ordered?

222

A: . . . Most probably now, instead of having only *Andrea Doria* at the bottom of the sea, there would be also the *Stockholm*.

The hearings adjourned for the Christmas holidays, then resumed in January. The original six weeks had stretched to four months.

It was clear now, as Underwood had suggested before the hearings, that both ships were to blame. Both would have to pay. The question was how much. In addition to the settlement, there were legal bills which were growing larger the longer the hearings progressed. In the words of Underwood's assistant H. Barton Williams: "It was determined that about every underwriter in the world was on the case. Therefore, taken as a whole, the two ships were insured by the same parties. The underwriters estimated the cost of attorneys' fees would exceed $3.5 million if allowed to continue."

It was no surprise that the hearings were suspended early in January. The shipping lines had agreed to an out-of-court settlement. The terms of the secret agreement were immediately leaked to an inquisitive press. The underwriters agreed to pay $1 million for the repair of the *Stockholm*'s bow, and $16 million for the loss of the *Andrea Doria*. Third-party claims were to be settled out of the $5.7 million bond.

Both sides claimed victory. The Italian Line pointed out that only $1.8 million of the bond was paid by it, while the *Stockholm* paid $3.9 million. The Swedish-American Line noted that $16 million was far short of the true value of the *Andrea Doria*.

The real victims were the dead, the injured, and those who lost their possessions. Over the next two years lawyers pressured the claimants to settle for far less than they had asked. The individual lawsuits were eventually paid for completely out of the $5.7 million bond. One man who had lost five members of his family originally asked for damages of $522,000. He received only $28,000.

In a larger sense the loser was truth. Without the full testimony of all the witnesses in a court of law, without the honest judgment of twelve independent men and women, the complete truth of what happened in the crucial hours leading up to the fatal collision at 11:10 P.M. remains obscured in that fogbank some nineteen miles west of the Nantucket lightship.

But despite this, the gnawing question continues to be asked, and is deserving of an answer:

What really went wrong the night of July 25, 1956?

16

FLASHBACK

No ONE, even those who were there, can say with certainty exactly what happened. Nevertheless, the recollections of the major officers of both ships, scores of surviving passengers, as well as a thorough study of more than six thousand pages of hearing testimony from the key crew members—and an overview from the perspective of almost twenty-five years—allow one to fit together several pieces of this puzzling event.

What emerges is a mosaic of miscalculation, misjudgment, and simple bad luck. A reconstruction of the events of July 25 reveals a series of mainly minor actions, and inactions, that taken individually were not calamitous.

But collectively, they added up to a tragic sum. Had any one fact been altered, the *Andrea Doria* and the *Stockholm* might have passed easily in the fog and continued uneventfully to their destinations. But it was not to be. The two ships seemed drawn together by a magnet of fate.

The last ten hours before the impact are the most significant. And of these, the last twenty-five minutes is the period when error and oversight conspired to cripple the beautiful Italian liner. What follows is a retelling of the most crucial

WHAT THE ANDREA DORIA SAW

FRANCHINI TESTIMONY·

At 17 miles distance, the pip was 4º north.

At 3½ miles distance, the pip was 15º north.

At 1 mile distance, the Andrea Doria saw the Stockholm 35º – 40º north.

CALAMAI TESTIMONY:

At 17 miles distance, the pip was 4º north.

At 5 miles distance, the pip was 14º north.

At 1.1 miles, the Andrea Doria sighted the Stockholm visually 22½º north.

MILES	15		10		5		0
			CALAMAI				
			FRANCHINI				
ANDREA DORIA HEADING							ANDREA DORIA

WHAT THE STOCKHOLM SAW

At 10 miles distance, the Stockholm saw the pip 2º north of its course heading

At 6 miles distance, the Stockholm saw the pip 4º north.

At 4 miles distance, Cartens estimated a passage distance of 0.6 to 0.7 miles.

At 2 miles distance, the Stockholm sighted the Andrea Doria visually, 20º north

MILES	0	2	4	6	8	10
STOCKHOLM					STOCKHOLM HEADING 91º	

THE ANDREA DORIA

On a course of 268º when it sighted pip.

When pip was 3½ miles distant, changed course to 264º

At less than a mile, turned hard left.

THE STOCKHOLM

On a course of 89º since 10:30 P.M.

Changed course to 91º about 10:50 P.M.

When ships were 2 miles distant, swung 20º south.

Swung hard right just prior to crash.

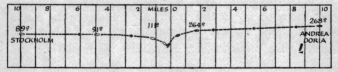

10	8	6	4	2	MILES 0	2	4	6	8	10
89º STOCKHOLM			91º		11º	264º				268º ANDREA DORIA

decisions of that day and night and a critique of what went wrong.

Wednesday, July 25, 1956. 1:37 P.M.

Captain Harry Gunnar Nordenson watched the Ambrose lightship pass his field of vision, about one-half mile to the north of the *Stockholm*. "Ninety degrees," he ordered. Another officer stepped in front of the helmsman and adjusted a set of blocks, like three large dice, to read: 0-9-0. The course would take the *Stockholm* due east to a point about one mile south of the Nantucket lightship. Then Nordenson would set a north-easterly course toward Scandinavia. The *Stockholm* routinely followed this track between New York and Nantucket whether it was going east or west. This was against the recommendation of the 1948 International Convention for the Safety of Life at Sea, which advised an eastbound course twenty miles to the south. Several shipping lines had an agreement to follow the southern route, but the course was voluntary and, in any event, the Swedish-American Line was not a party to the agreement. Nor, for that matter, was the Italian Line. Captain Nordenson was not accustomed to wasting time by swinging twenty miles out of his way to the south. He had crossed the Atlantic 423 times, and always followed this route. He wanted to get his 534 passengers to Gothenburg on time.

The sea, though apparently vast and open, is in reality a congested superhighway. Especially at critical intersections of heavily traveled routes, the possibility of encountering dangerous traffic is not remote. The ease with which Nordenson negotiated his exit from New York in the past was no guarantee of safety. The Stockholm, *in effect, was legally driving in the opposite direction on a wide, but potentially dangerous one-way street. Had Nordenson and the Swedish-American Line adopted the recommendations of the 1948 Convention, the* Stockholm *and the* Andrea Doria *would have passed each other safely at a distance of twenty miles.*

3:00 P.M.

The *Andrea Doria* was 160 nautical miles east of the Nantucket lightship. Captain Piero Calamai walked out on one of the bridge wings. Here, some eighty feet above the surface, he could view the horizon best. There was no mistake. A bank of fog stretched ahead of the bow. Calamai turned, strode back to the wheelhouse, and issued his orders.

He called to the engine room that they were in fog. "Reduce the speed," he said.

The engineers knew their duty. They reduced pressure in the boilers from forty to thirty-seven kilos per square centimeter, which dropped the speed of the ship from its cruising velocity of 23 knots to 21.8 knots. Reinforcements arrived in the engine room to stand by in the event that fast maneuvering became necessary. Stopping—or even slowing—a great ship is a difficult job requiring many sets of muscles to twist cumbersome valve wheels. Even with extra manpower the task cannot be done quickly.

Calamai, alert on the bridge, was confident that he could guide his ship safely through the thick fog at a speed of almost twenty-two knots.

In theory a ship should be able to come to a stop in half the distance of its visibility, but in practice few captains choose to lose time that way. Every extra minute spent at sea burns up additional fuel oil, and every hour late into harbor produces more disgruntled passengers. Since this particular fog was extremely dense, sometimes producing a situation of "nil" visibility, Calamai would have had to stop the Andrea Doria *dead in the water to comply with safety procedures to the letter. Because he was assisted by radar that could "see" through the fog, stopping the ship was unnecessary. Yet he did have the option of reducing speed significantly. He chose, instead, to make only a token reduction of 1.2 knots. Had the* Andrea Doria *been traveling through the fog at half its speed, it would have had precious time in which to maneuver away from the* Stockholm.

3:45 P.M.

The *Andrea Doria* was approximately 145 nautical miles east of the Nantucket lightship. Relaxing after a buffet lunch at the first-class swimming pool, passenger Robert Young indulged in a critique of the Italian ship and her crew. He was on vacation with his family, but as principal surveyor, or inspector, for the Western European division of the American Bureau of Shipping, he was always alert to the dangers of the sea. He could feel that the ship was rolling more than it had before, despite a calm sea. Young knew that near the end of the trip the ship's fuel and freshwater tanks were low. The captain could order the empty tanks filled with seawater, but it would be an expensive and lengthy job to pump the water out in New York before the ship could refuel. Young was concerned that the *Andrea Doria* was "tender," almost top-heavy.

The engineers had taken on seawater ballast in the freshwater tanks, but not in the fuel oil tanks. Therefore, those tanks, deep in the ship's bowels, were empty. When the tanks were penetrated on only the starboard side of the hull at impact, that side quickly took on water. The empty port side rose like a bubble to the surface. The result was an immediate, disastrous list. Had seawater ballast been in the used-up fuel tanks, the Andrea Doria *would not have listed so severely and the watertight compartments might have held.*

10:00 P.M.

The *Stockholm* was forty nautical miles west of the Nantucket lightship. Third Mate Carstens entered the chartroom to take radio direction finder bearings. In addition to its regular directional signal, the Nantucket lightship broadcast a special signal of four dashes in one minute, followed by two minutes of silence. It was a coded warning that there was dangerous fog in the area. Though the meaning of the radio signals was recorded in a manual on board, Carstens was unaware of it.

Carstens walked out on the bridge and saw that his mast-head lights were clear, not obstructed by any kind of fog. Above him and slightly to starboard the third mate could see the nearly full moon blazing down.

About twenty miles ahead of the Stockholm was a thick wall of fog, encasing the onrushing Andrea Doria. If Carstens had been aware of the fog, he would have called Captain Nordenson to the bridge, and he would have alerted the engine room to have extra men on duty in order to reverse the engines more quickly, should he encounter an emergency situation.

10:45 P.M.

The *Andrea Doria* was ten miles west of the Nantucket lightship. Second Officer Curzio Franchini yelled out to the other officers from the chartroom, where he was crouched over the dim radar screen.

"It's a ship. We can see a ship," he said.

"What's the distance and bearing?" Calamai called out to Franchini.

"Seventeen miles distance, and bearing four degrees on the starboard bow," Franchini answered.

The unknown ship was almost directly in the line of the *Andrea Doria*'s course.

During the next twenty-five minutes, as Franchini watched the radar screen, he did not plot the progress of the pip on the Marconi Locater Graph that sat nearby in a drawer. By connecting the dots he would be able to monitor the course of the ship and would note any changes. Instead, he merely followed the progress of the pip from one reading to the next.

It was not customary for the Italian officers to plot the courses of approaching ships on the Marconi Locater Graph, which sat unused in a nearby cabinet. But if Calamai had ordered his officers to do so, Franchini would have seen the other ship drifting in from the right on a course of direct confrontation with the Andrea Doria.

10:50 P.M.

The *Stockholm* was twenty-five nautical miles west of the Nantucket lightship. The ship was now three full miles off course to the north. Third Officer Carstens went forward to the wheelhouse and ordered helmsman Peder Larsen to shift course two degrees south, which would put the ship on a heading of ninety-one degrees. Then Carstens checked the radar. During the several minutes he had been busy in the chartroom, a pip had appeared on the screen. He estimated the unknown object to be twelve miles away from the *Stockholm,* and slightly to the left.

As the beam swept around the screen, Carstens transferred the changing position of the pip to a plotting board. If his calculations were to be valid, he had to be sure that the *Stockholm* was on course. There was no gyro repeater at the radar, so Carstens could not check the compass himself without leaving his place. He called out to the helmsman: "Larsen, the compass reading." Larsen yelled back, "Ninety," or one degree to the north of the set course.

Carstens traced the pip to a point now ten miles away.

"Larsen," the mate called, "again, the compass reading."

"Ninety-one," Larsen replied.

The mate connected the dots on his plotting board and calculated that the other ship would pass to the north at a distance of 0.7 to 0.8 miles, slightly less than the minimum of one mile ordered by Captain Nordenson.

Without a gyro repeater attached to his radar screen, and being the only officer on the bridge, Carstens had no alternative but to rely on the helmsman for the compass reading. Larsen, he knew, sometimes allowed the ship to yaw. If Larsen should err when he called the compass reading back to Carstens, even a tiny discrepancy would be critical. At a dis-

*tance of ten miles, an error of only three degrees in the com-
pass reading could show the* Andrea Doria *to be 0.7 miles
north of the* Stockholm, *when, in fact, she was dead ahead.*

11:00 P.M.

The two ships were seven miles apart. Aboard the *Andrea
Doria*, the reading of the radar screen had convinced Calamai
that his ship and the *Stockholm* would pass starboard-to-starboard. When two ships meet on the open seas, they tradition-
ally pass port-to-port, unless that would force them into a crossing course. Since Calamai thought the other ship was already
on the starboard side, to the right, there seemed to be no reason
to swing to the right for a port-to-port passage.

On the *Stockholm*, Carstens' plotting of the radar pip of the
Andrea Doria showed the Italian ship to be slightly to the other
side, by two degrees. Carstens was convinced that, if both vessels continued their courses, they would pass in the prescribed
manner, port-to-port.

*Each commander, interpreting his radar screen differ-
ently, came to an opposite conclusion. Each saw the situation as a mirror image of the other. Calamai thought he was
to the left of the* Stockholm. *Carstens thought the opposite,
that he was to the right of the* Doria. *In the last few minutes
before visual contact, both Calamai and Carstens maneuvered their ships with the help of radar in the belief that they
were moving away from danger. In actuality, at every turn
they were coming inevitably closer to collision.*

11:05 P.M.

The *Andrea Doria* was 3.5 nautical miles distant from the
Stockholm. "Steer four degrees to port," Calamai directed.

Calamai reasoned that the slight swing to the left would
open the gap between the two ships.

*If Calamai had made a dramatic course shift to the left—
thirty degrees or more—the radar of the approaching ship
would have reflected the action despite any possible minor
errors of deduction or perception. But a mere four-degree
change was not large enough to be readily apparent to anyone watching the Stockholm's radar screen. Equally important, a precautionary large course change at that point
would have avoided the possibility of a collision.*

11:07 P.M.

The *Stockholm* was two nautical miles distant from the *Andrea Doria*. On the bridge wing, lookout Ingemar Bjorkman
called, "Light on port."

Carstens stepped out to the wing to see for himself. The
other ship was slightly to the left. The mate and the sailor read
her lights easily. The forward lower light was to the left of the
higher masthead light, meaning that the ship was on a course
that would take it safely past on the port side. Nevertheless,
the passage would be closer than one mile. Carstens decided to
turn sharply to the right to give the other ship more maneuvering room.

"Starboard," he called out to Larsen. The compass indicator
moved about twenty degrees to the right. Carstens did not
order a blast of the ship's whistle that would have signaled his
turn to the other vessel.

The telephone suddenly rang in the wheelhouse. Carstens
turned his back on the approaching ship and left the bridge
wing in order to answer it.

*If Carstens had kept the approaching ship under contin-
ual observation, he would have seen that the lights were
changing even as he watched, which meant the* Andrea Doria
was shifting course in front of him. The Andrea Doria *was
moving into its left turn just as she became visible to the*
Stockholm *at the edge of the fogbank. But the overworked
mate could not keep the other ship under constant observa-*

233

tion. He had to supervise his helmsman and also answer the lookout's telephone. The telephone call unfortunately diverted Carstens from watching the lights at that crucial moment. In addition, had he remembered to signal his sharp right turn, the Andrea Doria *would have been alerted sooner.*

11:07 P.M.

The *Andrea Doria* was two nautical miles distant from the *Stockholm.* Calamai and Third Officer Giannini watched carefully on the starboard side. Calamai did not expect to see the other vessel until it was close, because of the fog, but he was puzzled that he did not at least hear the foghorn. Calamai did not realize that he was at the edge of the fogbank and that the other ship would have no reason to use the foghorn.

Suddenly Giannini saw a blur of lights off to the right.

The ships were about one mile apart when the vague glow of the approaching vessel separated into visible masthead lights. Calamai saw that the lower forward light was slightly to the right of the other. For an instant, Calamai thought the other ship would pass safely to the right.

Then Giannini focused his binoculars once more on the lights of the approaching ship. He was suddenly confronted with the ghastly realization that the lower masthead light of the other ship was rapidly swinging to the left of the higher masthead light. Incredibly, unbelievably, the other ship was turning directly toward the *Andrea Doria.*

Calamai had to act quickly, but there was little time. When collision is unavoidable, a ship should turn *toward* danger to minimize impact. But Calamai could not bring himself to concede the inevitable.

"Hard left," he yelled at the helmsman, Giulio Visciano. It was a last daring attempt to outrun a disaster by turning the *Andrea Doria* to the left faster than the *Stockholm* was turning right.

If Calamai had turned the Andrea Doria *directly toward the approaching* Stockholm, *the combined forward speeds of the two ships would have been greater. But damage possibly would have been sustained at a less critical area. By exposing the starboard side of his ship to the* Stockholm, *he opened the vitals of the great liner, including the empty fuel tanks, like a target.*

11:08 P.M.

The *Stockholm*, a ship sailing twenty miles north of the recommended course, unaware that it was at the edge of a massive fogbank, relying on the navigation of a busy young third mate forced to plot his course without the aid of a gyro repeater, turning sharply to the right in a maneuver it had failed to signal, pointed its reinforced nose directly at the *Andrea Doria*.

11:09 P.M.

The *Andrea Doria*, running almost at full speed through a thick fog, navigating on the basis of radar information it had observed but not plotted, having made a slight, barely noticeable turn to the left, now skidded forward in the water for perhaps half a mile before futilely attempting to turn away from danger.

11:10 P.M.

The bow of the *Stockholm*, angled forward on top like a sharpened blade, cut first into five passenger decks of the *Andrea Doria*, then continued to hit against the side of the ship, slicing her apart.

Below the passenger decks fuel tanks and deep ballast tanks ruptured. Five hundred tons of ocean rushed into the empty tanks and compartments on the starboard side. The *Andrea Doria* tilted sharply toward her right. The edges of A Deck sank beneath the surface of the ocean as she listed, destroying the watertight integrity of the ship. Water poured over the top of A Deck and rushed down into nearby compartments that were theoretically sealed off by the watertight doors, but were now exposed to the onslaught of the unleashed ocean.

The *Andrea Doria* had begun her descent into the sea.

The collision was one of the great tragedies of the sea, the cumulative result of this series of circumstances and decisions. Yet, for the great majority of those on board the *Andrea Doria,* the run of bad luck seemed to play itself out just in time. Even as the night hours of July 25, 1956, moved toward disaster and death, so the early-morning hours of July 26 produced a chain of fortuitous events that made the heroic rescue possible.

The *Andrea Doria,* gravely wounded, remained afloat many hours longer than observers thought she would. The same crowded sea-lane whose congestion contributed to the collision also assured the proximity of rescue ships.

The vacation replacement captain of the *Ile de France* made the honorable decision to turn his great ship around and bring the necessary lifeboats to the scene.

The damnable fog that cloaked the dying ship also accommodated the rescue by choosing a dramatic, and convenient, moment to dissipate.

Brave men from the hovering rescue ships worked in fear of death to save others. Though some of the men and women aboard the *Andrea Doria*—both passengers and crew—reacted with selfishness and cowardice, enough found the inner valor to save both themselves and those around them.

The story of the *Andrea Doria* may be viewed as a tragic accident that took the lives of fifty-one people and brought a giant ship to the bottom of the ocean. But at the conclusion of those fearful night and morning hours, 1660 men, women, and children were saved in what had become the greatest rescue at sea of all time.

EPILOGUE

Just as the long hours of darkness aboard the *Andrea Doria* produced a full range of emotions, so, too, the years that followed revealed the same diversity. Some passengers seemed to recover easily with no legacy of fear. Others were permanently shaken by the experience.

Sister Marie Raymond Baker, who escaped the *Andrea Doria* despite her crippled leg, now teaches piano at Holy Rosary Academy in Bay City, Michigan. "God sent me this accident to make me reevaluate my life," she says. "It's not what you have, it's what you are."

Marion Boyer, whose life was saved by his wife Malcolm's insistence on a final cup of coffee in the Belvedere Lounge, remained active as a director for Standard Oil Company of New Jersey until 1966. Today he and Mrs. Boyer live in retirement on the Sea Pines Plantation, Hilton Head Island, South Carolina. Boyer still has the room key from his demolished suite on the *Andrea Doria*. He never grumbles whenever his wife asks for another cup of coffee.

Jane Cianfarra underwent several operations for a fractured leg and hand. It was two and one-half months before she was well enough to visit her daughter, Linda Morgan, who was in traction because of her fractured kneecaps. Mrs. Cianfarra never recovered emotionally from her two-hour ordeal in cabin 56. Every year she suffered a severe depression on July 25, the anniversary of the collision. She died of a stroke on July 25, 1967, at the age of fifty-one.

Richardson Dilworth was not visibly affected by his heroic night on the *Andrea Doria*. Rather, he saw a chance to recoup the goodwill of his Italian constituents. He appeared on Philadelphia television shows praising the courage of the Italian crew. The next summer, in a demonstration of confidence, he and Ann returned to Europe aboard the *Cristoforo Colombo*. He was reelected mayor of Philadelphia in 1959, easily defeating Harold Stassen. He resigned to run for governor of Pennsylvania in 1962, but lost to William Scranton. Dilworth returned to an appointed office in the Philadelphia school system. He died of a brain tumor on January 23, 1974, at the age of seventy-five. Ann Dilworth still lives in the Philadelphia area.

Father John Dolciamore, whose life was spared by a late Scrabble game, is chief judge of the Matrimonial Court of the Chicago archdiocese. He has not played a game of Scrabble since July 25, 1956.

Liliana Dooner, whose desperate plunge off the stern of the *Andrea Doria* saved both her three-year-old daughter, Maria, and a thirteen-year-old girl, today has a paralyzing phobia about swimming at night. However, she still prefers ships to planes. Now Mrs. Richard Hughes of Hazlet, New Jersey, she is in the antiques business. She still has the flimsy purple half-slip she wore that night.

Maria Dooner has no memory of that desperate night in July, 1956. She is married to Thomas Socha, a supermarket manager in Elizabeth, New Jersey. They have a four-year-old boy, Tommy.

Alfred and Beverly Green today live in New York. Alfred is still active in his garment manufacturing business. The Greens own Meadow Hill Stable and the champion thoroughbred, Quiet Little Table. "People love to hear about the *Andrea*

Doria," Mrs. Green says. "I can become the center of attention at any dinner party."

Robert Hudson was sent to Savannah, Georgia, for surgery on his lacerated right hand. He wore a back brace for three years. Fully recovered from his injuries, in 1960 he returned to work as an able-bodied seaman, despite his nightmare escape as the last person left aboard the *Andrea Doria.* Today he lives in Port Arthur, Texas, and continues to travel the world on freighters.

Father Tom Kelly, who led a small band of brave men below the open decks to gather life jackets, left the priesthood in 1971. He married a former nun. He is a professor of sociology at Lake Superior State College in Sault Ste. Marie, Michigan. Each year he delivers a special lecture to his students on the varying reactions of people to stress, using his own experiences on the *Andrea Doria* as an illustration. In 1976 the college honored him with a Distinguished Teaching Award.

George P. Kerr returned to Europe to continue his work for Proctor & Gamble, Inc. For a time he lived in Genoa where, he says, "I can still remember seeing Captain Calamai walking the streets like a zombie." Kerr and his wife have taken many more enjoyable voyages on various Italian Line ships and live today in retirement in Locarno, Switzerland.

Kyrie Kerr, who escaped with her mother in one of the first lifeboats, is now Mrs. Robert Stone, the mother of two boys. She lives near Ipswich, England. She describes herself as a "typical English eccentric," who busies herself marketing homegrown vegetables and fresh honey from her beehives. Tucked away in the attic of her country home is a bright orange lifejacket.

After several operations on her knees and her left arm, Linda Morgan was released from the hospital to contemplate the miracle that spared her life when she was catapulted from her bed on the *Andrea Doria* to the bow of the *Stockholm.* Today she is married to San Antonio attorney, Phillip Hardberger. They have a daughter. "I'm not a very cautious person anymore," Linda declares. "My husband's a pilot. We fly all over. We hike and canoe and climb. I feel life is to be lived to the fullest. Life is precious. There's a very thin line between when you're living and when you're not."

Dr. Thure Peterson returned to his work as a chiropractor in Upper Montclair, New Jersey, after his wife's death on the *Andrea Doria*, but did not regain his robust energy. He remained in contact with Jane Ciarifarra until her death, and with the heroic steward, Giovanni Rovelli. Peterson died in 1971.

Paul and Margaret Sergio never returned to their beloved Italy. Back home in South Bend, Indiana, Paul resumed work in his shoe repair shop behind the Golden Dome of Notre Dame University. He could never forget the memory of how he refused the request of his nephew Rocco, who asked to sleep with him only a few minutes before the fatal crash. Paul Sergio died of bone cancer in 1972, at the age of seventy-two. Margaret's years were plagued with ill health. She suffered from high blood pressure and occasional bouts of pneumonia. She became terribly distraught whenever she discussed the *Andrea Doria*. She died in 1978, shortly after granting this writer an interview.

Mike Stoller's fortunes continued to rise from the moment he arrived in New York aboard the *Cape Ann* to learn that Elvis Presley had recorded his song "Hound Dog." Today he is one of New York's most successful songwriters. With his partner Jerry Leiber he wrote twenty additional songs for Presley, including "Jailhouse Rock." The two men produced a series of rock-and-roll hits for groups such as The Coasters, The Drifters, The Shangri-Las, The Dixie Cups, Procol Harum, and Steeler's Wheel. They are now writing a show for Broadway producer Bob Fosse.

After the death of his parents in deluxe suite 180, Peter Thieriot and his three younger brothers were raised by an aunt and uncle. Today Peter is vice-president of a family-owned business, the San Francisco Newspaper Printing Co., Inc., which prints both the *Examiner* and the *Chronicle*. "An experience like the *Andrea Doria* makes some of the less tasty things in life easier to deal with," Peter says. "An awful lot can happen and it doesn't seem like any big deal."

John Vali and Melania Ansuini, who met for the first time in the tourist-class Social Hall of the *Andrea Doria* only a short time before the collision, were married on March 10, 1957. A year later Melania gave birth to a daughter. They named her *Doria*.

Alba Wells returned to Birmingham, Alabama, with her husband, Charles, and her children, Henry, Shirley, and Rose Marie, to discover that neighbors had collected food, clothing, and toys for the children. Eight-year-old Shirley thought it was Christmas. Mrs. Wells returned to Italy for another visit a few years after her ordeal on the *Andrea Doria*. This time she flew. The trip to Europe was uneventful, but on the return flight the airplane encountered severe turbulence, prompting her traveling companion to remark, "Alba, I'll go to Italy with you again, but I won't ever come back with you."

Father Richard Wojcik returned to the Archdiocese of Chicago and met with Samuel Cardinal Stritch. Wojcik asked worriedly, "When I got to the *Ile de France*, I held a special Mass of thanksgiving, but some of the people had already eaten—did I do the right thing?" The cardinal replied, "You did well. Don't do it again!" Today Wojcik is a choral instructor at St. Mary of the Lake Seminary, Mundelein, Illinois.

Robert Young, the shipping inspector who had an early premonition of danger on the afternoon prior to the collision, is today president and chairman of the board of the American Bureau of Shipping.

For his heroic work in rescuing the passengers and crew of the *Andrea Doria*, Baron Raoul de Beaudéan was decorated as an Officier de la Légion d'Honneur. In 1957, he was given full command of the *Ile de France* until his retirement the next year. He lives today in Joie-les-Tours, France, with his wife of fifty-three years.

Sven Abenius, second officer junior of the *Stockholm* and commander of lifeboat number 8, today is a freighter captain for Brostroms, owners of several shipping lines and parent company of the now-defunct Swedish-American Line.

Johan-Ernst Carstens-Johannsen, who was in command of the bridge of the *Stockholm* at the moment of the collision, later served as an officer on the *Stockholm* and the *Gripsholm*, as well as other merchant ships until 1965. Today he is sales manager for Brostroms' trading division. When asked if he misses the sea, Carstens replies with a good-natured "No!"

Lars Enestrom, second officer senior of the *Stockholm*, who commanded lifeboat number 7, is now nautical superintendent for Brostroms, responsible for design and maintenance of safety, radio, and radar equipment for their ships.

Stockholm apprentice Per Hinnerson, who pulled many *Andrea Doria* passengers from the oily water into lifeboat number 8, later was a crewman on the Swedish freighter *Ryholm*. The *Ryholm* was rammed by a French freighter on the Elbe River and sank. Today he is captain of the *Ms. Prinsessan Birgitta*, an overnight ferry that runs between Gothenburg, Sweden, and Travemunde, Germany.

Harry Gunnar Nordenson remained as master of the rebuilt *Stockholm* for one more round trip between Sweden and New York. He then commanded the new Swedish liner *Gripsholm* until he reached mandatory retirement age in 1958. He now lives, age eighty-five, in Gothenburg, Sweden.

Guido Badano, junior second officer of the *Andrea Doria*, later commanded the *Leonardo da Vinci* and the *Cristoforo Colombo* before taking a brief sabbatical from the sea in 1976. He returned one year later and is now captain of the *Espresso Rosso*, an overnight ferry running between Leghorn, Italy, and Olbia, Sardinia. "The loss of the *Andrea Doria* was very sad," he comments. "It was like the feeling you get when a child dies. She was only three years old."

Professor Bruno Tortori Donati, the *Andrea Doria*'s physician, continued to work as a ship's doctor until 1964. Today he is chief physician of the Statal Lines of Finmare, the state-owned shipping companies of Italy, and lives in Genoa. "I have thought so many times of that night," he says. "I always thank God that I was too busy to be afraid."

Curzio Franchini, senior second officer of the *Andrea Doria*, subsequently served as officer and captain of several Italian Line ships including the *Rossini*, before taking a staff position in 1964. Today he is chief of the Genoa delegation of the Italian Shipowners' Association. "It was a very bad experience," he says of that dark night off Nantucket. "I don't like to remember it."

Eugenio Giannini, third officer of the *Andrea Doria*, later served as an officer aboard the *Cristoforo Colombo*, the *Leonardo da Vinci*, and the *Saturnia*. He left the sea in 1963 to pursue a business career. Today he is marketing director and stylist for Levorato, a menswear manufacturer in Padua, Italy.

Osvaldo Magagnini, staff captain and second-in-command of the *Andrea Doria*, later captained several Italian Line ships including the *Cristoforo Colombo*. He retired in 1963 and lives in Genoa. "Sometimes when I am a little sleepy," he says, "I ask myself, was it possible to do more? I have no answer."

Luigi Oneto, senior chief officer of the *Andrea Doria*, later commanded the *Cristoforo Colombo* and the *Michelangelo* before retiring in 1971. Today he is president of the Italian Union of Ship Captains and lives in the seaside village of Camogli, Italy.

Giovanni Rovelli, the heroic steward who labored alongside Dr. Thure Peterson in cabin 56 for five anguished hours, continued to work as a steward on Italian Line ships until he retired in 1970 at the age of sixty-three. He now lives in Genoa with his wife. His right arm, injured by the heavy jack that he and Dr. Peterson hauled aboard, still causes him great pain.

After the ordeal of his testimony, Piero Calamai, captain of the *Andrea Doria*, retired to his home in Genoa. He was, in the words of his daughter Silvia, "like a father who has lost his son." Not once in his remaining twelve years did he ever discuss the tragedy with his family. Then, on his deathbed in April 1972, in a final delirium, he cried out to his older daughter, Marina, "Is it all right? Are the passengers saved?"

The *Stockholm*, fully repaired, left New York for Gothenburg in December 1956. She remained in service on the same transatlantic route until 1960 when she was sold to an East German shipping firm and renamed the *Volkerfreundschaft*.

The *Andrea Doria* remains 225 feet beneath the surface of the Atlantic Ocean.

INDEX

ABOUT THE AUTHOR

WILLIAM HOFFER'S previous book, the highly praised *Midnight Express* (written with Billy Hayes), was made into a successful motion picture that was nominated for six Academy Awards. For his next book, he travelled extensively throughout Europe and the United States, interviewing survivors of the sunken cruise ship, *Andrea Doria*, and corroborating their stories. The result is *Saved!*, a book which the author feels is as authentic in its details as possible. Despite the important subject matter in both *Saved!* and *Midnight Express*, Mr. Hoffer still holds that "I write to entertain, not to deliver messages." In addition to writing books and magazine articles, Mr. Hoffer has held various editorial positions and has served as a director of the American Society of Journalists and Authors. He is presently living in Washington.